CHEKHOV—
THE SILENT VOICE
OF FREEDOM

CHEKHOV—
THE SILENT VOICE
OF FREEDOM

by
Valentine Tschebotarioff Bill

Philosophical Library
New York

Library of Congress Cataloging-in-Publication Data

Bill, Valentine Tschebotarioff.
  Chekov—the silent voice of freedom.

  Bibliography: p.
  Includes index.
  1. Chekhov, Anton Pavlovich, 1860-1904
Philosophy.   I. Title.
PG3458.Z9P483   1986   891.72'3   86-12196
ISBN 0-8022-2514-4

To C.R.

CONTENTS

PREFACE

Lopatkin is the central character in Vladimir Dudintsev's novel *Not By Bread Alone*, one of the early endeavors in Soviet literature to break away from the fetters of Governmental tutelage after Stalin's death in 1953. While inmate of a prison camp in Siberia, Lopatkin is assigned to work on a bridge under construction. Perched high among the bridge's trusses, the river rapids below and nothing but the sky above, he reflects: "The term imprisonment is inaccurate. A human being who has learned how to think cannot be completely deprived of freedom."

This thought has become a leitmotif of dissident Soviet literature in the post-Stalinist era. The perspective gained from this vantage point has moved the Soviet writer Vasily Grossman to look back at Chekhov in the light of freedom's function in Russian life and literature. His monumental indictment of Soviet reality, the novel *Life and Fate*, was completed in 1960, but was, naturally, barred from publication. Every copy of the manuscript found in the search of the author's quarters by the KGB was confiscated. Grossman died in 1964 and did not live to witness the escape of his manuscript abroad and the publication of the book in the West in 1980.*

* First in Russian, then in French and German translation and in 1986 in English in the United States.

What Grossman has to say about Chekhov in *Life and Fate* is a trenchant observation of utmost significance. He has one of his protagonists say: "Chekhov's path was the path of Russian freedom.... He was the first to say, as no one before him, even Tolstoy, had said: The most important thing is that people are people.... People are good and bad not because they are bishops, Russians, storekeepers, Tartars, workmen.... People are equals because they are people.... Chekhov is the standard-bearer of the highest banner raised in Russia during the thousand years of her existence—the banner of genuine, Russian democracy, of Russian human dignity, of Russian freedom. Our humaneness has always been sectarian, irreconcilable, and cruel. From Avvacum to Lenin our humaneness and freedom have been party-oriented, fanatical, ruthlessly sacrificing the human individual to abstract humanity.... genuine, humane democracy does not fit into our household."*

Grossman goes on to say that the Soviet Government "tolerates" Chekhov because they do not understand the essence of his work. Neither did Chekhov's contemporaries grasp the core of his creative thought. A famous essay by the philosopher Leo Shestov on Chekhov bears the title "Creation from the Void" ("Tvorchestvo iz nichevo"). It was published shortly after Chekhov's death in 1904 and is still quoted and referred to as the best that has been written on that subject. Shestov's argument rests on Chekhov's aversion to any set doctrines or accepted ideology: "Chekhov had no ideal.... An ideal presupposes submission, the voluntary denial of one's own right to independence, freedom, and force; and demands of this kind roused in Chekhov all that intensity of disgust and repulsion of which he alone was capable,"** In equally flamboyant style Shestov spoke of Chekhov's characters as people who had turned away from

* Pages 187-88 of the Russian edition, published by L'Age d'Homme, Geneva, 1980. The translation is my own.

** Leo Shestov, *Chekhov and Other Essays*, trans. Sidney Monas, Ann·Arbor, MI: University of Michigan, 1966, p. 35.

ends related to "the organized life of mankind," not believing that by changing outward conditions they could change their own fate as well. Every one of his protagonists marches along in utter desolation, bewildered, inert, helpless, and deprived of hope. Ideas and hopelessness cannot coexist. The only hero of Chekhov's, according to Shestov, is the hopeless man. He has nothing. He must create everything for himself; he is condemned to create from the void and this "creation from the void" is the only problem which occupies Chekhov's artistic imagination, Shestov tells us. But it is alien to human nature to attempt to create something out of nothing and so the only activity Chekhov's hero engages in is, as perceived by Shestov, "beating his head against a wall."

The longevity of this view of Chekhov as the poet of hopelessness—a number of recent studies of his thoughts are influenced by it—is due, in large measure, to the preeminence of formalistic trends in modern literary criticism. In declaring the primacy of form over content, of verbal structure over the image drawn or the idea expressed, in stressing that the "how" offers a new and sharper perception of the "what," the way was opened for a concentration on the poetic novelty of Chekhov's technique, the verbal structure of his stories and his plays, the plotless narrative, the minimal "action," the long silences in the plays, the countless innovative devices of word and sentence linkages, all weaving the marvelous aesthetic texture of his work.

Shestov's view of Chekhov's art fitted well into a school of literary criticism which strove to free the word from the supremacy of the idea and which assigned the literary hero the modest role of a compositional component rather than that of a psychological presence. If hopelessness was indeed the main attribute of Chekhov's heroes, then their stature was already reduced to a negligible entity by their creator himself. And if Chekhov was really "killing human hopes," if he was "infatuated with death and decay," if such concepts as "art, science, love, inspiration, ideals withered and died" as soon as he touched them, giving way to the Void, then there was all the more incentive and appeal to concentrate on the formal aspects of Chekhov's art.

But Shestov's Void was an optical illusion. It was not death, it was life that Chekhov was infatuated with. There was no Void, but there was an agglomeration of obstacles that Chekhov saw, a mass of chains, barriers, cages, which slowed an individual's growth, which threatened to paralyze him, and diminished the priceless gift of being alive.

Grossman's salute to Chekhov as the first Russian standard-bearer of freedom brings this vital aspect of Chekhov's art to the fore. It marks a turn from the "how" to the "what" in looking at Chekhov's work, in keeping with the hyperbolically but graphically expressed thought of John Gardner in *On Moral Fiction* published in 1978: "Fiddling with the hairs on an elephant's nose is indecent when the elephant happens to be standing on the baby." Grossman's tribute is in need of an extensive explication before the lonely figure of a single individual looming against the background of one thousand years of Russian history can be brought into a clear focus; before human destiny, as Chekhov saw it, can be understood.

I owe a great deal to the late Father Georges Florovksy, Professor of Theology at Harvard University, who lectured at Princeton University after his retirement. Through his personal interest in my project I gained invaluable insight into the nature of Russian Orthodoxy and a new approach to Chekhov's relation to religion. I am equally indebted to the late Professor Ira O. Wade, prominent Voltaire scholar and my one time departmental chairman. He read several draft chapters of this book and his comments on Proust helped me greatly in analyzing Chekhov's treatment of Time. My thanks go to my former departmental chairman Professor Richard Burgi, who assigned me to conduct a graduate course on Chekhov in the late 1960s, when the first thoughts for this book took shape. Princeton University's superb Firestone Library provided me with a unique environment for research and writing and I gratefully acknowledge the speedy and efficient help I received from their Interlibrary

Loan Division. I also owe a debt of gratitude to Ludmila Turkevich, Professor Emeritus of Russian Language and Culture, then Chairman of the Russian Department at Douglas College, Rutgers University, for valuable comments; and to Mrs. Arthur Sherwood, Literature Editor at Princeton University Press, for time and organizational suggestions generously given to me at various stages of the project. My heartfelt thanks go to my husband, Edward C. Bill, for repeated, meticulous readings of the manuscript.

I

The Roadblocks

"Freedom is a difficult condition. To remain enslaved is easier."

> —Nicolai Berdiaev, *On Human Slavery and Freedom*
> (*o rabstve i svobode cheloveka*)

A Masquerade of Freedom

The nineteenth century into which Chekhov was born was a truly unique and extraordinary period of Russian history. It was a century of great cultural advances and creative achievements, a golden age of literature, music, and painting. But it was also a century of harsh divisiveness and stupendous shifts in the composition of society, a somber era of social disintegration and growing economic imbalance. At no time before in Russia had so many currents of thought

15

and imaginative inspiration burst forth with such vigor and passion, filling each decade with new trends, conflicting ideas, and a large score of brilliant achievements. At no time before had so many new social groups appeared on the Russian scene, divergent in their goals, antagonistic to each other, and steering the country with ever-mounting momentum toward the upheavals at the opening of the twentieth century.

All this, the intellectual ferment and artistic bloom as well as the political turmoil and social blight, sprouted and grew in an environment dominated by a fateful problem the preceding century had created and been unable to solve: how to graft European ways of life and thought on the ancient feudal order of Muscovy. At no time throughout the eighteenth century had a clear and comprehensive image of Europe presented itself to the Russian mind. What appeared worthy of being emulated and transplanted to Russian soil was a series of highly selective, fragmentary aspects of European civilization, torn from their native soil, severed from roots that reached deep in to Europe's past.

Peter the Great saw Europe as a noisy, bustling, urban landscape, dotted with shipbuilding yards and factory smokestacks, teeming with streets of shops and warehouses and graced with a vast variety of centers of learning. Peter's gaze was riveted on the marvels of Europe's technology, industry, and military expertise. Eager and impatient to import these marvels to Russia, not prone to contemplative thought by nature, Peter failed to observe that the urban scene he so greatly admired had emerged after centuries of groping quests, searching thrusts, and fierce conflicts between two basic modes of human existence—servitude and liberty. Serfdom had been the distinctive feature of agrarian medieval Europe between the third and the twelfth centuries. Commerce and city life had deteriorated under the late Roman Empire, and had but slowly come back to life after the Crusades. The rebirth of urban centers in Europe, nurtured by a growing awareness of the potentials and aspirations of the human individual, contributed most to the disappearance of medieval serfdom. Within the walls of the city freedom ceased to be the monopoly of a privileged class of nobles and became the natural right of all urban inhabitants. City air made them free.

It is doubtful that Peter could have comprehended the importance of individual liberty as the foundation of European city life and as the lifeblood of its new economic and social order, even had he taken the time and shown an inclination for historical analyses. For he had been born and reared in an environment in which servitude permeated every aspect of life and serfdom had gained formidable proportions. The topography of the land itself was responsible for this salient feature of the country's history. It is a vast, flat plain merging in the West, without any natural obstructions, with the northern lowland of Western Europe, and is flanked in the East by the high, flat Central Asiatic plateau, which descends, in decreasing levels of altitude like a staircase, into the flat stretches of Southern Russia's steppes or prairies. From East and West this was an open road travelled for centuries by invaders, nomadic tribes such as the Polovtsy, the Pechenegs, and the Mongol-Tartars from Asia, and the Teutonic Order, Poland, Lithuania, Sweden, France and Germany from the West.

For centuries Russia saw herself as a besieged fortress, a military camp, and the minds of Muscovite men in all walks of life were dominated by the idea of submission to a higher central authority. To provide security from aggression was the uppermost reason for their existence. Each social class carried duties, each was differentiated by its obligations, but none conceived of itself as having any rights. Flight or violence, not legalized corporate resistance, was the only avenue of protest. Russia did not participate in the great cultural experiences of the West which came in the wake of the Middle Ages and gave the individual and his way of life a new direction. There was no Renaissance, no Reformation, no Enlightenment in Russia.

In the later part of the sixteenth century the peasants, heavy with discontent over the increasingly exacting tax burden, set out by the thousands to abandon their fields and to flee south to the fertile steppe regions not yet incorporated into the realm of Muscovy. To arrest this disasterous flight and the ensuing labor shortage, the Tsars resorted to issuing decrees which restricted the peasants' freedom of movement with increasing stringency. By the middle of the seventeenth century, under Peter the Great's father, Tsar Alexis, at a time when vestiges of serfdom were disappearing in Europe, a large percentage of the rural population in Muscovy found itself permanently attached to the soil and converted into serfs, burdened with a hereditary system of servitude.

This is what gave Russian serfdom such formidable proportions. It was not based on a system of small, disparate political units comparable to those of feudal Europe, but grew within the boundaries of a large and ever-expanding state, while duplicating the essential feature of European medieval agriculture. Farming was done by peasant communes almost entirely on a subsistence level using the three-field system, which greatly impeded the possibility of producing any sizeable surplus and revenue.

The Muscovite towns were incorporated into the fabric of this serf society, unable to develop beyond the functions of fortress and administrative center into autonomous bodies and promoters of personal freedom. In medieval Europe people seeking to escape bondage had fled to the cities. In Muscovy, they fled to the frontier. The merchants who inhabited the towns of Muscovy shared with the peasantry restrictions on the freedom to change their place of residence and onerous obligations to supply the treasury with funds. Trade was a state-imposed obligation as well as a voluntarily chosen way of life.

Far from starting Russia's Europeanization by loosening the fetters of bondage, Peter tightened them and grafted his imported innovations upon a foundation of servitude grown more rigorous than ever. Peter's aim was to transplant Western secular culture to Russia, to raise the productive forces of the nation, but it was a strong commercial state and a militarily mighty industrial empire rather than a conglomerate of prosperous citizens and free individuals that stood uppermost in his mind. Utter disregard for the welfare of the individual and the concept of personal liberty marked Peter's actions no less than those of his Muscovite ancestors.

Europe provided the pattern and the expertise for the organization of the large standing army, for the new navy, for the hierarchy of military and civil service ranks, for the numerous institutions of learning. European technology was employed in the establishment of Peter's new industrial enterprise—the shipbuilding yards, the iron works, the arms factories, and the cloth, sailcloth, and rope factories. European architecture shaped the contours of the new capital on the shores of the Baltic Sea. But the manpower needed to set and keep the wheels of Westernization in motion was provided by coercion and by new forms of bondage.

The education of the nobility, oriented toward technical and practical skills, was mandatory. This in itself amounted to an enforced cultural revolution, for secularization spelled a radical departure from ancient Muscovite traditions. The souls of the Muscovites were ruled by the religious tenets of the Orthodox Church. Education was regarded as a matter of moral discipline rather than of intellectual training. The educational ideal in Muscovy was learning how to live like a good Christian, not how to think. For knowledge was vanity and inquisitiveness a sin. The "classroom" was the example set by the paterfamilias in his daily conduct. Wisdom was measured in terms of charitable acts and moral excellence and was not related to the accumulation and assimilation of knowledge. Reading and writing, taught by local deacons and sextons, were looked upon as techniques, skills comparable to shorthand and typewriting, needed for certain clerical professions and ecclesiastical functions, but not for general education and mental discipline. Peter's contemporaries were thus, at best, barely literate. And to be forced to attend schools of mathematics, navigation, artillery, and engineering, staffed by imported European instructors, or to be commandeered to study at Western universities was, for Peter's nobles, a stupendous, laborious task.

Service of this forcibly educated nobility in military or

administrative posts was for life, while the rank and file of the armed forces was provided by a type of conscription, the recruiting system. The number of men needed by the army and navy was annually announced by the Government and levied from the rural population on the basis of one recruit from a specified number of peasant households. Separation of a recruit from family and home was for life. This gave rise to a new type of folk art, laments over the departure of a conscripted family member. The new industrial enterprises too gave rise to a new form of servitude, since there was no free labor to man the factories. Rural serfs by the score were transported to the ironworks in the Urals or the shipbuilding yards at Voronezh or the construction sites at Petersburg and permanently attached to their new place of employment.

Under Peter's successors the image of Europe that came to be imprinted on Russia's imagination changed perceptibly. It was no longer the picture of a busy, industrious, urban workshop, but rather the vista of a brilliant court, of palaces with elegant ballrooms and formal gardens, of theaters, opera, ballet, and aristocratic salons. In the middle years of the eighteenth century glimpses of the book-lined studies of the *philosophes* were added to the picture.

The absence of a law determining the order of succession had initiated this change. When Peter died, his throne lay in dispute for he had hesitated too long while assessing the competence of his possible successors to continue his reform work and had passed away without stating his choice. The seventy years that separated Peter's death from that of Catherine II brought a series of palace revolutions, sparked by the contested succession. Court intrigues and the bayonets of Peter's two Guard regiments, composed entirely of nobles, lifted in rapid succession various members of the dynastic family to the throne—Peter's wife (Catherine I), his niece, his daughter, a great-niece, two grandsons, and the wife of one of the latter. The reign of four of these rulers was brief. The seven decades were dominated by the personalities of three women who, among themselves account for sixty-four years of that period: Peter's niece, the dour, coarse, and indolent Ann of Courland; his daughter, the gay and frivolous Elizabeth; and the majestic, ambitious, and erudite Catherine II, born a German princess and the wife of Peter's grandson, Peter III.

The emergence and growth of a lavish, extravagantly luxurious court, held up for emulation before the nobility, distinguishes this period. Under Ann of Courland the scene was one of tasteless frivolity and endless rounds of garish festivities. Under Elizabeth, tastes and manners gained a considerable measure of refinement. French became the accepted language of the court. The Empress invited French theatrical ensembles and Italian operatic troupes to visit her realm and sought foreign assistance in the organization of the first Imperial theaters. Nobles educated under Peter the Great's stern and technology-oriented regimen felt out of place if they had not mastered the art of wearing fine clothes and dancing the minuet. Under Catherine II Russian nobles were encouraged to reach beyond the glittering superficialities of cultural amenities, to cultivate their minds along with their manners, and to become acquainted with the fruits of the French Enlightenment that Catherine held in such high esteem.

The benefits the nobility drew from the era of palace revolutions were vast, since each upheaval was staged by the Guard's regiments, which represented the flower of their class. The duties Peter the Great had imposed upon his nobles lightened and fell away, orders ceased, regulations were relaxed and lifted; honors, privileges, and titles ceased to be means of harnessing the nobles' energies in the service of the State and became prerogatives of their own standing. During the seventy years following Peter's death the nobles moved upward from privilege to privilege and from grant to grant, soaring to spectacular heights of prominence and power. Empress Ann rewarded the nobles for the support she had received from the Guards at her accession to the throne by reducing their previously lifelong military service to twenty-five years. Elizabeth conferred upon the nobles the right of criminal jurisdiction over their serfs and the lucrative privilege of selling and buying serfs apart from the land. Wealth was now measured in "souls" owned instead of land or money. Under Catherine II the privileges of the nobility reached their peak. The nobles were altogether freed from compulsory military service and were granted a charter that gave them the right of self-administration. The nobles of each province formed a corporation, elected their local representatives, and held the privilege of petitioning the Crown.

Catherine conferred similar benefits upon the towns. They too were given the right to form a legal entity, to elect local administrators headed by a mayor who could appeal to the provincial governor. But this attempt to stimulate urban life in Russia proved futile. A Government decree was incapable of creating an urban class in a society where serfdom reigned and a subsistence economy prevailed. The self-sufficient countryside could not provide a lucrative market for the products of urban crafts. And the merchant class continued to share the lowest rung of the social ladder with the peasantry instead of assuming the intermediary position of a "middle class" between the aristocracy and the rural population. The majority of Russian towns did not beckon like prosperous citadels but merged with the rolling and monotonous countryside "like small toys resting on the wide, wrinkled palm of an outstretched hand."

Serfdom in Russia had assumed proportions and features bordering on slavery, harsher by far than the conditions that distinguished European servitude in the Middle Ages. The freedom of the Russian nobility, however, became, in the later part of the eighteenth century, incomparably more extensive than any privileges ever enjoyed by any European social group. In the absence of any sense of responsibilities, lacking any counterbalance of duties, these privileges were a hideous masquerade of the concept of freedom that had evolved in Europe since the Middle Ages. The estate of a Russian nobleman resembled a small, autonomous domain where the owner ruled like a sovereign, holding those living on his land under his absolute power. The nobleman made his own laws and enforced them within the bounds of his realm; he held court, distributed fines and punishments of his own making, and sold and bought peasants at will, breaking up families or transporting whole peasant communes to a new site. He turned to France for a model of luxurious living which his native land was culturally unable to satisfy but which unrenumerated serf labor provided him the means to pay for. The manor houses, built in the style of European mansions, became the cultural and intellectual centers of the country. In them French was spoken—often with greater fluency than Russian, the music of European composers was played, the latest Parisian fashions were worn and copied, and the *philosophes* were read and translated.

Acquaintance with the ideas of the French Enlightenment was the final stage in the intellectual development of the eighteenth-century Russian nobility. It is difficult to assess whether the mental confusion created by this latest European import was more severe than the wrenching adjustments experienced by Peter the Great's nobles in the early part of the century. The compulsory education of Peter's nobles had pursued the definite, immediate, and practical purpose of providing the Tsar with the assistants he required. Dissemination of the ideas of the French Enlightenment among the Russian nobility in the later part of the century, however, had no comparable tangible purpose and produced the opposite effect of social alienation, of widening the chasm between the upper and the lower classes. The power of reason, the pursuit of knowledge as a tool for solving all human problems, and the striving for liberty and equality were the aims held up before the Russian readers of the French *philosophes*. But these were all abstract concepts which no one knew how to apply in Russia—in a country where human beings could be bought and sold at will and where equality before the law was a thing unknown.

When the French Revolution erupted and the caste system of the Ancient Regime was destroyed, making way for the ascendancy of a bourgeois society, the Russian devotees of Voltaire and his peers were scarcely capable of grasping the changes. Catherine II advocated, in a memorandum written in 1792, the dispatch of foreign troops "to rescue France from the bandits," to help restore the monarchy and maintain the Roman Catholic religion. "A principle to consider in this affair," she wrote, "is to be on guard against the frivolous and flighty spirit and the inborn recklessness of the French nation."

The social structure that emerged in Russia as the eighteenth century came to a close, its rigid simplicity, the stark division of society into free nobles and enslaved serfs, bore no resemblance to the European scene that had beckoned, for one hundred years, as the guiding source of so many varied modes of inspiration. The first warning that this ponderous and anomalous structure, resting on blatant injustice and inequality, could not endure had been the fierce and bloody peasant uprising led by Pugachev in 1773. It engulfed the entire southeastern region of the country and swept as far as the Urals, where industrial serfs joined the rural rebels in burning down mansions, devastating estates, and massacring landlords and masters by the score. A year of bloodshed and destruction passed before Pugachev was seized and executed, and peasant unrest continued into the following decades. The formidable task of dismantling the antiquated feudal structure of Russian society was bequeathed to the nineteenth century. And no issue dominated the lives of Russians in all walks of life as completely and as imperatively throughout that century as the question of how to break up the rigid mold, how to bridge the gaping chasm, how to gain the social cohesion that had been Muscovy's before the advent of Westernization. The cry "What should be done?" reverberated from decade to decade, and finally reached a crescendo in the title of one of Lenin's incendiary publications.

A Century of Mounting Maladjustments

Both distinctive features of nineteenth-century Russia, the growing and divisive complexity of society and the brilliance of its cultural achievements, sprang from the one central issue bequeathed by the preceding century: the conflict between servitude and liberty grown infinitely more complex now that Russia was no longer a novice in and an apprentice of Europe but an active participant in European affairs, drawn politically, militarily, economically, and culturally into the web spun by the acquisitive industrial society that had evolved there and was spreading so vigorously to all corners of the world, particularly to the American continent. Europe continued to act as the inspirational source for many a thought, achievement, and action, but the answer to the key problem in Russia, unique in its magnitude and unprecedented in human history—how to abolish the peculiar domestic form of serfdom, how to do away with feudal practices rampant on so large a scale, how to adapt to a market economy and an industrial and pecuniary order— could only be sought and found at home.

The first answer to the cry for action, the first hammer blow aimed at breaking up the rigid, anomalous social mold, was supplied by Catherine II's son Paul I, who succeeded her in 1796: curb the power of the nobility. But this was the answer of an unbalanced and thwarted man. Middle-aged when he ascended to the throne, embittered by years of neglect and seclusion forced upon him by a hostile and disdainful mother, Paul was bitterly resentful of everything Catherine's reign stood for. Determined to break the power of the nobility and to prevent further interferences in the question of Imperial succession, he issued a proclamation that henceforth the right of succession was to be lawfully transmitted from father to oldest son or, in the absence of sons, to the oldest brother of the deceased sovereign. Furthermore, Catherine's charter conferring upon the nobility the right of self-government was abolished. Though Paul's reign lasted but five years and ended, as he had feared it would, in assassination, the nobility never regained its former prominence. Its destiny, determined by the interaction of complex political, economic, and intellectual developments, was henceforth one of deepening decline. The monstrous, unbridled power attained by that class over the serfs in the later part of the eighteenth century, that grotesque caricature of freedom, was doomed.

Profound changes were taking place in the emotional and intellectual life of the aristocratic segment of Russian society. The failure of the French Revolution to vindicate man's rationality, the defeat of Napoleon on Russian soil through the heroic and concerted efforts of the Russian people, the spreading of romantic and nationalistic ideas that countered the cosmopolitan and mechanistic theses of the Enlightenment and stressed the uniqueness and plurality of individual cultures as living organisms—all these converged in a new way of seeing Europe. A small avant-garde within the nobility, defiantly rejecting further intellectual tutelage by the Government—a dependence this class had borne for a hundred years, sought to find its own way of interpreting the cataclysmic changes in contemporary Europe and its own answer to the question of what should be done to cure the diseased organism of Russian society. In a tragic paradox, perhaps brought on by its romantic aspirations, the new group leaped almost instantaneously from thought to action and entered upon the path of conspiracy and rebellion before its ideas had had time to mature. It began to lay the groundwork for a concerted and organized execution of conspiratorial plans. Perhaps the magnitude and kaleidoscopic swiftness of the new ideas born, the fierce aspirations voiced, and the political and economic changes instituted in contemporary Europe were more than the Russian mind could properly assess at the time. How should freedom be grafted to the body of Russian society? How should the serfs be freed, with land or without? Should Russia become a constitutional monarchy or a republic? Should she remain a centralized state or should the American principle of federalism be adopted? These and a host of related, unresolved questions assailed the conspirators, intoxicated with the magnitude of their projected reforms, yet lacking intellectual maturity, organizational experience, and unity of action.

The overthrow of the regime was attempted in December

1825 and proved abortive. The government responded with stern reprisals. One hundred twenty men were arrested and tried. Five were hanged, the rest banished to Siberia. And this tragic and noble group known as the Decembrists entered history under the name of the month when the revolt was staged rather than under the banner of their vague, contradictory, and crushingly weighty aspirations. Yet they were the founders of a new social group of utmost importance in Russian society and unique in the history of the human mind: the intelligentsia, a group of men aspiring to independent and reformatory thinking, free from Governmental supervision and in fierce opposition to it. What set them apart from European intellectuals was the fact that neither social origin nor material interests held the group together. Originally composed almost exclusively of nobles, the intelligentsia came to be complemented by members of lesser classes as the century progressed. To them all, thinking became an intoxicating experience, almost as important as living itself.

The preceding hundred years of secularization imposed on the Russian mind by the Government had not eradicated the centuries-old spiritual outlook of Muscovy. If the power of the Church had suffered severe setbacks under Peter the Great and his successors, if the dogmatic tenets of Orthodoxy had lost much of their previous preeminence, the moral and ethical Christian precepts underlying the dogma and addressed directly to the human individual had not. They now sprang to new life among the intelligentsia, enriched and revitalized by contacts with contemporary Western thought and the contention, formulated with such brilliance and diversity of arguments, that man was far more than a being of reason alone. But lacking a stable secular foundation on which to build and to grow, lacking the time-honored European traditions of skepticism, of objectivity, of dispassionate analyses and debate, mingling the quest for liberty with sentiments of compassion for the downtrodden, forever seeking an answer to the calls for action—how to alleviate the sufferings of the destitute, how to raise the masses from "the lower depths" of existence—Russian thought came to be marked by total devotion to an idea, not admitting any doubts, reservations, qualifications, or revisions. If reality proved an idea wrong—that is, inadequate for the pursuit of set ethical goals and practical reforms—it was discarded as emphatically and fiercely as it had been previously wholeheartedly and passionately adopted. Spectacular shifts and changes in prevailing ideas distinguished the evolution of Russian thought in the nineteenth century. And with mounting insistence demands were voiced by prominent leaders of the intelligentsia for a total destruction of the existing order rather than gradual reforms. The assassination in 1861 of Alexander II, who had raised in his own way the banner of freedom by liberating the serfs, luridly illuminated this trend.

If the emergence of the intelligentsia was an event of paramount importance in the evolving complexity of society, there was yet another trend of comparable significance in the early decades of the century, the growth of a bureaucracy. Each of the two sovereigns who succeeded Paul I, Alexander I and Nicholas I, assiduously built up this class, motivated by the need for a large corps of obedient civil servants to rule over an empire that now stretched from the Baltic to the Black Sea and to prepare for the abolition of serfdom in such a vast and diverse territory—a reform the Government had recognized as a matter of mounting necessity and the highest priority ever since the Pugachev uprising.

By the second quarter of the century one third of the population of Petersburg, the center of government, came to be composed of Government employees. From a city of palaces and private mansions the capital turned into a city of imposing official buildings, monuments, and parade grounds. In the provincial towns the houses of the mayor, the postmaster, the police officials, and other local dignitaries, not the residences of affluent merchants and traders, stood out as the most prosperous buildings in the community. The nobility provided a reservoir for the upper echelons of the civil service hierarchy, but the harmony between the Court and the nobles as a class that had prevailed in the later part of the eighteenth century was over. After the Decembrist uprising the Government never ceased to regard the newly emerged intelligentsia as a dangerous adversary to be watched and curbed.

Periods of cautious probing and preparatory planning alternated with decades of repression and hesitation before the Government finally proclaimed the Emancipation Act in 1861. At that time no word was probably repeated as frequently, as hopefully, and among as many different social strata of Russian society as the word freedom. But freedom from what? Freedom to do what? No concept proved more illusory and further from realization once the problem of shifting from a serf economy to a pecuniary order became fully apparent. When the Emancipation Act was implemented, it became evident that the peasant was far from free in practice even though he was declared free by law. For the land allotted to him by the Government he incurred a state debt which he had to pay in installments spread over forty-nine years. Only then would he, or his children, become the private owners of his land. Meanwhile, the land allotment was not turned over to him personally but to the commune of which he was a member, and the commune was made collectively responsible for the debts of its members. The commune became a fiscal and administrative unit filling the vacuum created by the removal of the authority of the landlord. It was no longer primarily concerned with the welfare of its members, but with the collection of monetary payments. The vitality of the commune depended on economic equality among its members, but the shift to pecuniary practices put an end to any equality, giving scope to the talents of the more astute and ruthless. The village elder, for one, now an official figure controlling the village funds, had ample opportunity for profitable personal transactions such as purchasing grain and cattle for a low price from a peasant in immediate need of cash and later reselling these items at a high profit.

The main effect of the Emancipation on the peasantry was a differentiation within its ranks: a minority, aptly named "kulaks" or "fists," who owed their upward movement to ruthless use of force and cunning, and a vast majority of destitute paupers. Since agricultural techniques in the village had hardly changed from the ancient three-field system which yielded no sizable surplus or produce for sale, peasant men by the thousands, in desperate need of money to keep up payments on their obligations, flocked to the factory gates and formed a vast reserve of cheap industrial labor, leaving cultivation of their land in the hands of the female members of their families.

The landowner too suffered depressive changes from the Emancipation. The transition from owning "souls" to handling money, the confrontation with a legally freed labor force, was an adjustment which only a minority of Russian landlords was able to perform. The average member of the landed gentry found himself at a loss as to how to treat hired help and how to extract financial profit from his land. A shortage of capital was only partly mitigated by the issue of redemption bonds to the landowners from the Government in payment for the land allotted to their former serfs. Many a landowner decided to sell his property, others mortgaged their land to the hilt. The differentiation within the ranks of the gentry became evident within the decade following the Emancipation. A deserted manor house or one badly in need of repairs, looming sadly in an untended park overgrown with weeds and brush, became a familiar landmark of the Russian countryside.

The commercial class emerged as the main beneficiary of the Emancipation. At last, its ranks steadily augmented by the kulaks who fought their way out of the village, it rose to a position of prominence and of rapidly expanding economic opportunities comparable to those the European bourgeoisie had enjoyed for more than a century. The plight of the peasant provided an ample reserve of cheap labor for factory and warehouse, while a stream of capital and a supply of modern machinery was readily offered by European bankers and industrialists eager to aid in the exploitation of Russia's vast and largely untapped natural resources.

The growth of Russia's industrial production began to

gather momentum after 1861 and reached a spectacular speed in the last decades of the century, surpassing the contemporary rate of European and even American advances. It was a triumphant march of the machine and owed much to imported technical improvements and progress in production methods. It was a march in which imported locomotives, steam engines, textile power looms, internal-combustion engines, and scores of other mechanical devices held the lead and were supplemented by a nascent domestic machine-building industry. The speed of mechanization led to a rapid differentiation within the ranks of the bourgeois class itself. For the new, powerful machines necessitated large capital investments which only the larger concerns were able to provide. As the nineteenth century neared its end, nearly half of the entire industrial labor force of roughly one and a half million workers was concentrated in the employ of large enterprises constituting only 4 percent of all industrial establishments.

An equally striking imbalance developed in the distribution of Russia's urban centers as a result of the coming of the railroad. For the construction of railroads did not come to Russia to supplement a network of commercial and industrial centers established in past centuries, as it had in Europe, but was telescoped into the same decades that brought the march of factory mechanization. The iron tracks spanned the land in long-distance transcontinental sweeps, converging in Moscow like the spokes of a wheel, linking the interior region with the frontiers at points of contact with Europe and Asia and connecting the forest belt of the North, the reservoir of construction material, with the black-soil belt of the South, Russia's granary.

Toward the end of the nineteenth century Moscow, with a population of one million people, was the only large city in the interior of the country. Most of the eighteen other large cities with a population of one hundred thousand or more stretched in a sweeping peripheral arc which began in the Northwest with Petersburg and its one and a quarter million inhabitants and ended with Nizhny Novgorod on the middle Volga in the East. These nineteen large cities housed six million people, or nearly half of the total urban population of European Russia. A large percentage of the other urban residents lived in small towns, many of them hardly distinguishable from good-sized villages. Bypassed by the railroads, all owed their state of neglect to the lag in the growth of domestic markets and of a local exchange of goods.

The result was that the coming of a pecuniary and industrial order to Russia and the formal abolition of serfdom failed completely to alleviate existing ills. Quite the contrary, it created new tensions, divides, and imbalances and aggravated social discord. The spirit of an acquisitive society, the idea of individual liberty as the lifeblood of economic and social life, the psychological atmosphere nurturing the quest for monetary gain which was flourishing in Europe and triumphant in America—none of this accompanied the abrupt and tumultuous advent of capital and machine in Russia.

The bourgeoisie, though not lacking in enterprise, practicality, and acquisitiveness, was wanting in solidarity. It gave little thought to itself as a class. The rapid differentiation within its ranks into large entrepreneurs and petty traders was only partly responsible for this attitude. Genealogically and socially closely linked to the peasantry, it retained many an ancient custom and belief rooted in that association. Paramount among these was the idea of the supremacy of the state, the state that for centuries had shaped the life of each component of Russian society. Both branches of the bourgeoisie, the large entrepreneur as well as the petty merchant, continued to look upon the Government as an omnipotent power, an institution not to be criticized or appealed to with demands for freedom of action, for laissez-faire, but a force to be allied with and obeyed. In spite of its constantly improving economic condition, the bourgeoisie was not yet prepared to raise its voice and attempt to play a part in the political life of the country, to say nothing of being ready to assume a posture of opposition or rebellion comparable to that of the French bourgeoisie.

Failing to see itself as a component part of society, as

dependent on the welfare of all other parts, the entrepreneurial class could not grasp the potential gains to be drawn from a prosperous working class and an expanding domestic market among that class and in the countryside—an idea so successfully applied by American industrialists and rooted in the Constitution of the United States, where resources were to be developed not for the benefit of one group or class but for the welfare of all. In a country accustomed to absolutism and autocratic rule the value of a command, the utility of force, the threat of punishment, and the techniques of coercion were better understood than the benefits to be derived from reciprocal consent, free agreement, and shared responsibility and prosperity.

But the greatest impediment the free spirit of an acquisitive society met was at the hands of the intelligentsia. While the Russian bourgeoisie was busily importing techniques and materiel for industrial growth, all the while neglecting to adopt the ideological foundations of the new machine age, neglecting to clamor for economic and political freedom, the Russian intelligentsia was actively opposing a way of life that stressed the statistics of profit and loss rather than humane concern for the condition of the poor. The intensity of this hostility was such that it prevented the formation of a united middle class in Russia, even after the reforms of the 1860s fostered the expansion of an exclusively "ideological" intelligentsia, striving for independent judgment and thought, into a "working" intelligentsia, men of liberal professions who were earning a living by intellectual work.

The reforms that followed immediately upon the Emancipation of the serfs opened a vast field of activity for members of the medical, educational, and legal professions. Most questions related to local community life in the countryside—schools, hospitals, dispensaries, road construction, fire insurance—became the concern of the newly formed Zemstvos, elected bodies of local landlords and members of the peasant communes. At the same time the judicial reform of 1864 introduced the jury system, justices of the peace, and a formal bar for lawyers. But even the "working" intelligentsia remained largely hostile to the world of business, industry, and finance.

The steps toward modernization undertaken by the Government were countered by policies of far graver portent that pointed in the opposite direction and greatly impeded the dismantling of the ancient structure of Russian society. One, already mentioned, was the retention of the peasant commune for another half century that was written into the Emancipation Act. Another was the Government's half-hearted support of the Zemstvos, its withholding of financial assistance. The Zemstvos' budget rested solely on taxing local real estate and their work was, hence, impeded by the same problem that plagued post-Emancipation peasantry and nobility alike—a scarcity of monetary revenues and the depressed state of Russian agriculture. The emerging network of schools and medical centers staffed with poorly paid and overworked pedagogical and medical personnel remained inadequate to provide the rural population with anything but the most rudimentary educational and health-care facilities.

By the end of the nineteenth century 80 percent of Russia's population was still agricultural, and it was the cruel face that life wore for these rural masses that held the professional attention and the artistic imagination of the educated segment of society. Folklore motifs, momentous events from the history of the people, and scenes from the blighted contemporary life of the peasants were recreated on the canvasses of Russia's painters. Folksong melodies and ancient church chants were woven into the composition of Russian musicians. But it was the men of letters who attacked most forcefully the machinery of a society that appeared unable to provide an equitable distribution of the means of existence, unable to secure material and spiritual nourishment for its people.

Chekhov's life span encompassed the most dramatic, critical stages of this century of mounting imbalances. He was born in 1860, on the eve of the Emancipation of the serfs, began to write in 1880, on the eve of the assassination of

Alexander II, and died in 1904, on the eve of the first revolution heralding the beginning of a new era of worldwide upheavals and the involvement of Russia in the bloody international vortex.

The range of his vision was extraordinary. No aspect of the mounting drama during his lifetime escaped his observant eye, no facet of divisiveness or malfunction remained beyond his notice, no locale languishing in stunted growth or flushed into thriving bloom was missing from the map drawn by his creative imagination. He knew them all: the small provincial towns bypassed by the railroad tracks and vegetating in somnolent stupor, the pulsing vigor of Moscow and of the large peripheral cities; the dilapidated country estates inhabited by perplexed and helpless owners, the bureaucrats, their egos monstrously swollen by the sense of power and of their own importance; the impecunious downtrodden, and self-effacing little clerks; the rural paupers starving in their villages or knocking at the factory gates; the shrewd and ruthless merchants and the rapacious kulaks avidly counting their profits; the doctors and teachers in their back-breaking predicaments and humanitarian concerns. Chekhov's ear was attuned to the infernal din and surging uproar of industrial endeavor and his creative thoughts reached out to ponder the effects of the formidable new machinery on man's natural environment as well as on man himself.

Freedom Coveted or Superfluous?

If the nineteenth century was a unique and extraordinary period of Russian history, the role of literature in that period was equally unique and extraordinary. The intellectual landscape was a teeming battleground with a fierce contest waged on several fronts and yielding explosive encounters. There was the spirited, at times acerbic, sparring between two generations of the intelligentsia; there was also conflict between individual groups of contemporaries defending opposing convictions. Even the views of a given intellectual could register, at times, radical and abrupt changes. But the most momentous and persistent confrontation occurred between the Government and the intelligentsia as a whole. Locked in the dualism of cautious liberalization and tenacious protection of the bastion of autocracy, the government staunchly and consistently defended its position against the intelligentsia. The idea of free inquiry, of unfettered expression of individual opinions and the right to criticize the government, was deemed incompatible with the principle of autocracy.

The official view was repeatedly reiterated throughout the century by prominent Government officials. In the early decades it was most forcefully formulated by Count Uvarov, Minister of Education, who proclaimed that his aim was "to prolong Russia's youth by some fifty years" and to shield her from the corroding influence of contemporary Western ideas—liberal as well as socialist. In the last two decades the official stand was cast into even harsher and more uncompromising terms by the powerful Chief Procurator of the Holy Synod, Konstantin Pobedonostsev, who disclaimed that any benefits could be derived from education. Since the majority of the population lived by the work of its hands, it was in need of vocational and physical training rather than intellectual development and stimulation. "The press," he thundered in his corrosive and strident eloquence, was "the organized judgment of others; parliamentarism the greatest falsehood of our times, and the idea of Liberty, Equality, Fraternity a monstrous generality in no way related to actual life."

The Government's arsenal in the combat consisted of a wide range of weapons, from wary vigilance and police surveillance of the enemy camp to arrests, imprisonments, trials, exile, and even executions. But no official measure affected the channels of Russian thought more deeply and decisively than the weapon of censorship, the Government's policy pursued throughout the century that no man was free to say what he liked in print, be it in books, pamphlets, periodicals, or daily newspapers, without prior official permission. This elevated the realm of literature to unprecedented importance. For it was harder for a censor to take exception to thoughts transposed into the key of fiction than to ideas expressed in a political, social, or economic vernacular. It was easier to voice criticism of the regime and of contemporary life if it was expressed by a poet, a novelist, a playwright, or a literary critic, even though, as Vladimir Nabokov expressed it, all had "to knock at the holy gate of the censorship to be let into the Heavenly Kingdom of Publication." Not one of Russia's prominent men of letters escaped the repressive interferences of the censor ranging from demands to delete a word or a paragraph or to change the turn of a plot to total rejection of a submitted manuscript, or even to the suspension of a journal's publication. And the personal lives of the greatest among these men were deeply affected by punitive and repressive actions of the Government. A glance at the fate of Pushkin and Dostoevsky will suffice. Following the clandestine circulation of his early poems against autocracy and serfdom, Pushkin was banished to Southern Russia in 1820 at the age of twenty-one, and remained under Governmental surveillance for the rest of his life. Dostoevsky, while a member of the Petrashevsky circle of young socialists, was arrested in 1849 and condemned to endure a sham execution before being sent to Siberia for four years of hard labor followed by five years as an army private.

Not entertainment, not artistic detachment, not esthetically and imaginatively pleasurable creations were expected from its writers by the literate segment of Russian society, but rather social and moral commitments, concern for the evils that fettered and crippled human beings, leadership in the combat against repression and ethically relevant answers to the question of how to live and what to do to bring light to the Russian "Kingdom of Darkness." While in nineteenth-century Europe prominent writers sprang largely from the middle classes and focused on secular issues and rational expression, the distinctive features of Russian literature of the century were the moral and spiritual problems and reli-

gious quests which elevated it to world renown. The heroes of
European novels moved in the milieu of a cruel but stable
and solidly grounded world. No tremors presaging the catas-
trophic quakes of the next century were in evidence. But the
Russian writers felt the underground rumblings with seis-
mographic sensitivity.

Dmitri Merezhkovsky made the arresting observation
that Russia had never produced a figure comparable to
Homer, Raphael, or Leonardo da Vinci, artists who harmoniously synthesized and embodied the creative forces of the
respective nations they sprang from. Tolstoy and Dostoevsky, he said, were "too complex, frightening, and muti-
nous" to be considered as representatives of Russia's creative totality, and Pushkin "was but a spark." An astute
observation this, illuminating the discordant complexity,
ferment, and turbulence of nineteenth-century Russia, its
atmosphere unconducive to inspirational serenity and tranquil creativity, but breeding instead a sense of uneasy foreboding, a penchant for encompassing critical assessments
and reflections about where the world as a whole was
headed.

The searching examination which Europe began to be
subjected to is a salient indicator of the course Russia's men
of letters chose to embark upon. Should Europe continue to
be a source of emulation as it had been in the eighteenth
century, a vigorous fount of new mores, gadgets, institutions, and ideas to be imported and copied? Or was Europe
perhaps an aging organism that had taken a wrong turn in
its old age? Should further entanglement with its decadent
culture be shunned? If we accept Merezhkovsky's view that
Pushkin was "but a spark," considering the tragic brevity of
his life span, the brilliance of that spark and the vastness of
the terrain it illuminated must be stressed. None of Russia's
writers has since given us a more dispassionate and sweeping, though pithy, terse, and succinct, view of the cultural
transformation the consciousness of Western man had
undergone after the passing of the Middle Ages.

Pushkin's four "Little Tragedies," all written within two

weeks during the wondrous burst of creative energy known as the "Boldino autumn" of 1830, rank among his greatest artistic achievements. In miraculous flashes of insight Pushkin apprehended the very essence and depth of the transformation Europe's spirit had undergone. He drew a detached, concise, composite image of modern man as he had emerged shedding medieval shackles, questing frantically for personal liberty, repudiating transcendence, extolling reason, propelled by an exuberant feeling of strength and confidence, seeking knowledge, adventure, pleasure, and gratification of all his desires.

The themes of the "Little Tragedies" are all drawn directly from Western history. The chief protagonist of the first dramatic work is representative of the changing European milieu. *The Covetous Knight* is a Flemish baron who has painstakingly and laboriously amassed a large fortune in the early days of the new, slowly burgeoning pecuniary economy. The main characters in the second and third works are culled from the annals of European culture— *Mozart and Salieri* and Don Juan in *The Stone Guest*. Finally, *The Feast in Time of the Plague* is Pushkin's "translation" of one scene from John Wilson's three-act play *The City of the Plague*, written in 1816 and set in London during the epidemic that ravaged that city in the middle of the seventeenth century.

The climax of *The Covetous Knight*, according to Dostoevsky one of the crowning achievements of Pushkin, is the baron's monologue delivered while he is revelling in the sight of his open trunks filled with gold coins. Each sentence is packed with titanic exultation. The baron's conscience is silenced. He is unmoved by the thought that each coin represents tears, blood, and sweat shed by the victims of his greed. He is intoxicated with the feeling of power which the sight of his wealth evokes. And as the heaps of gold gleam in the soft, flickering candlelight that casts mysterious shadows along the walls of the treasure vault, he utters a triumphant cry: "I reign supreme! What magic glitter!"

The symbols of man's proud withdrawal and intoxication

with his power in this dramatic work are solid and concrete—the subterranean treasure vault and the gleaming
heaps of gold. In the second of the "Little Tragedies" the
symbols of isolation are intangible and fluid. The haughty,
morose, withdrawn musician Salieri lives in an artificial
enclosure of dogged perseverance and assiduous application
mastering the technique of music, the "algebra of harmony." He is consumed by acute and pulsing envy of his
friend Mozart, the serene, carefree, and gregarious genius
whose effortless, dazzling, God-given creativity affronts the
plodding endeavors of the less-endowed mortal. Posing as a
heroic defender of art, as a loyal "servant of music," the
vengeful Salieri poisons the "useless" Mozart in order to
eliminate a rival whom he views as an obstruction of his own
reach for the rank of genius. Salieri's final words betray
neither remorse nor compassion for the victim of his crime.

Salieri's transgression is singular and vindictive. Don
Juan's is perpetual and all encompassing. In his boundless
freedom, in his scorn of Christian ethics, he recognizes no
law but that of gratifying his unlimited sexual desires.
Without scruples or remorse, knowing nothing of sin, he
lives in the intoxication of his momentary choice. After a
fleeting pause of regret remembering "the poor Inesa," who
was killed by her jealous husband, Pushkin's Don Juan
rushes to embrace Laura, heedlessly killing her present suitor, Don Carlos, on the way. Don Juan had already killed
Don Carlos's brother, the Commodore Alvaro, and the next
target of his mad pursuits is the Commodore's widow, Dona
Anna. He confronts her when she comes to mourn and pray
at her husband's sepulchre, which is adorned by the imposing statue of the deceased. Don Juan's invitation to the
statue to come stand guard at the door of Dona Anna's bed
chamber and watch him make love to her is far more than
the prank of a godless adventurer. The fatal confrontation
with the great stone figure of death is a last fearless, arrogant shout of defiance flung by an individual who deems
himself the equal of God.

The last of the "Little Tragedies" is a final hymn to the

roused secular energies of modern man, a final challenge to transcendence. The mood of resignation pervading John Wilson's play, the theme that death from the plague comes quicker and is easier to bear than death from many other causes, is missing from Pushkin's "translation." The scene is a rousing feast in honor of the plague held by a group of men and women in an open street in London, away from the desolation, the deadly emptiness, and the contaminated air of their respective homes. It is an exuberant and fearless feast extolling "the inexplicable fascination held by mortal dangers for the human heart"—the thrill of battle, of violent storms at sea, of destructive tropical hurricanes and the deadly breath of the plague—"a pawn of immortality perhaps!" In vain a priest attempts to break up the monstrous feast of these "godless madmen." His entreaties to disperse, to revert to mourning for the dead and to dwell on the beatitude of life hereafter, go unheeded.

Aside from the beauty of the expressive verbal economy, the dazzling brilliance of Pushkin's terse reflections on the European scene springs from the fact that the salient traits of a whole historical era—one that Russia had missed—are compressed and magically brought to life in his protagonists. With unsurpassed brevity and detachment the poet etches in a few powerful strokes the contours of the new human being that had emerged in Europe with the advent of the Renaissance, a being driven by a compelling quest for freedom. That there was no fertile ground for comparable urges in Russia, that servitude gripped his native land, Pushkin had expressed in his earliest creations, a prelude in verse to the abortive uprising of the Decembrists. His youthful, impassioned, poetic cries for freedom, equating autocracy with villainy, the gentry's mores with barbaric tyranny and the peasant's lot with slavery, had earned him the displeasure of the authorities from the start and sealed his fate. They laid the foundation for punitive actions and initiated an official surveillance that plagued the poet to the end of his life.

There is none of the condensed distillation of Pushkin's

thoughts on Europe in his image of Russia. It is a crowded canvas teeming with brightly differentiated figures drawn from all walks and spheres of life, each a unique human being, each blazingly alive, and each made immortal by the magic wand of its creator. The poet drew inspiration from every conceivable source accessible to his creative genius— from his own times and surroundings, from historical annals, from folklore, from mythology. His penetrating vision perceived ancient springs deeply rooted in his native soil and clashing with the hasty importations from Europe beginning with the days of Peter the Great. But the figure of the Tsar whose iron will set Russia on a compulsory and compelling course of Westernization towers over the prodigious variety of Pushkin's personages, an implacable, admirable, and redoubtable figure.

There are two works central to Pushkin's thoughts concerning Europe's impact on Russia's destiny and both rank among his triumphant achievements, alongside his "Little Tragedies" and their reflections on the rise of individual freedom in the Western world. One is *Evgeny Onegin*, begun in 1823; the other is *The Bronze Horseman* , written ten years later. Onegin's first name is also given to the protagonist of the latter work, who is pitched against the awesome bronze equestrian statue of Tsar Peter. Pushkin justifies this choice with a casual remark that the name "is agreeable to the ear" and, moreover, "a longstanding favorite of my pen." But there is a deeper connection. Both Evgenys are victims of circumstances born of Europe's impact on Russia. Onegin's character is deformed and his life is ruined by the superficial graft of Western culture on his consciousness, which is unable to assimilate the import into the domestic setting of servitude and to adapt it to native cultural roots; his emotions atrophy under his abortive education. The second Evgeny is smitten by one massive, devastating blow—he is driven to insanity and death by the violent flood that inundated Petersburg, the new link to Europe, in 1824. Military, political, and cultural exigencies dictated Tsar Peter's choice of the low, marshy, but ice-free estuary of the Neva for the new capital, though the locale was exposed to the danger of periodic floods and a challenge to human safety.

In the first work, a portrait of Lord Byron and a bust of Napoleon adorn the study of Onegin, both effigies frowning, no doubt, at the mental torpor and intellectual immaturity displayed by the room's occupant, that "Muscovite draped in Harold's mantle." Onegin lacks the drive and training to gain more than a random, superficial acquaintance with European thought. Not only ideas but all the luxurious amenities surrounding him are imported—the expensive accoutrements of his dressing room, his impeccable clothes that mask him as a "London dandy," his food (the truffles served with the rare roast beef, the pineapple, the champagne that grace his table). But this lifestyle rests on the shaky foundation of a disintegrating serf economy that is beginning to crack under the advance of a monetary order. Onegin lives on the free toil of his serfs and, following in his father's and his uncle's footsteps, on money borrowed by mortgaging his land with little concern over how to repay it.

Onegin is the new type of individual that Pushkin saw emerging in Russia in the early decades of the nineteenth century. The fruits of Western civilization were handed to him, almost literally, on a silver platter. But he has no understanding of the springs and roots that, for centuries, had nurtured these treasures. He knows how to spend money but he knows nothing about accumulating it, about the thrill of toil and perseverance, about "the magic glitter" of gold coins stored in treasure vaults, the allure of personal advance and power, the defiant exuberance of individual liberation. He does not even seek gratification of his desires any more, for his appetite was jaded at the early age of eighteen. He yawns his way through endless social entertainments and listlessly endures theatrical performances. Even his Don Juanesque amorous escapades have come to bore him and his heart has turned to stone. Not as a rival does he kill his friend Lensky in a duel, but in a thoughtless, senseless moment of ennui. As if in exasperation Pushkin parts with this misfit, dropping him at the feet of Tatiana, the woman who loves him. Onegin had coldly rejected her love when she had offered it to him as a young, naive, and trusting girl, ignorant at the time of the depth of Onegin's emptiness and inner deformity. Meeting her again some years later as a married woman who holds a prominent position in Petersburg society, Onegin is full of regrets and claims now to be in love with her, but is unequivocally and sadly rejected.

The second Evgeny is treated by Pushkin with great compassion. The obscure little clerk who holds an insignificant job "somewhere" loses his fiancée Parasha in the devastating inundation of Petersburg and his mind gives way under the double impact of grief and shock, witnessing the progress of the storm and the violence of its destruction. But the strains of sympathy are muted, for the poem is primarily an ode to the beauty of the new capital, a hymn of praise for Tsar Peter, for his vision, courage, and drive in creating the city, one hundred years earlier, taming the elements though sacrificing thousands of lives to overcome the adversities of its construction. Pushkin gives free rein to his admiration of the severe and graceful lines of this European transplant, this visionary dream turned to stone under the guidance of prominent foreign architects. And when the raging waters of the autumnal flood advance on their destructive course, it is triumphant majesty and power that Pushkin detects in the bronze statue of the Tsar, towering above the chaos as if undaunted in his westward course. But the Tsar's vision focused on a horizon of progress and reform of the nation as a whole, visible through the new "window to Europe," brushing aside concern for the welfare of individual human beings.

After the flood subsides "my poor, poor Evgeny," demented by the ordeal and in a state of amnesia, a helpless, abandoned, and destitute wreck, spends weeks and months wandering aimlessly about and gradually losing his human cast. When chance brings him to the foot of Tsar Peter's statue, his mind clears for a fleeting moment of sanity and in a flash of recognition Evgeny perceives the founder of the city in this perilous locale as the true source of his own

bereavement and disaster. But the burst of clarity, of seething bitterness and resentment, is instantly submerged again
in a renewed upsurge of madness and hallucinations that
the statue of the Tsar, enraged by the affront, is leaving its
pedestal and setting out to pursue the terrified, fleeing little
man, the hoofs of the bronze horse thundering along in a
wild chase. Can a greater contrast to Pushkin's Don Juan
and his ebullient, arrogant, mocking challenge of the Stone
Guest be imagined? In the following spring Evgeny's body is
found and buried on one of the small outlying islands of the
Neva estuary. The final lines of the poem devoted to this
burial ground ring, in their stark and grim simplicity, like a
dirge to human freedom.

And indeed, the theme of freedom and reflections on its
essence retreated for a time and the leading theme of pre-
Emancipation literature after Pushkin became not what
freedom could do to or for the individual, but what servitude
had done to human beings, to masters as well as to serfs.
Onegin's descendants are especially brought into the lime-
light. The absence of heroism, the absence of that exuberance and surging energy that Pushkin portrayed in his
European protagonists, distinguishes them all. The inertia,
the immobility of these frustrated men living in helpless,
impotent isolation from their native soil, has earned them
the epithet "superfluous men," and is mirrored in the devices
employed by Lermontov, Turgenev, and Goncharov. It is as
if we had entered a picture gallery, where verbal manipula-
tion is used to achieve the effects of painting.

Sardonically Lermontov calls his Pechorin—handsome,
cold, ruthless, and cynical, drowning his discontent in restless travels—"a hero of our times, a compound portrait of all
the vices of our generation." Turgenev's Rudin is capable of
charming and fascinating a circle of provincial gentry with
his musical eloquence, discoursing melodiously about philosophical platitudes gleaned during his sojourn at German
universities. But Turgenev is merciless in disclosing this
"tumbleweed's" inherent inability to take roots, to act, to
work, to make decisions. His senseless death is a final par-

ody of bravura—he is felled on the 1848 barricades in Paris while brandishing a red flag. Lavretsky, hero of Turgenev's *A Nest of Gentlefolk*, is another victim of his cosmopolitan upbringing and comes to resign himself to the modest goal of plowing his native Russian soil, "to plow it as well as possible."

And finally there is Goncharov's Oblomov in the novel of the same name—"oblomok" meaning debris, a fragment of waste—perenially draped in his dressing gown, spending his days in a prone position, believing that work is a scourge and happiness is rest and inactivity. Traveling, so widely practiced by European Romantics and by the older generation of superfluous men in Russia, is anything but enticing for Oblomov. Forced to move from the apartment he occupies, he is filled with the genuine distress that provides the key to the plot of the entire novel. This epitome of inertia is drawn with such artistic depth of penetration that it conveys the impression of a sculpture rather than of a painting. The figure of Oblomov grows far beyond the bounds of his Russian setting and becomes a universal symbol of human indolence and indecisiveness.

And then we enter another gallery, the horror chamber of Gogol's fantastic world of monstrous phantoms and hyperbolically drawn misfits inhabiting Russia's stagnating provincial towns, run by incompetent and corrupt officials, and the small, landed estates whose owners vegetate on the free labor of their serfs. Chichikov, the central character of *Dead Souls* , is trying to amass a fortune not by storing gold coins in subterranean treasure vaults but by purchasing and then mortgaging the "souls" of serfs deceased but still registered as living in the last census. But it is the owners he approaches with his fraudulent scheme whose souls have withered and atrophied in a bog of vulgarity, mediocrity, and triteness. With infinite care for realistic detail, heaping synonym upon synonym, stringing out attributes and situations that rise into the realm of ridicule, Gogol presents us with a procession of specters magically alive and real, each in the grip of one vice born of their environment, each endowed with a

manner of speech and behavior reflecting that vice, saturated with it. There is—to mention just the chief protagonists—the empty, dreamy sentimentality of Manilov,
the abysmal ignorance and stupidity of Korobochka, the
querulous arrogance of Nozdrev, the ludicrous and uncouth
coarseness of Sobakevich, and the passionate miserliness of
Pliushkin.

As the age of money and machine began to draw Russia
vigorously into its orbit after the Emancipation, freedom
failed to emerge as a driving force. The commercial class
itself lacked comprehension of individual liberty as the lifeblood of economic and social progress. The idea of the
supremacy of the State over the worth of the human individual, so brilliantly embodied in Pushkin's *Bronze Horseman*
in 1833, still held sway over the mentality of that class in the
later part of the century and prompted it to rely heavily on
the technique of coercion and the use of force. Hostility
toward the inhumanity and drive of these new beneficiaries
of European civilization, of the imported tools of technology
and finance, became the hallmark of three prominent writers who took a hard look at the world of Russia's merchants
and industrialists; the playwright Alexander Ostrovsky, the
satirist Mikhail Saltykov-Shchedrin, and the novelist Maxim
Gorky. All three regarded rural serfdom as superseded by a
new type of servitude—bondage to money and machine.

Hostility was evidenced, to begin with, by their choice of
locale and theme. All three shunned descriptions of the big
cities and of the large entrepreneurial class, and concentrated their attention on the small, sleepy, and stagnant
provincial towns bypassed by the growing transcontinental
railroad. All three writers peopled these towns with uncouth,
despotic, mercenary masters and their helpless, crushed victims. The hopeless uselessness and the harm perpetrated by
these communities is stressed by the names of the imaginary
towns: Idiotville, Sleepy Hollow, Thieftown, Cigarette-butt
town. How restrained and impartial Sinclair Lewis's "Gopher
Prairie" and even Charles Dickens's "Coketown" seem in
comparison to these contemptuous and abusive appellations.

The merchant and factory owner is seen as an unlimited autocrat who "reigns supreme" in his house, his store, and his plant. He issues orders and expects unconditional obedience and submission from everyone living under his roof. The sole purpose of his existence is to make money, to perpetually increase his wealth. He is unable to comprehend or to appreciate anything beyond the narrow confines of profit-and-loss arithmetic. No expedient, not even dishonesty, is neglected to increase profits. Like his sixteenth-century forefathers he distrusts knowledge and is suspicious of those who seek it. Knowledge, he maintains, does not increase wealth and may, on the contrary, have dangerous effects on people: it can impede their business prowess.

Gorky's novels and Ostrovsky's plays are weapons of social criticism as sharp as Saltykov-Shchedrin's satires. Central to the structure of their plots is the tragedy of the victims of this world of greed, dishonesty, depraved cruelty, and uncouth ignorance. A successful rebellion against or an escape from the crippling and soul-crushing bondage is the exception and does not hold the author's prime attention. But when they speak of the frustration, disasters, and defeat of the victims of brutality and oppression, the writing swells into a grim and accusing dirge. Katerina, heroine of Ostrovsky's drama *The Storm*, takes her life to escape the unbearable brutality and inflexible tyranny of her mother-in-law, the merchant widow Kabanova (from *kaban*, a wild boar). Foma Gordeev, the title figure of one of Gorky's novels, wages a losing battle trying to free himself from the chains of his father's business, a lucrative boat and barge enterprise on the Volga. After a final, violent outburst he is sent to a mental hospital from which he returns several years later, spent, worn, subdued, and incoherent.

Business achievements and financial successes are never commented upon as anything but fundamental mistakes and tragic failures. Gorky's Ilia Artamonov, an up-and-coming industrialist, boasts that he is not interested in winning the affection of his fellow townsmen for "he knows how to break people." But he bleeds to death from a ruptured blood vessel after straining to move an overturned piece of newly arrived machinery. "I was mistaken" are his last whispered words, "dear God, so mistaken!"

The vehemence of the rejection the bourgeois world met at the hands of Russia's writers was matched by the enthusiasm the intelligentsia mustered for the socialist ideas that filtered into Russia along with the scientific and technological imports of post-Emancipation times. The new generation of intellectuals, no longer exclusively composed of gentry in its social composition, poured scorn over the ideal and effete superfluous men of the past, over phrasemongers such as Rudin and corpulent hulks such as Oblomov. But this did not bring them any closer to the sense of personal liberation and exuberant ascent experienced by modern man in the West and so brilliantly sketched by Pushkin in his "Little Tragedies." Embracing socialism as the answer to solving Russia's divisiveness and imbalances meant substituting egalitarian ideals for the lure of freedom. "Give me equality or give me death" would have been a slogan readily accepted and increasingly popular among the intellectual circles as the century moved toward its end.

It was Turgenev who portrayed in his post-Emancipation novels, particularly in *Fathers and Sons* and *Virgin Soil*, the peculiar, evolving amalgam of Western rationalism and materialism with Russian maximalism and moral quests: the Nihilists of the 1860s and the Populists of the 1870s. The former were bent on destroying all irrational prejudices and social conventions impeding Russia's advance on the road toward a just, socialist society; the latter sought justice by heeding their awakened conscience and attempting to rescue the destitute peasantry. For centuries Russian culture had developed at the expense of the broad masses of the people. The time had come to repay that silent creditor, the peasant who was struggling for survival on a subsistence level in the village. By the thousands the Populists invaded the countryside, arriving as teachers, doctors, clerks, and heavy laborers, wearing peasant dress and frequently equipped with false passports.

The undisguised suspicion, incomprehension, and hostility of the peasantry only increased the fervor of these tormented moralists and led them to shift their efforts from peaceful educational endeavors to revolutionary tracts, political propaganda, and attempts to rouse the peasantry to violent revolt. When the reception accorded the Populists by the peasants continued to be hostile, the more radical segment of the Russian intelligentsia shifted, in the eighties and nineties, to Marxist doctrines and transferred their propaganda efforts from the village to the factory.

Like the intelligentsia, the industrial workers as a class had developed independently from Governmental control and supervision. They too were a class whose mentality and way of life had been molded by environment and circumstances rather than under State tutelage and pressure as had been the case with noble, merchant, and peasant alike. Seeing himself victimized by machine and by employer, the industrial worker proved receptive to the intelligentsia's propaganda of revolt and to Marxist prophecies that the prevailing order was doomed to collapse and give way to a socialist reign of equality and justice. The coalition between these two groups resulted in the formation of a new and formidable power steering the country toward the revolutionary upheavals of the twentieth century. It accomplished what the individual, "poor, poor Evgeny" in Pushkin's *The Bronze Horseman*, had been powerless to stage—to rise in a free, indignant rebellion against oppression by the State. At long last the statue came crashing down and the fury of the flood swept triumphantly over the land.

II

Tolstoy, Dostoevsky, and Chekhov

Russian literature had travelled a long distance from the extraordinary beauty and harmonious majesty of Pushkin's poetic voice, from his brief, detached, and brilliant flashes of insight into European history and culture to the tormented groans of the Populists and the harsh clamor for revolutionary violence rising as the nineteenth century neared its end. The highest peaks along that road were those of Tolstoy and Dostoevsky, universally regarded as the foremost literary figures in nineteenth-century Russia. Both were men of the second half of that century, when Russia was no longer a bystander or an apprentice to Europe, but a participant, a member of the European community. Both authors saw the country drawn in to the perilous course of Western civilization. Both have a direct and illuminating bearing on Chekhov.

In a brilliant lecture on "Chekhov as a Thinker" given in

the fall of 1904, the theologian Sergius Bulgakov stated that "after Tolstoy and Dostoevsky Chekhov is *the* writer of greatest philosophical importance."[1] This in spite of the fact that in format and style Chekhov's short stories are as far removed from the epic breadth of Tolstoy's novels as his fragile, musically orchestrated plays are from the feverish, dramatic dialogues which fill Dostoevsky's novelistic tragedies. This in spite of the fact that Chekhov's quiet voice, muted by restraint and understatement, never rose with the finality and peremptory insistence of Tolstoy's pronoucements or with Dostoevsky's urgent sense of foreboding and premonition.

In spite of the fundamental divergence in their conception of existence, both Tolstoy and Dostoevsky founded their literary creations on a loud indictment of a humanity grown materialistic, egoistic, and above all godless. Both claimed that without God man could not remain human and society could not be saved from decay. Both searched for a meaning to life that could not be destroyed by death, for a way to fuse human time with eternity. And both believed that Christ offered man such a way to reach for the heights of infinity, though Tolstoy denied the divinity of Christ as emphatically as Dostoevsky ardently strove to affirm it. The moral balance between freedom and equality was lifted by the two writers into the sphere of Christian precepts.

The customary division of Tolstoy's creative life into two distinct segments—one a period of fictional, novelistic productivity, the other a time of concentration on discursive, didactic writing—tends to obscure the remarkable consistency and continuity in his basic beliefs. From the earliest period of his intellectual development Tolstoy, a man of the second half of the nineteenth century, avowed his kinship with the ideas of the eighteenth-century Enlightenment, particularly with Rousseau's doctrine of the power of reason and belief in the innate goodness of man, an affinity he retained to the end of his life. "It is as if Tolstoy had no ties with the preceding generation, as if he had resolutely turned away from his fathers [the Romantics] and returned to his grandfathers."[2] The urge to found a new religion of Christ, "purged of faith and mystery, a practical religion which does not promise future bliss but gives bliss on earth," is expressed in Tolstoy's diary as early as 1855, long before he had begun work on *War and Peace*, his first major fictional masterpiece.[3]

The Gospel and Rousseau were the two great influences on Tolstoy's reformatory endeavors. Though it must be mentioned that the idea of liberty as formulated by Rousseau, his view of an individual's free will finding expression in *"la volonté générale,"* was curiously ignored by Tolstoy in favor of Rousseau's concept of equality. Tolstoy's insensitivity to the idea of freedom is attested by the fact that the problem of serfdom is generally ignored by him in his fiction as well as in his moral tracts.

War and Peace is a huge, crowded canvas thronged with characters almost as numerous and as individualized as life itself, yet Tolstoy's basic view of human existence and of the relation between the temporal and the timeless orders is clearly revealed even there. It is a delusion, he claims, to imagine that heroic personalities determine historical events. For absolute continuity is the main attribute of any motion, of the flow of time and of the march of history. It is wrong to look for the beginning of any event, for a beginning does not exist. An individual always stands in the midst of moving events which spring from such multiplicity and interaction of causes that no human intellect is capable of seeing, understanding, or controlling them. History moves onward through the infinitely intricate tide of the lives of ordinary men and women.

This egalitarian notion of historical evolution was supplemented by Tolstoy's adherence to Rousseau's equally levelling, rationalistic concept of man as an individual. All men are born good and every single one is equally endowed with the divine spark of reason. Reason is "a particle of God" and enables love, that essence of the human soul, to manifest itself and to do good. Tolstoy rejected, with Rousseau, evil as part of man's original nature. Evil stemmed from the atrophy of reason. To do evil was irrational and stupid. A vein of this conceptual thought that was to become dominant in the later period if Tolstoy's moral preaching also runs deep in *War and Peace*. On his deathbed Prince Andrey becomes its mouthpiece. "God is love and to die means that I, a particle of love, shall return to the common and eternal source.... To love all, always to sacrifice one's self for the sake of love, means to love no one, means to abrogate this terrestrial life," he thinks.[4] And the sense of impending entry into the realm of eternal brotherly union and impersonal immortality lifts the weight and shackles of temporal, individual existence and the fear of death from Prince Andrey's soul.

In his famous essay on Tolstoy, "The Hedgehog and the Fox," Isaiah Berlin presents a uniquely perceptive analysis of Tolstoy's shift from literature to polemical writing, of the conflict between his artistic gifts and his philosophical opinions. According to the Greek poet Archilocus, "The fox knows many things, but the hedgehog knows one big thing." Tolstoy believed in being a hedgehog, though by nature he was a fox. "No author who has ever lived has showed such powers of insight into the variety of life—the differences, the contrasts, the collisions of persons and things and situations, each apprehended in its absolute uniqueness and conveyed with a degree of direction and a precision of concrete imagery to be found in no other writer."[5]

It was in the early 1880s that a tormenting sense of guilt, comparable to the violent moral qualms that had given the Populist movement its impetus a decade earlier, assailed Tolstoy and transformed the "fox" into the "hedgehog." It was a stricken conscience that cried out that it was wrong to belong to the class of the rich, educated, and free and to live by the sweat of destitute, ignorant, and oppressed people; a tortured conscience that urged Tolstoy the writer to turn from fiction to didactic works and to start propagating directly and urgently how life should be transformed here and now. The fact that Tolstoy had already attained worldwide recognition as a foremost novelist helped to keep the censor at bay, though several of his most powerful attacks on the state of human affairs saw the first light of publication abroad.

Tolstoy the moralist stripped reality of its complexity and intricate maze of relations and interdependence and reduced it to a design of stark simplicity and rationality. Love and reason became the two cornerstones of his views on the human condition. He came to see life cleft into two antipodal segments—body and soul, carnal existence and spiritual experience, intelligence and reason, egoism and altruism. Intelligence is an attribute of carnal existence. It enables a man to apprehend the worldly, temporal conditions of his personal life, to follow the ever-shifting patterns of daily occurrences and trends—a web that is woven in time and space and shaped by egoistic motives and the pursuit of personal pleasures and advantages. Egoism Tolstoy considered as "a form of insanity." "The law of temporal and spatial existence is a struggle of all against each, of each against each and against all."[6]

Reason is the opposite of intelligence. It is an attribute of the spiritual self, it is oriented toward eternity. Reason releases a man from the temptations that intelligence puts in his way, frees the inborn human urge to do good, and permits brotherly love to manifest itself. "Love is the only rational activity of man."[7] This function of reason and love Tolstoy considered "the true life of man," taking place outside of time and space, for good never ceases to be good and is independent from our personal desires, preferences, or pleasures. "If a man lives renouncing his personality for the good of others, he enters even here, in this life, into that new relationship to the world for which there is no death."[8] In doing good we touch eternity.

The idea of love as an altruistic, self-sacrificing force led Tolstoy to assume an increasingly austere and ascetic view of sexual relations, in spite of his own passionate and virile sexuality. "I have long been tormented by the incongruity between my life and my beliefs," he admitted in 1897.[9] From extolling domestic felicity in *War and Peace* he moved to condemnation of adultery in *Anna Karenina*, and then even to censure of marital sexual relations in *The Kreutzer Sonata.* "Copulation generally is an act humiliating both to oneself and one's partner and therefore repulsive, an act in which man pays involuntary tribute to his animal nature," wrote Tolstoy in 1901.[10] This from a man who had fathered thirteen legitimate children and a number out of wedlock.

The role of Christ in human life was, according to Tolstoy, to have guided men toward an understanding of their own true nature, to have revealed that brotherly love was the essence of the human soul and that violence was contrary to this essence. Nowhere, to quote Tolstoy once more, did Christ preach the resurrection of the dead in the flesh or speak about His personal resurrection.[11] Christ's teaching was a set of simple guidelines for humanity on how to live as individuals and with one another. It initiated a new era in human history, deflecting the direction of human life from the animal to the divine, from the temporal to the eternal.

At the center of the Gospel stood the commandment to abstain from violence and not to resist evil. Yet it was the very commandment, according to Tolstoy, that the established Church as well as the secular order of modern society assiduously ignored and violated. Wielding this argument, Tolstoy directed violent and sweeping blows at Church, at State, at civilization per se, nihilistic blows far more virulent than the destructive energies the men of the 1860s had ever mustered in their attacks on the old, aristocratic pre-Emancipation society and its debris after the abolition of serfdom. Tolstoy accused the established Church of sanctioning such acts as war and the death penalty, acts contrary to the doctrine it was supposed to expound. The Church had ceased to regard Christ's moral precepts as obligatory and had replaced them with ceremonials which represented an "external cult of idolatry," though Christ's teaching was in itself "Protestantism, a denial of all external rites of worship."[12] It was these views that led the Russian church to excommunicate Tolstoy in 1901.

True Christianity Tolstoy found equally incompatible with existing State organs and institutions such as courts, prisons, police, armed forces, private land ownership, and wealth, all based on coercion, social disparity, and violating Christ's precepts of brotherly love, equality, and humility. "In its true meaning Christianity destroys the state—Christ was crucified for that very reason."[13] The entire fabric of modern society is arranged on the pagan concept of "an eye for an eye and a tooth for a tooth." Humanity has outgrown this social and political order of life, which originated in pre-Christian times and is no longer compatible with the new era initiated by Christ. Yet society continues to adhere to this pagan principle, to be divided into an affluent, idle minority and an oppressed, destitute, slaving majority. The affluent adhere to egoistic pursuits and lead a life infected with an incredible degree of self-deception and hypocrisy, in constant discord with their conscience, saying and doing what often represents the exact opposite of what they recognize as the guiding principles of the new Christian era.

Tolstoy struck out against material progress, technology, industrialization, against civilization itself as a destroyer of morality. Civilization was the source of the growing atrophy of reason, the weakening of man's natural impulse toward the good. Tolstoy maintained that the simple man who worked with his hands all his life retained his reason in all its purity and force. The further a human being was removed from modern civilization, the less there was evil in him and the more there was good. Tolstoy advocated a flight from the lineal path of historical time, a return to the cosmic rhythm of nature, to the cyclical turn of the seasons, a return to pastoral simplicity, to a collectively and uniformly shared frugality which would eliminate social disparity, promote abstention from violence, and permit a man to devote his earthly activities to the "true life" of rational behavior and the establishment of an eternal reign of good in this world, "a Kingdom of God" on earth.

The rich and disparate throng of living beings crowding the pages of Tolstoy's fiction, each vibrant with life, unique in personal attributes, and rendered immortal by the genius of its creator, was to fade and melt into an egalitarian community of Platon Karataevs—the peasant from *War and Peace* who "had no specific attachments, friendships or loves...but loved and lived in loving harmony with everything life brought him in contact with, especially people who happened to cross his path, whose life had no meaning as an individual life, whose life had meaning only as a particle of a whole which he was constantly aware of."[14]

Dostoevsky's creative development lacked the consistency and steady continuity of Tolstoy's. It also lacked any affinity with intellectual trends of a past era in the evolution of the human mind comparable to Tolstoy's kinship with the period of the Enlightenment. In his youth Dostoevsky was totally immersed in the ideological currents of his own times. He was a true representative of that peculiar, newly emerged, Russian version of intellectuals who were capable of becoming totally absorbed in thought processes to the exclusion of caution and objective appraisals of reality—a quality that later became so characteristic of his major fictional characters. During his affiliation with the Petrashevsky circle of socialists and prior to his arrest, trial, and exile to Siberia in 1849, Dostoevsky was a humanist who believed that socialistic schemes such as those of St. Simon, Fourier, and Proudhon would be capable of fulfilling the yearnings of the Romantic to create a new and better world. The author of *Poor Folk*, filled with compassion for the needy and the destitute, embraced utopian dreams that humanity, virtuous by nature and rational by inclination, would be capable of establishing a terrestrial paradise, a world more just and less cruel than the one created by God.

The youthful dreams were shattered during the four years Dostoevsky spent as an inmate among the 250 convicts of the prison compound at Omsk. In this world, dark with confinement and repression, a new valuation of reality began to form in Dostoevsky's mind. Though he retained to the end of his life his passionate hope in the power of mankind to solve its problems, he became steadily more convinced that trust in man's rationality was an illusion, that secular meliorism or revolutionary schemes based on egalitarian premises were not the answer. It was a fallacy to assume that man was bent on the reasonable pursuit of his own advantages. Within the prison walls of Omsk, as he observed men stripped of the power to exercise their own volition, a most powerful and irrational urge governing human behavior revealed itself to Dostoevsky's eyes: the yearning for liberty. To be deprived of freedom, to be unable to act on one's own will or whim, appeared, Dostoevsky discovered, as a worse affliction for a human being than any degree of physical suffering. This revelation manifested itself daily in numberless ways. The most telling was the value money assumed in the eyes of the convicts. Even the most insignificant amounts, frequently acquired by stealing or swindle, gained incommensurably in worth and power. Spending money, a convict could express his individuality, he could choose, bargain, he could show off. Spent recklessly on drinking bouts, wretched pittances provided the means to savor fleeting moments of illusory freedom, moments of "a remote phantom of liberty," liberty that the convicts craved with an intensity "bordering on convulsive spasms of insanity."[15]

If the question of freedom was the first central theme to form in Dostoevsky's new valuation of the actual world during his sojourn in Omsk, the second became the problem of evil, stemming from the observation that the arch-criminals among the convicts were stronger and survived better than the timid and resigned ones. It was a fallacy to believe that man was good by nature or that evil stemmed from a supremacy of the flesh over the spirit. Evil was an independent, real, powerful, metaphysical force in the world. Dostoevsky listened to reminiscent accounts of the most hideous crimes, the most monstrous murders, narrated without a trace of repentance, accompanied by the "most irrepressible, childlike, merry laughter." The convict Gazin, who resembled a huge, man-sized spider, had—so the rumor went—murdered a score of small children after subjecting them to slow torture and enjoying their terror and the feel of their warm blood on his hands.[16] There was the criminal Orlov, a man of tremendous will power and self-control, capable of enduring any torment, any punishment including flogging, fearing nothing on earth, proud of his strength and his crimes, contemptuous of anyone weak enough to believe that there was such a thing as a voice of conscience, and determined to escape from the Omsk prison as soon as an opportunity presented itself.

The New Testament was the only book Dostoevsky was permitted to own during the four years of his penal servitude. "Sometimes I read it to myself and sometimes to others. I used it to teach a convict how to read," he later reminisced.[17] In contrast to Tolstoy, who saw Christ's teaching as a set of rules intended to guide human behavior and who considered the commandment to abstain from violence and not to resist evil to be the core of the Gospel, Dostoevsky came to interpret Christ's words as a religion of freedom, a religion based on the moral responsibility of every individual for his actions. "By making man responsible, Christianity *eo ipso* also recognizes his freedom,"[18] his freedom to choose between good and evil, to act according to his conscience. This was a revelation of paramount importance considering that Dostoevsky was also discovering that to be deprived of freedom was the worst affliction man could be subjected to. Christianity offered what humanistic socialism neglected. Studying the gospel Dostoevsky arrived at the conclusion that attempts to establish man's dependence on his environment, on the flaws in the organization of society, would strip an individual of his independence, of all personal moral obligations, and would reduce him to absolute impersonality, to a state of abject slavery. "Four years of forced labor was a long school: I had time to convince myself."[19] Thus, the human individual, his inner life, the question of his spiritual condition, moved to center stage in Dostoevsky's vision, to remain there for the rest of his life. The disorders of the modern world were not rooted in the environment, not in material or social issues. They could not be righted by force. All stemmed from disorders in the consciousness of the individual human being, disorders that then spread to the social fabric of family and society, disrupting marital and filial relations and steering humanity toward a state of a dehumanized "ant heap."

Dostoevsky's major masterpieces were created after his return from Siberia in 1859, when he began to transpose his observations from the House of the Dead to the land of the living, to the realm of a nascent pecuniary, industrial, and urban order which was just beginning to be grafted on the ancient mold of Russia's agrarian society and predominantly natural economy. During repeated trips to Europe in the following two decades Dostoevsky was also able to observe the course of a mature monetary and urban society progressing under the banner of an individualistic laissez-faire doctrine. Unlike Tolstoy, Dostoevsky was far from condemning civilization as a destroyer of morality. In his imagination Europe, with its wealth of art treasures and priceless cultural monuments, had loomed as "the land of holy wonders." But he now discovered that this land of glorious achievements which he had so greatly admired from the distance of his Russian milieu had been torn from its Christian foundations, that the Europe of his dreams had turned into "a precious cemetery," as Ivan Karamazov would later say, and become the domain of a self-satisfied, terrifyingly pedestrian, increasingly irreligious and materialistic bourgeois society, dedicated to the ruthless pursuit of monetary gain and engrossed in selfish betterment.

Tolstoy saw wealth and money as social phenomena cleaving society and creating a privileged minority in which "the insanity of egoism" and hypocritical self-deception were rampant and the inborn rationality of man deformed. Dostoevsky's gaze remained fixed on the individual, that innately irrational being forever thirsting for freedom, prone to succumb to the lure of evil, and now held in thrall by monetary greed. Humanism had elevated that being to the center of the universe, denying that man was the image and likeness of God and proclaiming the supremacy of the human intellect. The secularized, pecuniary environment of the nineteenth century had opened new avenues of power and freedom to the consciousness of that godless man. It is these avenues, it is the nature of human freedom in its modern milieu that Dostoevsky explores. Tolstoy's artistic powers of insight into the breadth and variety of empirical reality is matched by Dostoevsky's genius for penetrating into the depths of the consciousness of contemporary man, to be a "fox" in the spiritual realm of human existence. But in contrast to Tolstoy the moralist, Tolstoy the "hedgehog," who honed his arguments to rational simplicity and presented them with great efforts at persuasiveness, Dostoevsky does not offer peremptory pronouncements, though his central theme is the same as Tolstoy's: man cannot remain human without God.

The dominant issue that Dostoevsky explores in his major novels is a vast trajectory of his own travail and tormenting doubts and reflections. Modern man has fallen victim to the belief that it is possible to live without God. The ideas forged and acted upon to probe into the dilemma of the autonomy of the human intellect versus the sovereignty of a Divine Being are the main protagonists in Dostoevsky's novelistic world. They are stripped of any element of abstraction, however. They are poetically incarnated in human flesh, they are fused entirely with human flesh, so that one melts into the other, in spite of the fantastic limits and the preposterous extremes they are carried to. It is the thoughts and voices of Dostoevsky's heroes that fill the pages of his novels, thoughts so crucial to life itself that men writhe under their crushing weight, voices that moan and weep or shout or whisper or pray more often than they speak. Dramatic confrontations, verbal exchanges, sparring dialogues, and brooding soliloquies dominate the flow of time and telescope complex dramatic plots filled with tumultuous events, with murders and suicides, into short spans of a few hours or days or weeks at most. Time becomes a function of human consciousness, it contracts or expands in accordance with the inner experiences of Dostoevsky's heroes.

A proud withdrawal and deliberate isolation from other human beings is central to the consciousness of godless man, who regards humanity as split between a statistical abstraction of ordinary people who like to obey and the concrete elite of exceptional individuals who are free of any constraints. "I do not need money," explains Arkady Dolgorukii, protagonist of *The Adolescent*, whose one goal in life is to become as rich as Rothschild, "or rather it is not money I am after, not even power. What I am after is something that can be acquired through power and only through power—a solitary and calm awareness of strength. This is the most complete definition of freedom...."[20] In the rarified atmosphere of this freedom and isolation Raskolnikov in *Crime and Punishment* murders the old pawnbroker, not for the money, not to become a benefactor of the needy, but to find out whether he has the daring of a Napoleon to transgress, the right to spill blood and the power to still his conscience.

At the summit of the tortuous climb of Dostoevsky's heroes who explore the landscape of their freedom stands Stravrogin, central figure in *The Possessed*. Endowed with prodigious strength and talents, he discovers that his intellectual as well as emotional drives are boundless but contradictory. He instills atheistic ideas in some of his disciples while inciting another to seek religious faith and yet another to organize a network of revolutionary conspirators. He is sensuously drawn to one woman while turning to another for help and compassion and seeking atonement for his evil deeds by marrying a cripple. He is incapable of limiting himself, he derives as much pleasure from doing evil as he does from doing good. His confession to Bishop Tikhon of having raped a twelve-year-old who then hanged herself is not the voice of a tormented conscience but, on the contrary, an affirmation of his boundless pride and lack of remorse. "Good and evil are but prejudices. I can be free of all prejudices, but at the very moment when I achieve that freedom I shall perish,"[21] he tells Tikhon, sensing that suicide is the ultimate recourse left to him to escape the great dehumanizing void of supreme indifference and emotional torpor in which he lives.

For Kirilov, Stavrogin's atheistic disciple, suicide carries an element of grandiose intent. Man invented God out of fear of death, he says. Time will be conquered and eternity fused with the temporal order when that fear is overcome. There will be freedom when it becomes irrelevant to live or not to live. Kirilov kills himself with the sole motivation of proving this new freedom. Suicide without a concrete reason is the highest point of self-will. "My self-will is the attribute of my divinity,"[22] he exclaims, but during the last minutes of his life he turns into a raving beast; we see him in a state of demented frenzy, convulsed by a spasm of savage fury and despair.

At a summit commanding a horizon even vaster and bleaker than Stavrogin's stands the imposing and tragic figure of the Grand Inquisitor in Ivan Karamazov's "Legend." Loss of faith in God is his secret burden. But he intends to use the freedom of his unbelief for the benefit of mankind. He has taken it upon himself to alter Christ's teaching by taking away man's freedom and by putting human conscience to sleep. For this is the only way to deliver humanity from suffering and to provide the millions of ordinary mortals who crave to be led and to obey with the happiness of an earthly paradise. Christ thought too highly of men when he rejected Satan's three temptations in the wilderness: to perform the miracle of turning stones to bread, to display the mystery of his divinity by casting himself down to be upheld by angels, and to accept authority over all the kingdoms of the earth offered to him by Satan.

Christ did not wish to bargain for men's devotion. He wanted free faith, not faith enforced or sustained by miracles or mysteries. But freedom is a terrible gift. A free decision of what is good and what is evil is an unbearable burden for weak, ordinary men. The Grand Inquisitor accepts Satan's offers. "We have corrected thy work," he says in his monologue addressing Christ, "and founded it upon miracle, mystery, and authority.... Who can rule men if not he who holds their conscience and their bread in his hands?"[23] But man cannot remain human without God. Behind the Grand Inquisitor's compassion lurks a diabolical contempt for men, those lowly and miserable creatures whose happiness he intends to secure by satisfying their physical needs only, by dulling their quest for inquiry and knowledge, and by curbing the independence of their actions.

Far more space is devoted in Dostoevsky's novelistic tragedies to the devastating drama of terrestrial omnipotence claimed by modern man than to the redeeming spiritual freedom offered by Christianity. But it is the sparingly presented domain of Faith that shines in the dark and illuminates here and there the vast and desolate terrain of unbelief and proud withdrawal. A faint glimmer of hope lights Raskolnikov's path on the last pages of *Crime and Punishment.* He has confessed because he has found the sense of isolation from other human beings which he experienced after the murder to be unbearable. "It is not the old woman I killed, it is myself I killed," he says. This is not remorse as yet, only the realization that his is not the grandiose self-will of a Napoleon after all. But the promise of repentance and of Raskolnikov's return to the community of men is implicit in the final scene, as he falls on his knees before Sonia and bows to the love, infinite compassion, patience, and humility which drove her to accompany him on his journey into penal servitude.

In his humility and innocence the saintly, fragile Prince Myshkin in *The Idiot* is "Dostoevsky's most Christ-like symbol."[24] He is a light diffused, hovering like a compassionate spirit, divested of rational capabilities, above a world dark with sexual passions and love of money. Afflicted by epilepsy, he experiences before the onset of a fit, "for a second, never more than one second," an intense feeling of harmony, of the highest synthesis of life. "In such a moment," he says, "I understand the extraordinary word [of the angel in the Apocalypse] that there will be no time."[25] But neither Myshkin's intuitive wisdom nor his all-forgiving pity and humility are able to stem the destructive currents which churn all around him and finally overpower and engulf him.

Without Myshkin Dostoevsky could not give us Father Zossima,[26] the great Christian healer who radiates light and dispenses comfort and loving sympathy to all those who come to seek his help. He stands at the center of the Karamazov world of seething passions and tormenting conflicts. "The Karamazovs are prisoners of life in time. The limits of time itself make them captives."[27] Zossima opens the prison gate and points the way toward liberation. He stands on the threshold from the temporal to the timeless worlds. He came to the priesthood at the age of twenty-five in repentance for eight years of riotous and debauched worldly living in arrogant pride which had turned him "into an almost wild, cruel, and ridiculous being." His autobiographical comments and exhortations recorded by his disciple Alesha Karamazov hold a pivotal position in the novel. It is in remorse, in a sense of guilt for past wrongdoings experienced by a reactivated conscience, that a break between past and present can be instituted and control over the temporal process achieved. Conscience is an expression of man's immortality. It is in repentance that we touch eternity and reach for humility, which is the highest form of freedom and the antithesis to arrogant pride. Zossima lives in that Christian freedom and in continued awareness of that harmony of cosmic interdependence which flashed through Myshkin's consciousness only for the briefest moment before he was seized with an epileptic fit. "Everything is like an ocean," Zossima believes, "everything is flowing and touching; a touch in one place sets off movement at the other end of the world.... And the roots of our thoughts and feelings are not here but in another world."[28] Zossima's burning torch is handed over to Alesha, who responds to the exhortation never to judge anyone and to the idea that loving humility is the most powerful force on earth; pure and chaste Alesha, who seems to love everyone for no given reason and who is endowed with a natural talent for kindling affection in all those he comes in contact with—the spiritual counterpart of Tolstoy's earthy Platon Karataev.

The figure of Christ had always held a deep fascination for Dostoevsky, even in the early years when he leaned toward socialistic and atheistic ideas. And the final, brightly glowing burst of radiance in his fictional world is the kiss bestowed by Christ in silent pity and compassion on the Grand Inquisitor's bloodless, aged lips in response to the lengthy, rationalistic monologue in defense of unbelief. Faith cannot be clothed and imprisoned in words. Silence is the symbol of eternity.

Chekhov's relations to Tolstoy are richly documented and discussed at length by both writers themselves as well as by literary critics in a number of comparative studies.[29] Chekhov's literary debut in 1880 coincided with Tolstoy's spiritual crisis, which led him to repudiate the worth of his literary achievements and to assume the role of a moral and religious reformer. Chekhov's devotion to Tolstoy was deep and lasting. Even before they met, he wrote: "Tolstoy is not a man, he is a superman (*chelovechishche*), a Jupiter." His first impression on meeting Tolstoy in the summer of 1895 confirmed that opinion. He spoke of having met "something unexpectedly huge." Three years later Chekhov said: "In my whole life I have never respected anybody as deeply, I might say, as unreservedly as I respect Lev Nikolaevich." The heroes of Tolstoy's novels were like close friends of Chekhov's. He spoke of Anna Karenina as "dear, beloved Anna." When mentioning Prince Andrey in *War and Peace* Chekhov deplored the state of medicine in those days. "Had he been my patient," he said, "I am sure I would have saved his life."

But whenever Chekhov felt Tolstoy's philosophic views impinging on his artistic insight, his criticism was blunt and severe. He disliked the portrayal of Napoleon in *War and Peace*, which Tolstoy created as evidence of an individual's powerlessness to move the wheels of history. "Whenever Napoleon appears, you feel the strain, you see all sorts of tricks in order to prove that Napoleon was more stupid than he was in reality.... Everything that Napoleon is represented as thinking or doing is unnatural, stupid, exaggerated, and irrelevant." *Resurrection* Chekhov considered to be a remarkable work of art except for the "unclear" relationship between Prince Nekhliudov and Katiusha. Nekhliudov's decision to marry Katiusha in order to expiate his guilt for having seduced her and sent her on the road to her subsequent misfortunes Chekhov found not true to life. References to the Gospel at the end of the novel he deemed arbitrary and out of place. "Why a text from the Gospel and not from the Koran?"

And yet, looking back in 1894 upon the eighties, the first decade of his literary career, Chekhov admitted that Tolstoy's philosophical and moral tracts had greatly influenced his writing—to an extent close to hypnotism—"for some six or seven years." He added, however, that he was now totally free of that influence. "Common sense tells me that there is more love of mankind in electricity and steam than in chastity and vegetarianism. War is evil and courts are evil. But it does not follow that I should wear bark shoes and sleep on the stove with the field hand and his wife."[30]

Even during those early six or seven years when Tolstoy's nearly hypnotic influence prevailed, Chekhov did not accept his philosophy in toto. To repudiate and condemn civilization was unthinkable for a man who had chosen medicine as his profession. For most of the first decade of Chekhov's career literature remained a handmaid, a means of financing his medical education and then, after his father's grocery business had ended in bankruptcy, of contributing to the support of his family. Medicine he called his "legal wife" and literature his "mistress." In 1887 he playfully signed a letter to his brother Alexander, "your loving brother and sister Antonius and Medicina Chekhov." It is also worth recalling that the prevailing literary climate of those days was particularly ill-suited for moral and philosophical discourse. A severe tightening of censorship followed in the wake of the assassination of Tsar Alexander II in 1881. The only flourishing periodicals were cheap, humorous magazines such as *The Dragonfly*, *Fragments*, or *The Alarm Clock*. The editorial policy of these sheets aimed at amusing the reader with light and easy humor in short, simple stories.

Nothing could be attacked, denounced, or criticized. It is here that Chekhov's literary debut took place.

Bubbling over with creative energy and drollery of vision, aided by his medical schooling and scientific training, he applied himself to an examination of the state of health of contemporary society. And the stories which bear the mark of Tolstoy's influence are those exposing the malaise of hypocrisy and pretense, of discord between human actions and words on one hand and the dictates of a conscience cognizant of Christian precepts on the other. More often than not the simple plot in the early stories is comic or even irresistibly ludicrous, masking the underlying serious theme. A tone of hilarity is added by Chekhov's farcical choice of names which can only partially be conveyed in translation. We meet the goldsmith Khriukin (*khriukanie* is a pig's grunt), the police inspector Ochumelov (Off-his-Head), the district foreman Kozoedov (The Goat Eater), the merchants Khikhikin (The Giggler) and Potroshilov (The Disemboweler), the shopkeeper Osheinikov (Dog Collar), the Frenchman Pas de Quoi, the Portuguese singer Don Lai (Don the Bark), the songstress Dubadola Svist (Dubadola Whistle), and hundreds more.

At times, Chekhov's condemnation of hypocrisy is expressed in terms harsher than Tolstoy's. The story "In Court" (1886) contains strong echoes in setting and in plot of the trial scenes in Tolstoy's *Resurrection*. An atmosphere of cold boredom and indifference permeates the courtroom where the legal machinery is relentlessly and monotonously grinding away, impervious to human tragedies which are here seen to be "as commonplace as deaths are customary in hospitals." The defendant is the peasant Kharlamov, accused of having murdered his wife. The soldier guard who escorts him happens to be his own son Prokhor. Kharlamov hotly denies his guilt. Suddenly circumstances appear which point at his son's possible involvement in the crime. These are observed by all present in the courtroom, but the trial goes on as scheduled. In *Resurrection* Tolstoy grants Katiusha a reversal of an unjust verdict. After Nekhliudov's intervention she is freed of her conviction as a murderess. But Chekhov leaves little doubt that no such intercession is in store for Kharlamov and that his son's possible guilt will not be investigated.

"The Name Day Party" (1888) is Chekhov's most powerful indictment of hypocrisy. "From start to finish of the story I protest against falsehood," wrote Chekhov. And indeed the word "lie" appears practically on every page. A celebration of the name day of Olga Mikhailovna's husband is in progress. The pregnant hostess is wearing a tight corset in order to conceal her condition. She tries to hide her discomfort, fatigue, and boredom with her guests under a smile that hardly leaves her face. Conversation during dinner is conducted with great animation, though no one is genuinely interested in the topics discussed. The husband, Petr Dmitrich, is deeply worried about a lawsuit pending against him but conceals his anxiety under a mien of calm and carefree self-assurance. Olga Mikhailovna is irritated by her husband's unwillingness to share his worries with her. As the day progresses, her irritation mounts, particularly as she watches Petr Dmitrich flirting with their lady guests. Her anger reaches a pitch bordering on hatred but she carefully conceals her emotions, pretending to enjoy herself and to tend cheerfully to her duties as a hostess. After the guests' departure Olga Mikhailovna is seized with premature birth pangs and a miscarriage is the price paid for the lengthy perpetration of pretense and absorption in false values.

The story "Nice People," published two years earlier than "The Name Day Party," bears evidence that disagreement with Tolstoy was also beginning to gain in importance as a creative stimulus for Chekhov. The nice people are a brother and sister, the satirically drawn mediocre and obscure literateur Liadovsky and his grief-stricken, widowed sister Vera Semenovna, who spends her days idly and reverentially watching her brother write. The background of the story mirrors the impact of Tolstoy's moral injunctions to contemporary society. It is set in the 1880s, "when people were beginning to talk and to write about non-resistance to evil, about the right to try people, to dispense punishments, to wage war; when some people in our set were beginning to do without servants, to retire to the country to till the soil, turning vegetarian and abstaining from sexual love."[31]

Vera Semenovna is puzzled by the idea of non-resistance to evil and asks her brother to explain it to her. His blunt answer that it would give full rein to criminality and lead to complete chaos does not satisfy her and she ventures to raise timid doubts. Way into the night the two continue to argue "without understanding each other. If an outsider had overheard them, he would hardly have been able to figure out what either of them was driving at."[32] The dialogue breaks down and the issue of non-resistance to evil itself remains unresolved. But Vera Semenovna begins to sense her brother's stubborn conceit and narrow-mindedness. The estrangement finally leads to a complete break between the two "nice people." Central to the story is the inability of the two to respect each other's thoughts and to maintain a living relationship.

During the late 1880s, when Chekhov was beginning to free himself from Tolstoy's influence, he wrote three more stories arguing with the man he so greatly admired. All three are set in the realm of fancy, a most unusual choice for Chekhov the realist. "Without a Title" and "The Bet" were each first published as a "Fairy Tale," and the fable motif of "The Cobbler and the Devil" is implicit in the title itself. All three stories deal with issues central to Tolstoy's philosophy. "Without a Title," set in the fifth century, describes how the ascetic monks of a desert monastery succumb to the lure of urban secularism and defect, to a man, to a distant city rank with corruption and debauchery. "The Cobbler and the Devil," on the contrary, exposes the empty and illusory pleasures of wealth, while the hero of "The Bet" arrives at a complete renunciation of worldly goods and at contempt for all the fruits of civilization. One is tempted to assume that Chekhov deliberately chose to transpose these Tolstoyan issues into the key of fantasy and to treat them in this curiously inconclusive and contradictory manner in order to give free play to all possible pros and cons and to contend with Tolstoy's quest for final answers and solutions.

By the time the two met, in 1895, Chekhov was no longer under Tolstoy's intellectual spell. A number of photographs of their meetings have come down to us. One is particularly revealing. It was taken in September 1901 in Gaspra in the Crimea, where Tolstoy was recuperating from a serious illness. Chekhov was living in nearby Yalta, where he had built a house. Both are seated on a veranda by a coffee table. Tolstoy's right hand is raised in a gesture of pleading persuasion; he looks intently at Chekhov, his whole posture expressing the desire to make a convincing case of whatever he is saying. Chekhov, slightly stooped, clearly showing the ravages of the tuberculosis that was to bring him to his grave less than three years hence, his hands quietly folded in his lap, his eyes lowered, is listening silently, reserved, respectful, but apparently not convinced. One can almost hear Tolstoy's sermonizing and feel Chekhov's reticent silence.

Tolstoy, by thirty-two years Chekhov's senior, was genuinely fond of the younger man as a person and as an artist. He greatly admired his talent, the novelty of his art of the short story, the originality of his language and style, but he believed that "medicine was hampering him," deplored what he called Chekhov's inability to distinguish between good and evil, his "godlessness," and disliked those works of Chekhov's in which he thought that these flaws and deviations from his own views were particularly evident. The stark and grim realism of Chekhov's "The Peasants" (1897), its glaring contrast to Tolstoy's idealization of rural simplicity, aroused Tolstoy's indignation. He dubbed the story "a sin against the people."

Most of Chekhov's best creative achievements fall into the period when he had freed himself from Tolstoy's influence and struck out on a path that led him further and further away from Tolstoy's egalitarian striving for simplification of life and the establishment of a rational Kingdom of God—

of Love—on earth. Much as Chekhov admired and loved the fictional characters created by Tolstoy the artist, he could not accept the role Tolstoy the moralist assigned to the individual in his philosophy—a role of passivity, the role of a particle merging harmoniously, like Platon Karataev in *War and Peace*, with a larger monolithic whole and sacrificing one's self for the good of others. The following verdict of Chekhov is the most arresting on the subject: "Tolstoy's philosophy is, perhaps, the epitome of altruism, but it is not applicable in real life. There are millions of instances when people should and must react to an insult with an insult. The struggle for the sacred rights of the individual must be waged everywhere and it would be immoral if it were otherwise."[33]

The further Chekhov moved away from Tolstoy, the more he strove to elevate the individual above the level of egalitarian uniformity, to lift him to a lofty position of irreplaceable worth and absolute value, the more he moved in the direction of Dostoevsky, who also had ended up placing the individual in the center of his vision. The roots of this striving reach deep into Chekhov's personal experiences as a youth and adolescent, when he was endeavoring to free himself inwardly from his father's oppressive and despotic willfulness and to develop a sense of personal dignity and inner independence. In reply to a letter his fourteen-year-old brother Mikhail had signed, "Your worthless and insignificant little brother," in April 1879, at the age of nineteen, Chekhov wrote these oft-quoted words: "You know where you should acknowledge your insignificance? Before God perhaps, before intelligence, beauty, nature, but not before men. Among men one must acknowledge one's dignity. You are not a crook, you are an honest man. So respect your own honesty and remember that an honest man is not a nonentity. Do not confuse 'being humble' with acknowledging one's insignificance."[34]

The goal toward which Chekhov moved from the earliest stages of his moral self-education—a goal Dostoevsky had found to be the strongest motive governing human behavior—was the achievement of a sense of personal freedom. He described this painful and laborious process as "the squeezing of slave blood out of my system, drop by drop." The term "slave blood" refers not only to the effects of the despotic disposition of his father, but also to the fact that his grandfather had been a serf. Toward the end of the 1880s that goal, in Chekhov's own words, was nearly reached: "Only now am I beginning to develop a sense of personal freedom." And the concept of freedom begins to assume a meaning reaching far beyond the limits of personal existence and experience. "Hypocrisy, stupidity, and tyranny reign not only in merchants' homes and police stations," Chekhov wrote in October 1888 to his friend the writer Pleshcheev. "I see them in science, in literature, among our youth.... I consider labels and tags to be prejudices. My holy of holies is the human body, health, intelligence, talent, inspiration, love and *the most absolute freedom* [italics mine], freedom from violence and lies, no matter what form the latter two might assume."[35]

When Dostoevsky died on January 18, 1881, Chekhov's literary career had barely begun; a dozen or so stories had been published. The two had never met and comments by Chekhov on Dostoevsky are as sparse and laconic as those on Tolstoy are numerous, extensive, and supplemented by scores of personal impressions and exchanges. Comparative studies of the two authors are likewise few.[36] To his friend, the editor and writer Suvorin, Chekhov wrote on March 5, 1889: "I have bought Dostoevsky in your store and I am reading him now. He is good, but terribly long and immodest. There are many pretentions."[37] On another occasion Chekhov commented that Dostoevsky's talent was "without question very great, but at times he lacked flair (*chut'e*)."[38]

Such reserved and scant comments are understandable, considering that moderation, restraint, and understatement were clearly emerging as the distinctive features of Chekhov's art. His sober, scientifically trained, and disciplined mind was examining society under the microscope and scalpel of his medical schooling and recording its observations with selective brevity and terseness of expression—devices originally developed to fit the format of the humoristic journals where Chekhov's literary career began. And these features were greatly at odds with the visionary premonitions and mystical pitch of Dostoevsky's massive novelistic tragedies, most of them written in a feverish, breathless style with a creditor bending over the author's shoulder.

And yet, in the spring of 1890, Chekhov embarked on an expedition to the penal colony on the island of Sakhalin on the eastern periphery of Siberia. This in many ways voluntarily duplicated the Siberian experiences in a prison compound which Dostoevsky had endured under duress over forty years earlier. The experience proved as decisive in Chekhov's subsequent creative development as Dostoevsky's sojourn within the prison walls of Omsk had been. The trip was preceded by two months of intensive study of Sakhalin's geography, climate, soil, natural resources, economy, indigenous population, and state of criminal law and administration. Sighing with fatigue and mental strain, having read a total of sixty-five books and articles on Sakhalin, Chekhov complained of developing a "mania Sakhalinosa." His friends were at a loss to understand the motives for undertaking the perilous five-thousand-mile trip, the readiness to endure the discomforts of covering that distance by river boat and horse-drawn carriage (construction of the Trans-Siberian Railway had not even begun). It took Chekhov three months to reach Sakhalin in July 1890. Was he running away from an unhappy love affair? Was he perhaps imitating Tolstoy and withdrawing from art in the name of a more fruitful service to mankind?

Chekhov himself stated a number of reasons for the trip. Dissatisfaction with his literary production was one of them. He needed more self-discipline, he said. "I must put some gunpowder under myself.... I must become my own animal trainer." Sakhalin was "the ninth circle, the ultimate boundary of human misery.... We should make pilgrimages to places like Sakhalin, the way the Turks go to Mecca.... It is evident from the books which I have read and am reading that we let *millions* of people rot in jail, we let them rot to no purpose, without arguing, barbarously.... The famous decade of the sixties [when the liberation of the serfs and a series of related reforms were carried out] has done nothing for the sick and the incarcerated, thus violating the principal commandment of Christian civilization."[39]

Chekhov spent three months on Sakhalin and personally conducted a census of the population. He stated that he had talked to every single one of the ten thousand convicts and "colonizers"—the latter convicts who had completed their hard-labor penalty and were serving the second part of their sentences as settlers. Upon his return to Moscow in December 1890 he exclaimed: "My brief past on Sakhalin seems to me so enormous that when I want to talk about it, I do not know where to begin." He then set out to write a documentary account of the trip. *The Island of Sakhalin*, first serialized in 1893 and 1894 and published in book form in 1895, Chekhov labeled "a convict's gown" which he proudly hung in his "belletristic wardrobe." Though the book is a scholarly work, with detailed statistical tables covering every aspect of the composition of Sakhalin's population, with geographical and meteorological information, it is also a work of art, fully comparable to Dostoevsky's *House of the Dead*.

The clanging of chains and shackles rings on every page devoted to the inhabitants of the island. For bondage does not stop at the doors of the overcrowded, filthy prisons with their ill-fed and ill-treated inmates, but actually permeates every stratum, every group of Sakhalin's society. Hard labor begins after hard labor, says Chekhov. For the "colonizers" invariably come out of prison with impaired health, hard pressed to squeeze a subsistence out of the barren, cold soil. Neither are they able to exploit the rich opportunities for hunting and fishing, activities requiring the endurance and self-reliance of free individuals. The island is a natural habitat for sable, fox, and bear, Chekhov found, and the periodic runs of herring in the spring and salmon in the summer are spectacular.

The women on Sakhalin engage in prostitution or illicit

liaisons. The pale, thin, constantly hungry children are list-
less and child mortality is high. Even the wardens dwell
within the same confinement as the imprisoned, the guards
and supervisors sinking into a morass of drink, gambling,
fornication, and indifference toward their wards. Morality
on the island is turned inside out. Murder among convicts
goes unpunished, since it is considered a normal occurrence
within prison walls. But attempted flight—even assistance
offered to a fugitive—is punished as a grievous crime.

Like Dostoevsky before him, Chekhov returned to Russia
with a vast store of evidence that to be deprived of freedom is
the ultimate calamity to befall a human being. Though the
theme of Sakhalin itself appears in the pages of Chekhov's
fiction but in passing, the impact of the trip on his writing
was tremendous. Shortly afterwards began the mature
period of his creativity. And Sakhalin became the prism
through which Chekhov examined his native Russia, view-
ing innumerable manifestations of the same thwarted human
potentialities and suppression of liberty which he had found
in such tragically concentrated form on Sakhalin.

There can be little doubt that, when Chekhov spoke of
Dostoevsky's "pretensions" and lack of modesty, he had the
polarization of themes in mind, the concentration on fantastic extremes of human consciousness which, to Dostoevsky,
constituted the prime essence of reality. To swing between
diametrical opposites, to speak in terms of doom and salvation, either to lead heroes to perdition or to grant them a state
approaching sainthood, to oscillate between the disastrous
freedom claimed by godless man in his proud isolation and
the redeeming freedom and human communion offered by
Christianity—to all these Chekhov with his sober, disciplined mind was completely averse, though the concept of
freedom itself was as central to him as to Dostoevsky. But it
was not the freedom of sinners and saints; it was the freedom
of the average individual human being that concerned him,
freedom brought down from the lofty heights of spiritual
reality to the pedestrian level of workaday existence, the
freedom that was essential for the richest possible development of personal characteristics, of every aspect of human

life, and indispensable for the growth of civilized human beings—in short, the freedom that Russia had seen so little of during her long and pain-filled history.

In his personal pronouncements and correspondence after Sakhalin Chekhov continued to hold the banner of freedom high, as he had done before, as quoted in the letter to Pleshcheev. As to the scope of Chekhov's activities on behalf of human welfare and the release of blighted human potentialities, it has been admirably and succinctly described by Simon Karlinsky: "Anton Chekhov's life was probably more filled with direct involvement in valid social and humanitarian activity than that of any other writer one could name. His life was one continuous round of alleviating famine, fighting epidemics, building schools, and public roads, endowing libraries, helping organize marine-biology laboratories, giving thousands of needy peasants free medical treatment, planting gardens, helping fledgling writers get published, raising funds for worthwhile causes and hundreds of other pursuits designed to help his fellowman and improve the general quality of life around him."[40]

But to place the concept of freedom in a pivotal position in creative writing presented special problems. To preach, to sermonize, to try to influence directly the reader's mind would be tantamount to violating the very concept itself. And Chekhov's literary efforts centered on eliminating this pitfall by activating a reader's perception and granting him the full freedom to discover the author's intentions for himself, unaided by directional signposts or signals. At times, Chekhov appears to camouflage his most important thoughts behind a facade of neutral, casual titles: "On the Road," "In Exile," "The Student," "A Case from Practice," "On Official Business." Even in the documentary *Island of Sakhalin* a direct reference to the concept of freedom occurs but twice, and is tucked away the second time in a footnote: "The natural and unconquerable yearning for the highest good—for freedom—is here considered to be a criminal inclination, and flight is punished with hard labor and flogging, like a serious criminal offense."[41]

A writer must never offer solutions, Chekhov said; he must

never become a judge, he must remain an objective observer who limits himself to stating the problems of human life. Chekhov strove to engage the reader's imagination in retracing the creative act, to participate with the author in the psychological and moral analysis of a literary work. If you want to touch the reader's emotions, Chekhov advised a budding writer, remain as cold as possible. An author can weep and suffer with his hero, but he must do it so that the reader will not be aware of it. "The more objective, the more powerful the impression." Emotional experiences must not be described, but conveyed by the hero's actions, gestures, facial expressions, or intonations. Diffusion (*rasplyvcha-tost'*) must be avoided at all cost. Brevity and laconism are essential in order to avoid blurring the reader's vision and dulling his attention. Comparing the work of a writer to that of a sculptor Chekhov said: "To make a face out of marble means to remove from that piece of marble everything that is not a face. Remove everything that has no relevance to the story. If in the first chapter you mention a rifle hanging on a wall, in the second or third chapter a shot must be fired with that rifle. Otherwise do not mention it."[42] Carefully chosen details must be assembled and combined to form a clear, sparse, and objective picture that the author holds up to the readers, leaving them to think about the meaning of that picture, to evaluate it, and to become the jury that passes its own judgment on the literary work.

These were indeed exacting demands Chekhov made on the Russian public, a public that believed that ideological messages were the prime aim of literature, that sought firm and clearly voiced guidance from its writers, that was accustomed to hear ready, if contradictory, answers to the question of how to cure the country's ills, how to live, and what to do. Unaccustomed to thinking unaided by readily visible props, the literate segment of Russian society remained unresponsive to the novelty of Chekhov's art. He was accused of betraying the humanitarian traditions of Russian literature, of being the bard of hopelessness, of a "twilight world," of a dying era, of having no ideals, of being weak, passive, and indifferent to the plight of the people, of offering the reader no ideas and no conclusions. He had no principles, said the populist Lavrov. "As soon as Chekhov touches on such topics as art, science, love, inspiration, ideals, the future, they instantly fade, wither, and die," wrote Leo Shestov in his famous treatise "Creation out of the Void," published in 1908, four years after Chekhov's death.[43]

If the Russian public was unable to grasp the role of freedom in the arsenal of Chekhov's literary devices, it was even less prepared to perceive that the same concept—that "highest good" in human existence, as the unobtrusive comments in *The Island of Sakhalin* spelled it—was central to his creative thought as well and lay at the core of the major topics of his writing. The primary melody of freedom, woven into the harmonic texture of his literary polyphony and played in a rich array of variations, passed unheeded and fell on deaf ears. Yet it is the role freedom played in Chekhov's work that sets him apart and awards him an exceptional and unique position in nineteenth-century Russian literature, a literature with such extraordinary functions in an equally extraordinary period of the country's history.

The variations on the melody of freedom touched on the same central issues that moved Tolstoy and Dostoevsky: the theme of time, of human divisiveness, of conscience, of love. Chekhov stood between the two giants—Tolstoy, the moralist who urged and preached what ought to be, and Dostoevsky, who shouted of what will be. Abandon industrialization, science, technology, abandon civilization itself urged Tolstoy—go back to pastoral simplicity, touch God by living in love and peace, sharing equally the gifts of the land and the toil. Warnings came from tormented Dostoevsky, premonitions of a world soon to be drowned in bloodshed, wars, revolutions, violence, hatred, all caused by human beings who had severed their ties to God and declared their supremacy and power to rule their destiny alone. And there was Chekhov between the two, speaking quietly and softly, not of what ought to be or what will be, but of what *is*. There is an entry in his notebook: "Men will become better when you show them what they are like."[44] And what he wanted to show was how little freedom there was among men—freedom, which is the highest good in human existence.

Freedom was Chekhov's "holy of holies." If this was his most original attribute in Russia's literary world, its source must be sought in the fact that he was the only writer in nineteenth-century Russian literature who combined familiarity with scientific methods, through his medical training, with intimate knowledge of religious beliefs and practices, acquired during his youthful years under the pressure of his pious and devout father. Science and religion are the two great irreconciled forces in our modern world. There is the reality of our time-space world open to rational, factual exploration and there is the reality of an eternal world accessible only through intuitive apprehension. Cognizant of the intersection of the divine and the natural order, of mystical intuition and conceptual comprehension, Chekhov's vision of reality encompassed them both and spelled out their roles for an unfettered development of human potentialities. No author had as much respect for the power of reason as Chekhov and none was as keenly aware of its limitations.

Few statements are as erroneous as Tolstoy's contention that medicine was hampering Chekhov as a writer. But equally misguided was Merezhkovsky when he stated that Chekhov "ignored Christ"—a view shared by many of Chekhov's contemporaries and echoed in various forms by most modern critics. There are two key figures in Chekhov's fictional world that illuminate this issue—the doctor and the priest. These introduce us to Chekhov's treatment of the theme of freedom.

Notes

All quotations from Chekhov's works are based on the latest Soviet edition, in thirty volumes (1974-1983), of his writings and letters. Quotations from his letters are preceded by "L." All translations are my own.

[1]   This lecture was printed in Moscow as a pamplet in 1910. It has become quite difficult to locate; p. 12.

[2]   Boris Eikhenbaum, *The Young Tolstoy*, trans., ed. Gary Kern, Ann Arbor: Ardis, 1972, p. 11.

[3]   Ibid., p. 46

The following footnotes are from three editions of Tolstoy's works and are indentified by year: *1913, 1928* or *1960*. a) *Polnoe Sobranie Sochinenii* (Complete works), Moscow, *1913*, 20 vols. b) *Polnoe Sobranie Sochinenii*, Moscow, *1928-58*, 90 vols. c) *Sobranie Sochinenii* (Works), Moscow, *1960-65*, 20 vols.

[4]   *Voina i mir* (*War and Peace*), *1960*, Vol. VII, Part IV, 1, Ch. 16, p. 74.

[5]   Isaiah Berlin, "The Hedgehog and the Fox," 1953, repr. in his *Russian Thinkers*, New York, 1978, p. 51.

[6]   Tolstoy, "O zhizni" ("About Life"), 1886-87; *1913*, Vol. XVII, Ch. I, p. 218.

[7]   Ibid., Ch. XXII, p. 264.

[8]   Ibid., Ch. XXXI, p. 291.

[9]   Tolstoy's Letters, sel., ed., and trans. R.F. Christian, New York, 1978, Vol. II, p. 561.

[10]   Ibid., p. 598.

[11]   Tolstoy, "V chem moia vera" ("My Religion"), 1884; *1928*, Vol. 23, Ch. VIII, p. 391.

[12]   Ibid., Ch. XI, p. 438.

[13]   Tolstoy, "Tsarstvo bozhie vnutri vas" (The Kingdom of God is within you), 1890-93; *1928*, vol. XXVIII, Ch. 10, p. 186

[14]   *Voina i mir* (*War and Peace*), *1960*, Vol. VII, Part IV, 1, Ch. 13, p. 60.

[15]   F.M. Dostoevsky, *Sobranie Sochinenii*, 10 Vols., Moscow, 1956-58; Vol. 3, *Zapiski iz mertvovo doma* (*Notes from the House of the Dead*), p. 473.

[16]   Ibid., p. 437.

[17]   In *The Diary of a Writer*, trans. Boris Brazol, New York, 1949, Vol. 1, p. 9.

[18]   Ibid., p. 12.

[19]   Ibid., p. 9.

[20]   Dostoevsky, Vol. 8, *Podrostok* (*The Adolescent*), Part I, Ch. 5, 3, p. 98.

[21]   Stavrogin's Confession, F.M. Dostoevsky, *The Possessed*, trans. Constance Jarrett, New York: Modern Library, 1936, p. 712.

trans. Constance Jarrett, New York: Modern Library, 1936, p. 712.

[22] Dostoevsky, Vol. 7, *Bessy (The Possessed)*, Part III, Ch. 6, 2, p. 644.

[23] Dostoevsky, Vol. 9, *Brat'ia Karamazovy (The Brothers Karamazov)*, Part II, 5, p. 324.

[24] George Panichas, *The Burden of Vision, Dostoevsky's Spiritual Art*, Grand Rapids, MI.: W.B. Eerdman's, 1977, p. 51.

[25] Dostoevsky, *Idiot (The Idiot)*, Vol. 6, Part II, Ch. 5, p. 257.

[26] Panichas, p. 87

[27] Ibid., p. 171.

[28] Dostoevsky, *Brat'ia Karamazovy (The Brothers Karamazov)*, Vol. 9, Part II, 6, Ch. 3, pp. 400-401.

[29] V. Lakshin, *Tolstoy i Chekhov*, Moscow, 1963, 2nd ed. 1975. Logan Speirs, *Tolstoy and Chekhov*, London, 1971. *Chekhov i Lev Tolstoy*, coll. essays, ed. D. Opul'skaia and others, Moscow, 1980.

[30] L., V, pp. 283-4.

[31] V, 417.

[32] Ibid., 418.

[33] *A.P. Chekhov o literature*, ed. L. Pokrovskaia, Moscow, 1955, 310.

[34] L., I, 29.

[35] L., III, 11.

[36] "Dostoevsky i Chekhov", by Volzhskii, in *Russkaia Mysl'*, 1913, second pagination, pp. 33-42. "Chelovek v khudozhestvennom mire Dostoevskovo i Chekhova" (Man in Dostoevsky's and Chekhov's Artistic World), E.A. Polotskaia, pp. 184-245 in *Dostoevskii i russkie pisateli* (Dostoevsky and Russian Writers), coll. articles, Moscow, 1971. "Chekhov i Dostoevskii," in *Problemy traditsii i novatorstva v russkoi literature, 19 i nachala 20 vekov*, ed. M. Ia Ermakova and others, Gorky, 1981.

[37] L., III, 169.

[38] *A.P. Chekhov o literature*, p. 309.

[39] L., IV, p. 32.

[40] Simon Karlinsky, *Anton Chekhov's Life and Thought*, Univ. of California Press, 1975, p. 26.

[41] XIV-XV, p. 324.

[42] L., III, 273.

[43] Lev Shestov, "Tvorchestvo iz nichego" (Creation from the Void), in *Nachala i kontsy* (Beginnings and Endings), Petersburg, 1908, p. 5.

[44] XVII, 90.

III

The Doctor and the Priest

From the earliest beginnings of Chekhov's literary career hardly a year went by when a doctor was absent from the pages of his fiction.

"What Is Most Frequently Portrayed in Novels, Stories, Etc.?" is the title of a short, humorous sketch published in March 1880, the second product of Chekhov's imagination. The lengthy enumeration, gleaming with silliness, which answers the title's question ranges from a countess to a dog, with briefly stated attributes of each—"traces of faded beauty" of the countess and "inability to talk" as the dog's only shortcoming. The figure of the doctor is the only one given a whole descriptive paragraph. His face bears a worried expression and he generates "hope of a crisis." He is often bald and carries a cane with a knob. "And where there is a doctor, there is also rheumatism from righteous toil, migraine, inflammation of the brain, care of a wounded duelist, and the inevitable advice to take a water cure."[1] Another example of a doctor sharing in the foolery and hilarity streaming in sparkling profusion from Chekhov's early pen is "An Advertisement of Doctor Chertolov— specialist in female, male, and infants' diseases, in chest, back, neck, and cervical ailments and many others. Office hours daily from seven a.m. to midnight. Needy patients treated free of charge on February 30th, April 31st, and June 31st; on February 29th with a substantial discount."[2]

It is mostly across a sunny landscape of laughter, comic or trivial misadventures, and chance encounters that the fictional physicians and medical assistants move during the first seven years of Chekhov's literary career, those early years of prolific and facile output. Most of the doctors and assistants are, like their creator, young, witty, physically fit, gregarious, prone to drink, and fond of good food. But rather than represent a fictional self of Chekhov, they appear as targets of critical comments on the state of the medical profession that the author wishes to voice. All biographical material on Chekhov reveals his meticulous attention to his patients, his unrelenting endeavors to alleviate suffering, and his persistent disregard of remunerative considerations. And the strain of criticism that runs alongside the hilarity in the early stories is directed against physicians' violations of their function as healers—carelessness and indifference toward their patients and preoccupation with financial gain.

The assistant doctor Ivanov in "Trial" (1881) listens to a long tirade of accusations flung at him by a well-informed observer: "Who came close to performing an autopsy on the drunken carpenter last year instead of on a corpse? Had he not come to, you would have ripped his belly open. And who mixes castor oil with hempseed oil?... And who killed Malania? You gave her a laxative and then an astringent and then again a laxative and that was more than her body could bear. It's dogs and not people you should be treating."[3]

The country doctor in "June Twenty-Ninth" (1882) regales

his companions at a hunting party with numerous anec-
dotes and boasts that he could make millions if he chose to
collaborate with literary editors. When he claims to refrain
from such a tempting venture because the press tells nothing
but lies, the narrator, who is also a member of the party,
counters with derogatory comments on the medical profession: "And what about your medicine? Medicine?! What is it
worth? Don't *you* tell lies? All you do is take money. What is a
doctor? A doctor is a preface to a gravedigger."[4]

Perhaps the most striking figure of a doctor in Chekhov's
early works is the young, brilliant, and highly successful
Toporkov in "Late-Blooming Flowers," one of the few longer
works of that period. It appeared in four installments in the
fall of 1882. Some of Chekhov's contemporaries claimed to
see, behind the portrait of Toporkov, features of G.A. Zakharin, a famous diagnostician and clinicist of the School of
Medicine at Moscow University, known for the pomposity of
his manner and his businesslike attitude toward his patients.
With a strong dose of melodrama, parodying the plot and
style of the cheap serialized novels currently popular with
the readers of *The Alarm Clock*, *Fragments*, and their like,
Chekhov indicts Toporkov for the cold and heartless treatment of his patients and his love of money. He leads him to a
mawkishly staged admission that he is pursuing the wrong
goals, a conclusion couched in effusive theatricality but realized too late to yield felicitous results. It would be curious to
know whether Toporkov's repelling and revealing habit of
swallowing noisily was a product of Chekhov's imagination
or a trait observed in Zakharin. "Toporkov swallowed very
loudly. Apparently he did not stand on ceremony and drank
the way he liked. It seemed as if each swallow was hurled
down a precipice where it splashed against something large
and smooth."[5] In spite of his shortcomings Toporkov exemplifies the central function of a doctor in the early stories—
that of a healer. When two of Toporkov's patients recuperate
and revel in a sense of well-being, Chekhov comments:
"They feel and understand health, which is something that
an ordinary well person neither feels nor understands.

Health is freedom, but who besides released prisoners enjoys a sense of freedom?"[6]

The event that led Chekhov to reexamine the original priority of medicine over literature in his career is familiar enough. It was a letter of March 25, 1886, which he received from the noted novelist Dmitri Vassilievich Grigorovich, by thirty-eight years his senior. Grigorovich wrote of Chekhov's outstanding talent—he had particularly liked the recently published story "The Hunter"—and urged his young protegé to devote more time to thoughtful preparation for writing, to stop publishing hastily jotted-down thoughts and impressions, for "to neglect your talent would be a great moral sin." Chekhov responded gratefully and enthusiastically, promising to follow Grigorovich's advice. In 1887, sixty-four short stories by Chekhov were published; in 1888, the number fell to nine.

Though Chekhov continued to be a practicing physician, a reexamination of the relationship between medicine and literature was taking place in his consciousness, medicine moving to assume the function of an important tool of literary creativity. Much later, in 1899, at the zenith of his creativity and success, Chekhov wrote to a former classmate in medical school: "Without doubt, the study of medical sciences had a serious influence on my literary activity; it has considerably widened the sphere of my observations, enriched me with knowledge the true value of which for me as a writer can only be understood by a person who is a physician himself."[7] Chekhov the doctor came in close contact with a large and varied number of people from all walks of life—peasants rich and poor, merchants, petty traders, civil servants of all ranks, landowners big and small, intellectuals, professionals, artists. He entered their houses not as a guest when everything was tidied, cleaned, and polished, but at moments of crises, when illness, accident, or death had struck and led people not only to neglect the customary attention to their surroundings and appearance, but to drop the protective mask of conventionality from their inner selves as well. Chekhov the writer began to use medicine in the same way a sculptor uses anatomy as a preparation for carving and chiseling the human body. Chekhov the doctor not only knew the anatomy of the human body, but was also cognizant of the crucial relationship between psychic and physical factors as well. The contact with sick, pain-stricken people developed in Chekhov the writer an acute feeling for human suffering and emotional distress.

Among the drastically reduced number of stories written in 1888, in response to Grigorovich's prodding, was "An Attack of Nerves." A young student, Vassiliev, is persuaded by two friends to accompany them to a district of houses of ill repute, which Vassiliev knew until then only from hearsay. He is revolted by the garish dress, the cynical language, the impudent gait, the drunkenness, the bored, indifferent and grotesquely made-up faces of the prostitutes, and comes close to a nervous breakdown and suicide after realizing that "everything that is known as human dignity, personality, image, and likeness of God was here defiled down to its very foundations."[8] A friend's description of Vassiliev's character applies to Chekhov himself: "He is a talented person. There are literary, theatrical, artistic talents, but he has a special talent—a 'human' talent. He is endowed with a keen, magnificent feeling for pain in general. As a good actor reproduces the movements and the voice of another person, so Vassiliev reproduces in his soul someone else's pain...."[9]

Chekhov's extraordinary ability to get into the skin of a vast number of people he came in contact with became a salient characteristic of his art. Commenting on the wealth and thronging variety of characters presented on the pages of Chekhov's fiction, the Soviet writer and critic Korney Chukovsky let his imagination muse on what a terrible crush and congestion would occur if by some miracle all the people portrayed in Chekhov's works should suddenly come to life and burst forth onto a street in Moscow: "...all these policemen, midwives, actors, tailors, convicts, cooks, pilgrims, teachers, landlords, bishops, circus acrobats, civil servants of all ranks and departments, peasants from North and South, generals, bathhouse attendants, engineers, horse thieves, monasterial servants, merchants, choir members, soldiers, matchmakers, piano tuners, firemen, prosecutors, deacons, professors, shepherds, lawyers—for even the largest city square could not hold such a dense populace."[10] And every single individual in that vast throng carried his own distinctive, vivid traits in appearance and behavior—his speech, gait, gestures, habits, moods—thoughts and actions his alone—every one a unique and inimitable human being. To the very end of his life Chekhov treasured the range of vision granted to an observant physician. A few months before his death on July 2, 1904, momentarily forgetting his physical debility, he expressed the desire to volunteer as a physician and to be ordered to the front in the war with Japan: "A doctor is able to see more."

What does a doctor's vision convey? How does it and how should it function? This question is examined in two works of Chekhov's, the play *Ivanov* and the story "The Princess," both written in the late 1880s, those transitional years when medicine was developing into a literary tool. Ivanov, central character of the play, is the victim of a psychic disorder which Chekhov diagnoses as being a typical malaise afflicting the average Russian intellectual of his day: a penchant for brief spells of animated agitation and high spirits which are invariably followed by lengthy stretches of depression, fatigue, apathy, boredom, and inability to face reality and to cope with it. Ivanov, as we meet him, is no longer in love with his terminally ill wife Anna, shies away from his worsening financial problems, and hesitantly draws toward the young and rich Sasha, who is in love with him and hopes to marry him after Anna's death.

In spite of his shortcomings, Ivanov is not portrayed as a villain. He is confused, ineffectual, irresolute, and helpless, but he is basically a decent person. It is his wife Anna's doctor, L'vov, who bears the brunt of Chekhov's censure. L'vov prides himself on being "an honest person" and appears to divide humanity into those who are scoundrels and those who are not—an antipode to Chekhov's distaste for tags and labels. Sasha dislikes him intensely: "He cannot ask for a glass of water or light a cigarette without displaying his extraordinary honesty. When he walks or talks, there is a large sign on his face, 'I am an honest person.' "

"Human cruelty fills me with indignation," proclaims L'vov. He accuses Ivanov of wishing for Anna's death and the chance to marry rich Sasha. "In my capacity as a physician I demand that you change your behavior toward your wife. It is killing her," he flings at Ivanov, who feebly answers that "there are too many wheels, screws, and valves in each one of us to permit passing judgment on the strength of first impressions and a few outward symptoms."[11] But on Ivanov's and Sasha's wedding day, a year after Anna's death, L'vov considers it to be his duty "as an honest man" to open Sasha's eyes and to declare, for all to hear, that Ivanov is a scoundrel. Unable to bear the insult, Ivanov shoots himself. After finishing the play Chekhov wrote to Suvorin: "If the audience should leave the theater under the impression that people like Ivanov are scoundrels and doctors like L'vov great men, I shall have to go into retirement and hurl my pen to the devil."[12]

From this indictment of a mindless and shortsighted approach to people and its destructive consequences, from this examination of what a physician's behavior should not be, Chekhov turns in "The Princess" to an account of astute, humanitarian observations supplied by a doctor. The heroine of the story is a wealthy woman who engages in a number of charitable ventures. Her generosity seems impressive at first sight. She has built a house for homeless old women and organized a school where she personally wished to teach and arranged to feed the infants whose mothers worked in the fields. But the doctor Mikhail Ivanovich, whom the princess engages in conversation in the garden of the monastery which she honors with her visit, paints a very dismal picture of her activities. In the five years since she saw the doctor last, she tells him, she has married, become a "princess instead of a countess," had to sell three of her landholdings to pay her husband's debts, and then sought a divorce. "It is

frightening to look back," she sighs, "so many changes, all
sorts of misfortunes, so many mistakes!" She is surprised
when the doctor readily agrees that she has indeed made
many mistakes, for she does not expect him to know anything about her intimate life. And she urges him to tell her
what he knows about her mistakes.

He bursts out with an agitated and lengthy tirade of scath-
ing accusations. Her main mistake is that her whole lifestyle
is based on "revulsion to people," on reviling the human
personality. All her servants and employees are treated with
coldness and haughty contempt. Her philanthropic activities he calls "a puppet show, a comedy, a game of brotherly
love." The inmates of her home for aged women are treated
like human beings only on the days of her inspection visits.
The schoolboys she intended to teach all ran away after a
short while and had to be whipped or bribed to attend. And
the mothers whose infants she wanted to feed had to be
ordered to take turns leaving their children for "the princess's amusement." "Everyone ran away from your good
deeds...because in all your ventures...there was not a trace of
love and compassion. There was only the desire to play with
living dolls and nothing else.... Whoever is incapable of dis-
tinguishing human beings from lapdogs should not engage
in philanthropy."[13]

A bitter note of personal slight and resentment is added to
the doctor's outburst. He had been in the employ of the
princess's father and had then continued to work for her and
to minister to her own needs and the needs of those living on
her estates—"conscientiously, eschewing holidays and
vacations, earning everybody's devotion within a perimeter
of a hundred versts." And then, five years ago she had
suddenly dismissed him without a word of explanation. The
doctor's tirade is charged with emotion and couched in savage words and vivid images, but the reader is left to assess
independently its possible bias as well as the likelihood of its
justification. The princess experiences a mere passing feeling of discomfort over the doctor's harangue. Before she
leaves the monastery on the following day, the doctor

approaches her with apologies for "all the foolish things he said to her." She graciously proffers her hand to be kissed and departs "savoring the ultimate delight of forgiving offenses and of smiling pleasantly at enemies."

From the early function as a healer and the later role as an observant critic, from this exposure of an individual's lack of sensitivity and humaneness, Chekhov's doctor moves in "A Dreary Story" (1889) to a broader issue. In fact, the protagonist, Nikolay Stepanovich, is perhaps the most significant figure in the long gallery of members of the medical profession in Chekhov's fiction. His role is not that of a healer or an observer or a critic voicing his comments or formulating his diagnoses from an outside vantage point. His is the inside story of a man dedicated exclusively to science, a retrospective assessment of a long and successful career as a physician and a scholar. It is an exploration into the relationship between rational and nonrational elements of human consciousness. It would appear that Nikolay Stepanovich could look back with joyful satisfaction upon his life, for he has seemingly achieved everything that his youthful dreams had envisioned. "I was given more than I dared to hope for. For thirty years I was a popular professor, had excellent colleagues. I enjoyed honors and fame. I loved, married out of passionate love, had children. In short, when I look back, my life seems a beautiful, accomplished composition."[14]

And yet, the adjective in the title of the story is symbolic of Nikolay Stepanovich's situation. In the entire range of his works Chekhov never drew a character closer to a complete state of happiness in the earlier stages of his life and further removed from it at its close. When he was a young student, Nikolay Stepanovich reminisces, the sounds of an accordion from a distant pub or the jingling of bells of a passing troika were enough to fill not only his heart but even his stomach, legs, and arms with a feeling of happiness. "I would listen to the accordion or the receding bells and picture myself a doctor, and each picture was brighter than the preceding one." But what Nikolay Stepanovich tells us now provides a mournful, discordant finale to "the beautiful composition" of his life. As we listen, every revelation of his thoughts, feelings, fears, doubts, and unexpected discoveries adds a new facet to a picture of a total disintegration of his self.

He had devoted his great intellectual talents and large powers of industry exclusively to science. Even as he speaks to us, he confesses that nothing interests him except science; not literature, not the stage, nor any other of the creative arts. But he has come to feel the blighting effects of bringing everything before the bar of reason and of ignoring the many nonrational facets of human life. He never tells us his last name, which in Russia is known to every literate person and abroad is mentioned from university lecterns with the adjectives "famous" and "honorable" appended. But we learn that he has come to dislike this popular name of his and that he feels "cheated by it."[15] "I am every bit as dim and ugly as my name is brilliant and beautiful," he says at the opening of his narrative. He describes his deplorable physical condition, his sunken chest, narrow shoulders, trembling head and hands, the myriad of wrinkles that cover his face when he smiles. He is ill, suffers from insomnia, and knows as a physician that he has but a few more months to live. But he assesses his physical debility as a side effect rather than as the major cause of his distress.

His misery stems from a malfunction of his will, his consciousness. Accustomed to exercise his mind with analytical directness and precision, he puts his own self to a test by asking, "What do I want?" For he believes that desires and not actions are the key to a person's character. "Tell me what you want and I will tell you who you are," he says. The test brings the following answer: "I'd like our wives, children, friends, and students to love us as ordinary people and not as bearers of our name, our brand, our label. What else? I'd like to have helpers and successors. What else? I'd like to wake up a hundred years from now and to have a glimpse at what is happening in science. I'd like to live another ten years or so. And what more? Nothing more."[16]

Nikolay Stepanovich longs for a personal union with his fellow men and for an integration of his own life into the

universal stream of existence. As he examines the results of
the test he has subjected his own self to, he is struck by the
paucity of his atrophied desires. "I clearly see that something vital, something very important, is missing in my
desires. In my passion for science,...in all my thoughts, feelings, and the conceptions which I form about everything,
something is missing that would bind all these things into a
linked system."[17] He realizes that every one of his thoughts
and feelings is leading a separate existence and that his
judgments about science and about all nonrational facets of
human existence are not knit together by a unifying idea,
"the God of living man." He lacks the feeling of cosmic
harmony and interdependence from which Dostoevsky's
Father Zossima drew his luminous serenity.

The absence of a comprehensive inner vision Nikolay Stepanovich assesses as the true cause of his nightmarish
anguish. He has come to be trapped, imprisoned within the
confining walls of rationalism, relying exclusively on the
function of his intellect. Everything that once made his life
significant and brought him joy has become meaningless.
And with what consummate artistry Chekhov paints the
steps that carry Nikolay Stepanovich toward an ultimate
understanding of his plight, of his bondage! How chilling to
see the ties of affection, solicitude, and intellectual rapport
which bound him to the world dropping off one by one,
leaving him stripped of emotions and concern, less and less
able to proffer love and sympathy, to offer help, to take
interest, and sinking to greater and greater depths of helpless, despairing solitude!

His colleagues and students bore him. He tries to cut short
his assistant's visit by staring at him as though trying to
hypnotize him with the thought "Go away, go away!" In the
middle of a lecture he will feel the urge to stretch his arms
toward the audience and to complain loudly. "I want to
shout that I have been poisoned; new thoughts, hitherto
unknown, are poisoning the last days of my life and continue
to sting my brain like mosquitos."

His wife, once a lithesome, beautiful, and intelligent girl,

Nikolay Stepanovich sees transformed into an old, stout, clumsy woman who irritates him with her preoccupation with petty budgetary worries. He refers to his son, who holds a minor army post in Warsaw, merely as "our officer" and grudgingly subsidizes him with a small monthly allowance. He has grown cold and indifferent toward his daughter Liza as well. He dislikes her worthless suitor Gnekker. But the telegram informing him of their elopement fails to shock him. "I read the telegram and it frightens me only for short a while. What frightens me is not what Liza and Gnekker have done, but my own indifference to the news of their marriage.... Indifference is a paralysis of the soul, it is premature death."[18] And it is the same lack of genuine concern, the detachment from the broad current of life, the entrapment in cognitive capabilities which prevent Nikolay Stepanovich from offering any help to Katia, the young woman whose guardian he used to be. Once incapable of sharing her enthusiasm for the theater, he is now equally incapable of suggesting remedies when she comes to realize her lack of talent, her inadequacy as an actress. Sobbing, clutching, and kissing his hand, she cries for help: "You are my father, aren't you? My only friend? You are clever, well educated, you've lived a long life! You've been a teacher! So do tell me. What should I do?"[19] But Nikolay Stepanovich's only answer to this pitiful cry of desperation is that he honestly does not know what she should do; and he then suggests that they should have lunch together.

"A Dreary Story" was the last significant work of Chekhov's written before his departure for Sakhalin. Several epistolary statements written upon completion of the story indicate that Chekhov was aware of having dealt with "a new theme."[20] But was he aware at the time *how* new the theme was and how central Nikolay Stepanovich's diagnosis of his own fettering and crippling disease—the discovery that indifference is a paralysis of the soul, that it is premature death—would become during the post-Sakhalin, mature period of his creativity? After Sakhalin Chekhov's microscope examined the virus diagnosed in "A Dreary Story," penetrating into layer upon layer of human existence, attacking it with ravaging virulence. As the image of the doctor had shared, alongside a vast throng of figures from all walks of life, in the hilarity and innumerable witty thrusts of Chekhov's early stories, so the figure of the doctor plays a comparable role in his serious, mature works; the doctor is afflicted by the same predicaments which beset protagonists drawn from other social groups, predicaments affecting man's will, conscience, capacity to communicate, ability to love, and attitude toward the natural environment. The doctor continues in his role as healer, observer, diagnostician, but a new facet is added to his functions—a facet already indicated by Nikolay Stepanovich—that of a victim succumbing to the disease spawned by spiritual paralysis. All this will be discussed in connection with the analysis of the broad issues they form a part of, with Ragin and his demise in "Ward No. 6" and Startsev in "Ionych" reaching a terminal condition looming mournfully before the reader.

By 1900 Chekhov's tubercular condition had worsened perceptibly, gravely impairing his physical stamina and creative powers. And the alcoholic Chebutykin in *The Three Sisters*, written in that year, is the last in the long sequence of prominent doctor figures in his fiction. Chebutykin deserves to be mentioned at this point not only because he stands as the final link in the chain, but because he is sorrowfully singled out by Chekhov as a tombstone, lifted to the position of a phantom, hovering precariously on a borderline of human life. He is the deadly germ Indifference personified, raised to the level of a parody of existence. "Nothing matters" is his motto and he wishes he did not exist. In fact, he muses, "Perhaps I am not a person, but I only pretend that I have arms and legs and a head; perhaps I do not exist at all and it only seems that I walk, eat, sleep."[21] When Andrey, the sisters' dissolute brother, who is vainly trying to ward off obesity, asks him for a remedy for short breath, he is unable to provide one, for he does not remember anything. "People think that I am a doctor, that I know how to treat all sorts of diseases, but I know absolutely nothing. I have forgotten everything I knew."[22] A few days before he speaks in the third act, he had been summoned to minister to a sick woman, but she had died and he admits that he is responsible for her death—a realization that does not move him in the slightest. He is present, in the capacity of a second and an attending physician, at the duel between Baron Tuzenbach and Solenyi and reacts with utter indifference to Tuzenbach's death. "One more baron or one less baron—what is the difference?" is his view. After announcing the tragedy to the three sisters he draws a newspaper from his pocket and reverts to his favorite pastime of reading trivial bits of information. Humming his nonsensical "Tarara-bumbia" before the final curtain, he provides a dirge counterpointed to the voices of the three sisters, which blends in a poetic melody of joyous hope and longing.

The strict rules of worship and church attendance imposed by Chekhov's pious and devout father on all members of the family held a prominent place among the fettering bonds which prompted Chekhov to speak of striving for personal freedom as a laborious process of squeezing slave blood, drop by drop, out of his system. "I have received in my childhood a religious education and a religious upbringing, with church singing,[23] with reading of the Epistles and of the Psalms in church, with punctual attendance of matins, with the duty to help at the altar and to ring the church bells," reads an oft-quoted statement by Chekhov made in 1892.[24] "And so? When I now think of my childhood, I see it in rather somber tones: I have no religion now. You know, when I and my brothers would sing in the middle of the church the trio 'Let My Prayer Rise unto Thee like Incense...' or 'Song of the Archangel,' everybody would look at us with tender emotion and envy my parents; we, however, felt like young convicts." The assertion that he had no religion was repeatedly professed by Chekhov throughout his life. As late as 1903 he stated that he invariably felt perplexed at the sight of "an educated believer." This has prompted critics in the past and in the present, in the Soviet Union as well as in the West, to

speak almost unanimously of Chekhov as an atheist or as an
agnostic at best, and to neglect an examination of the figure
of the priest and the function of religious rites and symbols
in his fiction.

The story "A Nightmare" (1886) introduces us to this vital
topic. The landowner Kunin has been entrusted by the
responsible authorities with the task of assisting in the
organization of a parish school in the district where his
estate is located. Kunin summons the local village priest,
Father Iakov, to discuss the project. Step by step the figure of
the priest unfolds before the reader as apprehended by
Kunin, a sophisticated and self-assured man in whose heart
"there remained a small particle of religious feeling, feebly
glimmering alongside other nursery fairytales." Kunin's
first impressions are highly unfavorable. The face of the
young, puny, narrow-chested priest is coarse, snub-nosed,
and red-cheeked "like a peasant woman's," framed in straight
shoulder-length red hair and uneven tufts of a sparse and
untidy beard. The skirt of his worn and patched cassock is
spattered with mud. Kunin's displeasure mounts observing
Father Iakov's awkward stance, undignified timidity bordering on servility, and apparent lack of interest in or even
comprehension of the issues concerning the parish school
project. A flicker of animation lights the priest's features
only when tea and cookies are brought in by a butler. But
Kunin's disapproval turns to disgust watching Father
Iakov's greedy appetite and seeing him surreptitiously slipping a cookie in his pocket. "What a strange, uncouth fellow"
is Kunin's verdict at the end of this first encounter.[25]

The second meeting takes place in the squalid, dilapidated
village church which Kunin decides to visit on the following
Sunday. He is struck by the fact that the congregation
appears, at a first glance, to consist exclusively of old people
and children, but looking around more closely he realizes
that he mistook young people for old. "However, he did not
attach any particular significance to this small optical
illusion"[26]—a hint that Kunin's first impressions might be
erroneous and his vision faulty. His antagonism to Father

Iakov deepens as he watches his inept conduct of the service. Seemingly handicapped by youth and inexperience, the priest's voice, gait, and gestures lack the dignity and composure which Kunin deems essential for a member of the ecclesiastical profession. No less disheartening proves a visit to Father Iakov's ill-furnished, destitute home after the service. Kunin's hopes to be served some tea are dashed after mysterious, whispered consultations conducted by the host behind a partition—probably with his wife, thinks Kunin—from which the priest returns flushed and perspiring, too agitated and embarrassed to be able to conduct any semblance of a conversation with his guest. Upon his return home Kunin, guided by a feeling "close to hatred of Father Iakov," writes a letter to the bishop denouncing the priest as too young, leading—it seems—an intemperate life, and "failing to meet the standards which the Russian people, in the course of centuries, have come to expect from their spiritual leaders."

Kunin spends the following week away from his estate and is informed, upon his return, that Father Iakov has come daily during his absence trying to see him. "He must have really liked my cookies," sardonically thinks Kunin. He receives the priest on Sunday. This time not only the skirt of his cassock but his hat as well is spattered with mud. Kunin clearly indicates his desire to cut the meeting as short as possible. After painful efforts to overcome his timidity, trembling and white-faced, Father Iakov finally blurts out the purpose of his visit. He had heard that Kunin had recently dismissed his clerk and offers his services as a replacement, for ten rubles a month, which is one half of the former clerk's salary.

Haltingly, overcome with mounting agitation and despair, he reveals his agonizing plight to the astounded Kunin. He spends one half of his miniscule yearly salary of 150 rubles as a contribution to the ecclesiastical training of his younger brother and for the support of his own predecessor, the ailing and retired village priest Father Avraamy. Hunger is Father Iakov's constant companion. It impedes his performance of religious rites. Thoughts of food prevented him from comprehending Kunin's comments concerning the parish school during their first meeting. The cookie slipped into his pocket was intended for his wife, whom he pities with all his heart, an educated, well-bred young woman "used to having tea, white bread, and bed sheets." There was no tea in his house to offer upon Kunin's visit. Now pacing the room and gesticulating, now stopping and staring wildly at the floor, as if oblivious of Kunin's presence, Father Iakov confesses that he is too proud to ask for help, to go begging, and too proud to let Father Avraamy resort to such practices, which would be degrading to their cloth. He is ashamed of his poverty, of his hunger, of his tattered clothes, though he realizes that pride is a sin and an unseemly sentiment for a priest.

Suddenly coming to, as if ashamed of his outburst, Father Iakov falls silent and, remembering his host's initial, clearly conveyed unwillingness to spend much time with him, abruptly takes his leave from a stunned and horrified Kunin. Watching from a window, Kunin observes that the priest has no horse. He sets out on foot, in deep mud, on the four-mile trip home. And it dawns on Kunin that Father Iakov has walked that distance every day for a week in a vain attempt to see him and to reach for a pitifully small betterment of his financial condition. But then the view from the window yields an even more crucial revelation and a final glimpse of Father Iakov's character. Kunin sees the coachman Andrey and the boy Paramon rushing forward to receive a blessing, jumping across puddles and spattering the priest with mud. "Father Iakov took off his hat and slowly blessed Andrey, then he blessed the boy and stroked his head."[27] All the mud obstructing the path of daily life has not marred the priest's human sympathy and selfless devotion to his fellow men. Does the title of the story relate to the nightmarish impasse of Father Iakov? Or to Kunin's faulty vision? Or does it express individual helplessness in a drama rooted in far-reaching contemporary issues? Probably a mingling of the three.

The abysmal poverty of Father Iakov is an exception

rather than the rule in the gallery of ecclesiastical figures drawn in Chekhov's fiction. Father Christopher, prior of a small-town church in "The Steppe" (1888), is even engaged in a major commercial transaction, en route to a distant town to sell wool on behalf of his young son-in-law, who is unsure of his own financial skill. As we meet him, on an early July morning at the outset of his trip, he gazes with serene wonderment at the steppe bathed in sunlight that unfolds all around him. His smile is so broad that it seems to reach to the brim of his hat. The smile and the pleased amazement never seem to leave his face. As the hours pass and the temperature rises, "a pleasant thought appears to be stuck in his brain from the heat." At the first rest stop this pleasant thought begs to be released and Father Christopher addresses one of his three travelling companions, the nine-year-old boy Egorushka, who is being sent by his mother to enroll in the distant town's school. It turns out that the priest was thinking of the extensive theological and secular education he himself received in his youth. To set an example for Egoruskha, he tells the boy of composing poetry in Latin at the age of fifteen, of mastering the reading of Greek and French, of studying philosophy, mathematics, and history. He was blessed with a remarkable memory and hoped to continue his studies at the theological academy in Kiev, but yielded to his parents' entreaties and entered an active ecclesiastical career instead. He has never regretted this decision, he says, for obedience is superior to fasting and prayer. And it enabled him to provide his parents with a happy old age and to bury them with honor.

When Father Christopher lies down after this discourse to take a mid-day nap, a happy smile hovers on his face and the smile is still there when he wakes up. Toward evening the travellers stop at a wayside inn and Father Christopher confides to the Jewish proprietor, Moses, that he is the happiest man in his local town, perfectly content with his lot and wanting nothing. He is in his seventies and afflicted by some physical debilities, which, however, do not bother him too much. Suddenly he recalls the medical treatment for short breath suggested by his oldest son, who is a doctor—"a compressed air cure!"—and the memory of this suggestion, which he considers to be utterly ludicrous and preposterous, sends him into choking spasms of laughter and brings tears of merriment to his eyes. With all the erudition and intellectual training Father Christopher had received in his youth, he cannot summon faith in such clinical treatment of human ailments.

When the travelers reach their destination and Father Christopher succeeds in selling the wool advantageously, his radiant smile does not signify satisfaction with his personal success, but anticipation of the pleasure the profit will bring to his son-in-law. Before taking leave from Egorushka he reverts to his admonitions to the boy to devote all his energies to comprehensive studies so that he will understand everything. "Learn Latin, French, German," he advises, "geography of course, history, theology, philosophy, mathematics...." Father Christopher links these admonitions to precedents drawn from biblical sources and church history: "The holy Apostles spoke all languages—therefore you too learn languages; Vassily the Great studied mathematics and philosophy—therefore you do too; Saint Nestor wrote history—therefore you too study and write history. Follow the saints' example."[28] But Father Christopher's final and most expressive plea to Egorushka, spoken in an urgent whisper, is to shun conceit bred by erudition. " 'Woe to you if, after becoming a scholar, you should choose to neglect and to scorn people stupider than you are...woe! woe!' he repeated, his hand raised and his voice grown thin."[29]

If the motif of a smile is continuously linked with the figure of Father Christopher in "The Steppe," the deacon Pobedov's salient characteristic in "The Duel" (1891) is the fact that he is forever ready to burst into peals of laughter at the slightest provocation, radiating gaiety and good will toward all throughout the narrative, particularly toward the two sparring chief protagonists, the zoologist Von Koren and the young civil servant Laevsky. Antagonism between the two reaches its climax in a duel. Von Koren professes to being a sociologist as well as a zoologist, for these two sciences, he claims, are one. Natural selection should operate in human society as it does in the animal world—the weak must be destroyed. He loathes and despises Laevsky as a prime example of weakness and uselessness slated for annihilation, particularly since he is attractive to women and therefore threatens to multiply his species. Von Koren succeeds in drawing Laevsky into an open quarrel and a duel is set.

Although the deacon feels that his position forbids his presence at such a heathen spectacle as a duel, he cannot resist the temptation to be present. On the way he reflects on the hatred Von Koren and Laevsky feel for each other. If only they had endured the want he, the deacon, remembers from his childhood, how eagerly they would forgive each other's shortcomings and come to value the good qualities each one of them possesses. They should direct their hatred and anger, Pobedov thinks, toward those places where whole streets are drowned in ignorance, greed, filth, abuse, and screams.

Pobedov (the name is derived from *pobeda*, victory) saves Laevsky's life by suddenly springing from the bushes screaming, "He will kill him!" just as Von Koren aims to fire. The scream shatters Von Koren's concentration and the bullet misses its target. Nine years later, in *The Three Sisters*, Pobedov's antipode, Doctor Chebutykin, the spectral embodiment of indifference, will do nothing to prevent Tuzenbach's death in the duel with Solenyi and will react with mindless behavior to the wanton destruction of human life. The experience of the duel has a profound, salutary effect on Laevsky, and even Von Koren admits that a remarkable change has taken place in his adversary—a change he had not considered possible. When the two part as friends, Pobedov explains exultantly, addressing Von Koren: "Today you have won a victory over the greatest foe of mankind, pride!"[30]

Two weeks after publication of "The Nightmare" there appeared "On Easter Night," an unduly neglected story

offering crucial insight into those creative processes of
Chekhov's imagination which had already yielded the figure of Father Iakov and were later to bring forth the images
of Father Christopher and the deacon Pobedov and to reverberate throughout a number of other important works. It is a
story spun of fragile, interwoven threads of poetic and numinous inspiration. Set on the night of the celebration of the
Resurrection, it speaks of light and of darkness, of sky and of
earth, of the unison between the temporal and the eternal
worlds. Nature itself sets the tone. The narrator, the author,
is about to cross the River Goltva on a rope ferry to attend the
midnight service in the monastery on the opposite bank.
Usually a quiet, unassuming stream, the river is swollen by
the spring thaw to the dimensions of a large lake. The sky is
densely strewn with stars of all sizes. They have all come out
"in celebration," polished, radiant, and festive, and all are
reflected in the water, bathing in the dark depths and shivering with the faint ripples of the current. As if to stress the
majestic concord of stars and water, which is inaccessible to
man-made illumination, a rocket suddenly cleaves the darkness, shoots upward in an arc, and dissolves into crackling
sparks "as if it had crashed against the sky." The church
bells, on the other hand, blend harmoniously with the environment. When at midnight the first peal begins to ring, low
and rich, it is as if "the hoarse voice of darkness itself had
uttered the sounds."[31]

The arrival of the ferry to pick up the narrator coincides
with these solemn sounds heralding the joyous Easter ritual
on the other bank. The ferry is operated manually by a rope
pulled by the novice monk Ieronim. The rope is the only link
between the bank sunk in darkness, where the narrator is
waiting, and the opposite shore, which is beginning to be lit
by the festive glow of candles and of barrels of tar set afire.
Only the contours of Ieronim's tall figure, clad in a cassock,
are visible to the narrator. In a sad, muffled voice the monk
confides to his passenger that he is unable to participate in
the joy that is currently enveloping "sky, earth, the nether
world, and all living creatures," for his friend, the deacon

Nikolay, not yet forty years old, has died that day. As the ferry starts to move across the river, Ieronim unburdens his heart and unfolds the enormity of his loss. But every time he reveals a facet of the tragedy, he lets go of the rope in his agitation and the ferry stops, as if suspended between the sky and the earth, between the stars twinkling above and their reflection below. Glowing and wistful praise of Nikolay's gentle nature and kindness and his concern for Ieronim dominates the first break in the ferry's progress. Nikolay would get up in the middle of the night, according to Ieronim, when the novice monk was ferrying, and call to him across the water to dispel his loneliness and anxiety.

The next break in the ferry's progress is the longest. In fact it is so prolonged that the narrator finally feels compelled to urge Ieronim to return to the rope. During this interval Nikolay's most important feature is described, his extraordinary talent for writing canticles or hymns of praise to the saints. Ieronim explains that a hymn of praise must, of course, conform to the traditional structure, to ancient norms and guidelines set centuries ago by ecclesiastical authorities. But the most important aspect of Nikolay's writing was that there was beauty and sweetness in it, that everything was harmonious, brief, and thorough. There was gentleness, tenderness, delicacy in every line, not a single coarse, harsh, or inappropriate word. And each line was adorned "with flowers, or lightning, or wind, or sun or all objects of the visible world." Nikolay even created new expressive words of his own—not to be found in daily speech or in books, adds Ieronim, hiding his face in his hands in awe and shaking his head in transport and tremulous wonderment.

Nikolay's hymns touch on a crucial aspect of the Russian Orthodox religion, the unique role Orthodoxy assigns to the saints in every aspect of its religious practices and traditions, in liturgy and iconography. Galleries of holy figures traditionally surround the image of Christ at the center of the iconostasis, the screen of icons separating the sanctuary from the rest of the church. And the canonical lives of individual saints, incorporating hymns of praise for their exploits and songs of joy over their achievements, form an integral part of the liturgical services. As the religious image of a saint is not a portrait but an icon, so the story of his travails and exploits is not a historical documentation, but a selection of biographical material aiming "to offer concrete evidence that everything that the Gospel demands of us not only *can* be achieved, but also has been achieved time and again."[32] This role of the saint as beacon of Christian ideals upheld for active emulation and not for intercession on behalf of passive supplicants offers an example of the fundamental stress Orthodoxy places on inspiration rather than on discipline, appealing to the volitional individual striving toward the ideal of spiritual perfection, rather than setting rigid norms of conduct. "Orthodoxy does not persuade or try to compel, it charms and attracts. Such is its method of working in the world."[33] It was this method that Dostoevsky's Grand Inquisitor rejected in his monologue addressing Christ in Ivan Karamazov's "Legend."

When Ieronim resumes pulling the rope, he continues to talk, but his speech is changed. The nostalgic and rapturous agitation is gone. The long sentences laden with emotion are replaced by brief, staccato statements answering negatively the narrator's question as to whether Nikolay's hymns were ever published. No one in the monastery was interested in his work, says Ieronim. Some laughed at it, others even considered it a sin to write new hymns. He, Ieronim, was the only one to appreciate and to know them. Once more overcome with emotion and letting go of the rope, Ieronim bursts into a final wail of grief, lamenting his loneliness and sense of abandonment, for he is now slated to live among people who lack his dead friend's uncommon sensitivity and gentleness and is relegated to the tedious and unending duty of servicing the ferry. When the ferry finally emerges from the darkness and the tranquility of the river and beaches on the noisy, bustling bank bathed in festive lights, Ieronim, who has to continue ferrying, admonishes the narrator to listen carefully to the words of the Easter hymn—"Nikolay's favorite"—which will presently be sung in the monastery church. "It will take your breath away."[34]

The narrator is swept into the general turmoil and mood of exultation of the milling crowd. Hordes of people surge to and from the church gates, continuously going in and coming out. He is struck by the pervading restlessness, "as if people were searching for something." Inside the church, though, no one seemed to be trying to grasp the meaning of the chanted texts and "no one's breath was taken away" by the words of the Easter hymn. A mental image of Ieronim's figure rises before the narrator: he would be humbly standing by a wall, bending forward, the way he bent over the ferry rope, and eagerly taking in "the beauty of the holy phrase." All that was lost on those present his sensitive soul would have avidly absorbed "to the point of ecstasy, to the point of his breath being taken away. And he would have been the happiest man in the church."

This mental vision of Ieronim prompts the narrator to try to get a glimpse of his departed friend's body. He peers through the windows of a row of monk's cells adjoining the church, but sees nothing. On hindsight he claims to be glad not to have seen the body of the deceased. It would have blurred the image of this lovable, lonely poetic figure that had already formed in his mind. "I picture him a timid, pale man with soft, meek, and melancholy features. His eyes must have shone not only with intelligence, but with tenderness as well, and with that barely restrained childlike rapture which I detected in Ieronim's voice when he quoted to me passages from the hymns."[35] Did the narrator perhaps think at this point, of Ieronim's quotation relating to the Saint Nikolay the Wonder Worker: "an angel in appearance, but in substance a man?"

Both visions, of Ieronim in church and of the dead Nikolay, dissolve in the gray light of approaching dawn and rising mist, the stars dimmed, the sky turned morose and a grayish blue, the trees and the young grass seemingly asleep. As the narrator boards the ferry for the return trip, he has his first clear view of Ieronim—a tall, narrow-shouldered man of about thirty-five, with large, rounded features and an unkempt, wedge-shaped beard, his eyes half-closed and list-less, an expression of infinite sadness and exhaustion on his chilled and dew-covered face. Throughout the trip he pulls vigorously and silently on the damp and, "it seems, sleepy" rope, which at times disappears in the mist, and he does not take his eyes off the rosy, dark-browed face of a young mer-chant woman who stands near the narrator and shivers from the misty dampness. There was little sensuousness in his stare, comments the narrator. "I think that Ieronim was trying to find the soft and delicate features of his deceased friend in the face of the woman." The religious experience of the past night, the sense of God's nearness manifest in all parts of creation, spills over into the gray and chilly dawn. The world as seen by the narrator-author is still one; fatigue envelops trees, grass, the ferry rope, as well as the people; fog wafts over the passengers, over the river, and shrouds stretches of the rope; Ieronim no longer speaks of his dead friend and the poetic and spiritual beauty of his hymn, but his eyes, cast beyond his ecclesiastical milieu, continue to express the emotions that moved him during the night and search the features of the young woman, who happens to be crossing the river with him, for traces of affinity with Nikolay.

To be sure, the gaiety of a deacon Pobedov, the serenity of a Father Christopher who will admonish Egorushka "to fol-low the saints" are born of the same religiousness so vividly expressed in Nikolay's hymns and so keenly felt by the monk Ieronim. They all spring from the same intuitive apprehension of a spiritual reality. But this apprehension of God being present all around man in this world can be experienced by anyone. "The intersection of the divine and the natural occurs not only at every moment of time in the life of every man, but also throughout the universe at every space-time point of the natural order."[36] But religiousness is not a synonym for religion. The two may indeed be greatly at odds, if religious myths, images, and rituals cease to function as symbolic tools facilitating man's free ascent from the realm of reason and cognition to spiritual, intuitive communion with God, and assume the character of rigid instruments and perfunctory rites of worship, as Tolstoy claimed they inevitably were. This is what the narrator thought was happening inside the walls of the monastery and church during the Easter service in "On Easter Night," where a restless crowd seemed "to be searching for something" and "no one heeded the beauty of the holy phrase." And this is what Chekhov himself experienced in his youth and rejected and what earned him the reputation of being irreligious.

Images of religious rites perfunctorily executed and of meaningless priestly utterances abound in Chekhov's works. The figure most frequently commented upon is probably the village priest in "In the Ravine," "consoling" Lipa after the funeral of her murdered infant. Lipa is waiting on the guests at the copious funeral repast. While preparing to put a pickled mushroom in his mouth the priest addresses Lipa: "Do not grieve over the babe. For of such is the Kingdom of Heaven."

The most significant scrutiny of institutional religion, however, is provided in "The Bishop" (1902), Chekhov's next-to-last story. In the tranquil simplicity and penetration of its subject, in the limpid prose and rhythmic cadences of its style, it is one of his crowning achievements. A spring-drenched town reverberating with the ringing of church bells during Holy Week, full of bright sunshine and bustling street scenes alternating with magic moonlit vistas of urban and monasterial landscapes, supplies the background. The narrative is punctuated by the traditional sequence of religious services from the eve of Palm Sunday through Maundy Thursday and Good Friday to Easter Sunday. The theme, Chekhov said, had germinated in his mind for some fifteen years.

No one can fail to perceive the parallel between the protagonist, Bishop Peter, and the professor Nikolay Stepanovich in "A Dreary Story." Both have reached a high rank in their respective professions, ecclesiastical and medical. Both are ill and sense approaching death. Both look back nostalgically to a vanished, happy past and both feel trapped and isolated in circumstances from which they are powerless to extricate themselves. Even the words used by Bishop Peter to express his distress echo those of the renowned physician, who laments that something vital, something terribly important, is missing from his inner self. "Sitting in the darkened sanctuary, tears streaming down his face, the Bishop reflected that here he was; he had achieved everything accessible to a man in his position; he had faith and yet not everything was clear to him, something was still missing.... He still seemed to lack something of utmost importance...."[37]

Nikolay Stepanovich bemoans the contrast between the brilliance, the fame of his name and the deplorable condition of his body and the atrophy of his emotional involvements. Bishop Peter's predicament stems from his prominent position in the clerical hierarchy, which weighs on him like an oppressive and confining burden. Though modest by temperament and mild in manner, he constantly feels that the reverence and awe generated by his rank erects an insurmountable barrier separating him from all those around him. "In his presence everyone, even the older senior clerics, quailed and prostrated themselves." People's pettiness, backwardness, and ignorance irritated him. "How well he understood the behavior of the diocesan bishop who had written, in his youth, 'Studies on the Freedom of the Will,' yet now seemed to have forgotten everything, engrossed in trifles and no longer thinking about God!"[38] The higher clergy in the entire diocese is swamped with bureaucratic correspondence. Whole days have to be spent in handling trivial matters of red tape.

Illness and fatigue have rendered Bishop Peter irritable and impatient. He frets over the timidity and stupidity of the petitioners he has to deal with. Recently one of them, the elderly wife of a village priest, had seemed to be so awed and frightened that she was unable to utter a single word and left without stating what she wanted. The triviality of the petitions he handles annoyed him and at times he would throw one on the floor in a fit of anger. Is it possible that Chekhov is here consciously building a contrast to the compassionate rapport between Dostoevsky's Father Zossima and the peasant women who came seeking his help and consolation? Zossima, at death's door like Bishop Peter, yet able to radiate love and to dispense comfort freely and to assuage deep sorrow and alleviate tragedies far removed from the realm of the trivial?

Moments of peace Bishop Peter experiences only when he is in church or lost in reminiscences. In deliberate contrast to the natural environment of the story, bright and warm with the glow of spring, haze is the key image pervading these moments. During the service on the eve of Palm Sunday, sounds and sights melt into each other, the prayers and the singing, the glow of candlelight, the church doors, the faces of the worshippers all merge and blend "as if in a fog." Through the haze of the blurred faces Bishop Peter has a glimpse of a woman in the crowd who resembles his mother, whom he has not seen for nine years. Suddenly tears begin to stream down his face; he does not know why, since he feels serene and at peace. And in an inexplicable rapport with him, here and there someone in the congregation begins to cry "until gradually the whole church was filled with quiet weeping."

Is Bishop Peter's weeping a foreboding? Or a momentary escape from the bondage of his rank? Upon returning to his monasterial home quarters he is told that it was indeed his mother he had seen in church. She had just arrived for a visit. But his joy in greeting her on the following Palm Sunday evening is marred by her show of deference and awe for her illustrious son, which equals that of his customary entourage. Hardly daring to sit down in his presence, addressing him with the formal version of "you" instead of the familiar "thou," she holds her affection and delight in seeing him at bay behind a facade of stiff and meaningless chatter. When the Bishop returned, weakened by illness, exhausted by long hours in church, and overcome by a renewed sense of loneliness occasioned by his mother's incomprehensible reserve, his mind wanders again into the past, as it had on the previous night, trying to recapture the happy years of his childhood and youth. He had remembered a miracle-working icon carried in a procession, how "the air was vibrant with joy and he—at the time known as Pavliusha—followed that icon bareheaded and barefoot, blissfully happy with his innocent faith and his innocent smile."[39] But now the sounds from the adjacent room that keep intruding upon the hazy flow of memories intensify the Bishop's sense of isolation. He hears his mother prattle freely and gaily with his attendant Sisoy, normally a disgruntled and morose man who no longer knows why he had become a monk and who has never made it clear whether he believes in God. A favorite expression of his own making is one of dislike and displeasure. By arbitrarily inserting the consonant "d" into the Russian *ne n-d-ravitsia* (I do not like), he gives it an additional phonetic resonance of disapproval and uses it freely to express his attitude toward his surroundings and toward the people he comes in contact with.

Under the ministrations of this warped and inept cleric— chest and back rubs with candle grease and with vodka mixed with vinegar—Bishop Peter's condition grows rapidly worse. After the Maundy Thursday service, close to collapse, he is overcome by an uncontrollable urge to break out of his confinement and isolation. Falling into bed, "he felt ready to give his life, if only he could be spared the sight of these miserable, cheap shutters and low ceilings, to escape this oppressive monasterial smell. If only there were one single person he could talk to, unburden his heart to." While Sisoy is administering another rub, the Bishop, barely able to speak, whispers: "What kind of a bishop am I? I should have been a village priest, a sexton...or a simple monk.... All this is crushing me....it is crushing...."[40] Doctors hastily summoned on Good Friday morning, after the Bishop had an intestinal hemorrhage, diagnose that his ailment is typhoid fever.

Within an hour after the hemorrhage he seems to shrink in size and to age. He thinks that he is thinner, "weaker and more insignificant than anyone else," and that pleases him. When his mother sees the change in him and realizes that he is dying, she falls on her knees and starts to kiss his face, his shoulders, his hands. The wall separating them crumbles. She forgets that he is a bishop; he is again her child, her son, her Pavliusha. The Bishop can no longer speak or focus, but he feels that he is now "a simple, ordinary man, walking briskly and gaily in a field, tapping with his stick, and above him there stretched the wide, sun-drenched sky, and he was as free as a bird and he could go wherever he wished."[41] Father Iakov in "A Nightmare" comes to mind, trudging along on a muddy road, the coachman Andrey and the boy Paramon rushing toward him to receive a blessing.

It has been mentioned in discussing Tolstoy's and Dostoevsky's strikingly disparate conceptions of life that both converged in the fundamental conviction that man cannot remain human without God. While hoping to avoid the danger of oversimplification, it appears reasonable to state now that Chekhov's view on this issue was that man is human and that God *is* all about us in this world. As a tool of literary creativity medicine aided Chekhov the writer in forming his view of the irreplaceable worth and value of each individual human being. Science and technology held high priority in Chekhov's scale of values in mankind's progress. But his works bear witness to his religiousness as well. An untrammeled development of man's potentialities depends, besides intellectual advance, in equal measure on individual volitional striving toward spiritual growth and on intuitive apprehension of the divine order perpetually intersecting the phenomenal world.

How did the throngs of human beings created by Chekhov, the throngs that "the largest city square could not hold, should they all suddenly magically come alive," respond to the challenge of free will, of individual endeavor and liberty, that the images of the doctor and the priest evoke? How did they respond to Chekhov's silent call, buried deep in his fiction, to shed shackles, to destroy bondage, to break down

dividing walls, to reject restricting tags and labels, to ignore
the barriers of rank, to be as free as a sea gull, as free as
migratory birds, to find a way to break out of a cage?

Notes

[1] I, 17.
[2] I, 100.
[3] I, 97.
[4] I, 227-8.
[5] I, 405.
[6] I, 401.
[7] L., XVI, 271.
[8] Chekhov had written the story in commemoration of the writer Vsevolod Garshin, who had committed suicide that same year.
[9] VII, 216-7.
[10] Korney Chukovsky, *Sovremeniki*, Moscow, 1963, p. 9.
[11] XII, 54-6.
[12] L., III, 114.
[13] VII, 243.
[14] VII, 284.
[15] Originally Chekhov intended the story to be titled "My Name and I."
[16] VII, 307.
[17] Ibid.
[18] VII, 306.
[19] VII, 308.
[20] L., III, 239 and 244.
[21] XIII, 160.
[22] Ibid.
[23] In an amateur choir organized by his father.
[24] L.,V, 20.
[25] V, 63.
[26] V, 64.
[27] V, 12.
[28] VII, 98.
[29] VII, 99.
[30] VII, 453.

[31] V, 94.

[32] V.I. Kliuchevsky, *Sochinenia*, Soviet 8 vol. edition, 1956-1959, Vol. II, "History of Russia," Lecture XXXIV, p. 254.

[33] Sergius Bulgakov, "The Orthodox Church," in *A Bulgakov Anthology*, ed. Zernov and Zander, Philadelphia: 1976, p. 133.

[34] V, 99.

[35] V, 102.

[36] Walter T. Stace, *Time and Eternity*, Princeton, NJ: Princeton Univ. Press, 1952, p. 96.

[37] X, 195.

[38] X, 194.

[39] X, 189.

[40] X, 199.

[41] X, 200.

IV

The Tyranny of Time

The Hold of the Tyranny

Both Tolstoy's and Dostoevsky's treatments of time were dominated by their respective concepts of eternity. According to Tolstoy the moralist, the "true life" of man, doing good, took place outside of human time; it was an act of communion with eternity. Tolstoy's summons to establish a reign of good, a "Kingdom of God" on earth, called for a flight from the morally destructive historical progression of civilization and a return to the healing folds of the perpetually revolving, cyclical cosmic time of nature. Dostoevsky's gaze was riveted on the drama of godless man denying the existence of eternity, wrestling with human time, trying to conquer it, to free himself from it, to shake off the burden of the past, of memories, of conscience, of remorse, proclaiming

116

that "there will be no time" once the fear of death is overcome and the censure of murder lifted.

There are none of the mystical flashes of a higher reality
experienced by Dostoevsky's Prince Myshkin in Chekhov's
fiction. Neither is there a figure comparable to Father Zossima, but the feeling of the constant interpenetration of the
temporal and the eternal world is ever present and his concept of time encompasses both realities, constantly blending
the tangible and explicable with moves and impulses sprung
from beyond the realm of rationality and outside the reach of
words. Neither flight from time nor contests to overpower it
are at issue, though Chekhov's temporal horizon was vast
and the theme of time no less central to his work than Tolstoy's or Dostoevsky's. Anticipating Proust's contention
that "the mighty dimension of Time is the dimension in
which life is lived," Chekhov's characters are swept along in
the endless stream of existence and integrated into the universal process of life moving ever forward, a life in which
every living being is in a constant state of change and in
which nothing endures but time, in which there is nothing to
flee from and nowhere to go but forward—in time.

Chekhov employs numerous artistic devices to convey the
intrinsic continuity and the all-embracing, endless flux of
life. Tragic events receive no more emphasis than trivial
happenings. Poetic themes and prosaic images, emotional
experiences and the material milieu in which they occur, all
are treated with equal concern. His heroes are constantly
presented in the midst of ordinary household paraphernalia
and engaged in common routine activities. Death itself is
reported casually and briefly, as if speaking of a drop of
water disappearing in the ocean. And after death a character is quickly forgotten, Chekhov tells us, be he as prominent
as Bishop Peter in his next-to-last story or as insignificant as
the literateur Liadovsky in "Nice People." The absence of
endings, of denouements, also suggests the endless flow and
constant interdependence of all aspects of human existence.

When commenting on the temporal movement of the
external world, Chekhov uses tangible, visible signposts to

stress its inexorable progression. A sudden realization of how rapidly children have grown may release a sense of wonder at the swiftness of the march of time. The two nieces of Aleksey Laptev in "Three Years" (1895) were ten and seven years old respectively when they came to live in their uncle's house after their mother's death. At the end of "Three Years" Laptev is met upon his return home by the two girls. "How they have grown, he thinks, and how many changes during these three years."

Children's growth may also give an indication of the lengthy time span covered by the narrative itself: We are not told in "About Love" (1898) how many years Alekhin and Anna Alekseevna have known each other, but we know that at the time they met her first child was six months old and that toward the end of their painfully indecisive relationship she has two children old enough to greet Alekhin with shouts of joy whenever he appears.

The physical decline of the sixty-two-year-old Sorin in *The Sea Gull* (1896) is accentuated by his regression from walking with a cane in the first act to being wheeled in a chair in the second, to suffering a spell of dizziness in the third, to facing being bedridden in the fourth. The obesity and lack of vitality of Doctor Startsev in "Ionych" (1898), which grows in proportion to his professional success, is reflected in his giving up walking long distances in favor of riding in his own two-horse carriage and later—short of breath and barely able to move—in his elegant troika.

The fifty years of Iakov's married life in "Rothschild's Fiddle" (1894) are set off by a willow tree. Iakov's dying wife remembers sitting in its shade by the river in the early days of their marriage with their infant child who died. After his wife's funeral Iakov, walking along the river, recognizes the same willow tree, grown old as well, disfigured by a huge hollow in its trunk and studded with crows' nests. The trees blooming in the month of May at the opening of *The Cherry Orchard* (1904) will be chopped down at the autumnal finale of the play. The many symbolic functions of these trees— representing life and death, youth and age, the poetry of a bygone era versus the prose of a mercantile present and the vision of a new beautiful future—are all indicative of the march of time.

But when Chekhov speaks of the continuity and ceaseless temporal flux of the inner world of his characters, all tangible measurements and causal motivations are removed. Chekhov's treatment of man's consciousness and the domain of his free will is singularly suggestive of Henri Bergson's thoughts on the evolution of the inner life of the self, the belief that all changes and movements in the realm of personal consciousness, including arriving at decisions, permeate and penetrate one another, blending into an organic, indivisible whole like a musical composition in which every separate note merges into the next to produce a continuous melody. This excludes the principle of causality. And Chekhov's references to the emotional experiences of his characters and to the actions springing from them are frequently accompanied by the statement that they cannot be explained or that they remain incomprehensible even to the characters themselves. For they spring from a constantly changing totality of psychic experiences.

It is particularly significant that the two greatest dramatic events of human consciousness and will, murder and suicide, are removed by Chekhov from the realm of causality and determinism, denying them the right to function as probing stones of human self-will and reason, a right claimed so passionately by so many of Dostoevsky's godless protagonists. Murder in Chekhov's world is committed without being premeditated and suicide is discussed without stating the reasons for it. Matvey Terekhov, the victim in "The Murder" (1895), is quietly eating boiled potatoes which he has seasoned with vegetable oil when he is slain by Aglaia, wife of his cousin Iakov. Both Aglaia and Iakov are religious fanatics, but Matvey, once a member of a religious sect himself, has reformed and never tires of criticizing his cousin's fanaticism. "Eating vegetable oil is a sin, you are breaking the fast," say Aglaia and Iakov to Matvey. A brief and angry brawl ensues and Aglaia brings the bottle of vegetable oil down on Matvey's head, followed, at the urging of Iakov, by an iron. Only when the ironing board collapses under the weight of Matvey's body does Iakov understand what has happened and fear grips him. "But nothing was as gruesome for Iakov as the boiled potatoes soaked in blood which he was afraid to step on..." In "In the Ravine" (1900) Aksinia is seething with rage when she finds out that her father-in-law has changed his will in favor of his second daughter-in-law's infant son. But the actual murder of the child, Aksinia's pouring a bucket of boiling water over the boy, is drawn as a sudden, mad outburst of uncontrolled and unpremeditated villainy.

Suicide in Chekhov's works is discussed without analyzing motivations. In an early story, "A Story without an Ending" (1886), the narrator is summoned to the side of a man who had attempted to shoot himself after his wife's death. The wound turns out to be superficial and the would-be suicide, eager for comfort and companionship, draws the narrator into a conversation. He confesses that he himself does not understand what led him to try to end his life. "Man will never understand the psychological subtleties of suicide. Where are the reasons? Today a reason forces one to reach for a pistol and tomorrow that same reason seems not to be worth a damn.... Take me, for instance. Half an hour ago I longed passionately for death, but now that this candle is burning and you are sitting by my side, I have no thoughts of death. Try and explain this change."[1] What contempt Dostoevsky's Kirilov would have poured on this statement!

The suicide of Ivanov at the end of the play bearing his name (1887) is anticipated from the first act; it is repeatedly alluded to by Ivanov himself and hinted at by other members of the cast. But this is not a causal build-up. In his helplessness and inability to cope with life Ivanov is censured by Chekhov from the moment the curtain goes up, and is doomed by his creator. The fatal shot is a death sentence imposed by the author himself and the whole play a necrologue to a literary type which, Chekhov hoped, would henceforth be eliminated from Russian literature. "I nurtured the daring hope," wrote Chekhov in a letter in January 1889 "to summarize everything that has been written so far about whining and pining people and, with my Ivanov, to put a stop to such writings."[2]

In "On Official Business" (1899) the magistrate Lyzhin is called to investigate the suicide of the insurance agent Lesnitsky in the village of Syrnia. Lesnitsky shot himself in the village headquarters "to the complete surprise of everyone," after having ordered a samovar and arranging on the table the parcels of food he had brought along. In the course of the narrative we hear that Lesnitsky came from a once well-to-do family, but was left destitute after his father's death. We learn that his pride suffered from the decline of his fortune. We also learn that he left a wife and a child. We get a glimpse of his appearance as well. The magistrate suddenly remembers that he once met Lesnitsky casually. He recalls his quiet voice, his pale face, his dark eyes which had an unpleasant look about them, his clumsy boots. But the psychic processes which led to the suicide Chekhov does not touch upon.

Treplev's suicide at the end of *The Sea Gull* is prepared for by his abortive attempt to kill himself in the second act. We are well aware of the hopelessness of his love for Nina and of his dissatisfaction with his own creative achievements. But his final step toward death is merely preceded by laconic stage directions: "For two minutes he silently tears up all his manuscripts and throws them under the table, then unlocks the door at the right and leaves."

The lack of temporal causality prevails not only in moments of deep inner crisis experienced by Chekhov's characters, but also when minor emotional experiences or states of mind are the topic. In "Peasants" (1897) the stillness and the creaking of the cradle remind the old Chikildeevs "for some reason" that life had come to an end. Why a patch of gooseberries looms so largely in Nikolay Ivanovich's dreams in "Gooseberries" (1898) cannot be explained. Neither can the fact that Cleopatra in "My Life" (1896) is concealing her serious illness. Every stirring in the inner life of Chekhov's characters, every change in the stream of their consciousness, is accompanied by the remark that it takes place inexplicably.

When Chekhov wishes to arrest the mobility of the inner world of his characters and to relate a moment in this ceaselessly moving stream to the equally fluid and changing outer world, we often hear a clock strike or we see a character glancing at his watch. For a brief moment in the conventional measurement of time the consciousness of the protagonists and the external world in which they live are fused, before resuming their separate courses.

At the opening of *The Three Sisters* (1900) on a radiant spring day, the clock strikes twelve. Exactly a year ago, says Olga, their father died and the clock then struck also. Then it was very cold and snowing, now it is warm and sunny. Then Irina lay in a faint, now she is radiant and happy. The swift passing of time, the rapidity of change, thus forms the overture of the play and establishes the rhythm that will carry the three sisters onward in the evolution of their dreams and longings. The antipode to the sisters and the thirst for life is the old alcoholic doctor Chebutykin, that epitome of indifference who was in love with the sisters' dead mother, yet who can no longer remember whether she in turn loved him also. The two episodes involving him with a clock enhance his lifelessness and remoteness from the sisters' frame of mind. When, in the third act, he drops and breaks the antique china clock which belonged to the sisters' mother, he in unmoved and incapable of remorse. "Maybe I did not break it and it only seems that I did. Maybe it only seems to us that we exist and actually we do not?"[3] Chebutykin seems almost beyond the bounds of a world where the striking of a clock can attest to the movements of life. The second episode strengthens this impression. In the fourth act Chebutykin looks at his own watch and states that "it is antique and rings." He winds it and it strikes. But this is not a tolling of the hour, for there is no connection between this exhibition of chimes striking and Chebutykin's subsequent remark that the first, second, and fifth batteries will be leaving "at one o'clock sharp."

In "Three Years" Fedor Laptev urges his brother Aleksey in a heart-to-heart talk to start a career in politics. The family's wealth would seem to guarantee considerable success and honors easily won, he implies. Aleksey is not interested in this proposition. While he hesitates, not knowing what to say, his indecision and silence are accentuated by a time reference: "Fedor took out his watch and looked at it for a long, very long time, with strained attention as though he wanted to catch the movement of the hand...."[4]

In "Ionych" Startsev is impatiently waiting for a nocturnal rendezvous with Ekaterine Ivanovna at the local cemetery. He is struck by the peaceful silence, the softness of the moonlight, the lifelessness all around him, though "in each dark poplar, in each grave one could feel the presence of a mystery promising a quiet, beautiful eternal life." The chimes of the cemetery chapel cut into this train of thought and give it a new direction: Startsev suddenly has the feeling "that someone was looking at him and for a moment he thought that there was neither rest nor peace here but dull anguish of nonexistence, a suppressed despair."[5]

The merchant Lopakhin in *The Cherry Orchard* is probably more acutely conscious of conventional time measurements than any other character of Chekhov's. His glances at his watch, his references to hours and to dates, are significant signposts related not only to the stream of human consciousness, but to the entire process of change and flux which is symbolized in the beginning of the play by the bloom of the cherry trees and at the end by the physical destruction of the orchard. "What time is it?" is his opening remark in the first act. The train bringing Madame Ranevskaia, owner of the cherry orchard, home from Paris, is two hours late, he continues. He intended to meet her at the station but fell asleep sitting up in a chair. This is a symbolic overture, for the minds of Lopakhin and Ranevskaia will never meet. His proposal for staving off the impending auc-

tion of the estate and saving the family from ruin is introduced by Lopakhin with a glance at his watch and the
remark that "there isn't much time to talk." His suggestion
to chop down the cherry orchard, to tear down the old house
and cut up the land into lots to be leased for summer cottages, falls on deaf ears and is dismissed as nonsense both
by Madame Ranevskaia and her brother Gaev. And again
Lopakhin glances at his watch: "If we don't come to a decision, on the twenty-second of August the cherry orchard and
the whole estate will be sold at auction." Gaev's subsequent
childish babble and display of utter incomprehension of the
gravity of the situation induce Lopakhin to look at his watch
once more: "Well, it's time for me to go." "There is no time to
lose!" he exclaims in the second act, driven to distraction by
Ranevskaia's and Gaev's continued inability to face reality
and by their rejection of his scheme because of its "vulgarity." In the third act Lopakhin opens his triumphant
account of the auction and of his purchase of the cherry
orchard with a precise time reference: "The sale was over at
four o'clock. We missed the train, had to wait till half past
nine." And the departure of the old owners of the estate in the
fourth act is heralded by Lopakhin's admonition to hurry
because "the train leaves in forty-six minutes, so you ought
to start for the station in twenty minutes."

All artistic devices employed by Chekhov in his treatment
of time exhibit his sense of temporal continuity. It is when he
examines the function of the past in the lives of his protagonists that he finds "the mighty dimension" turned into
tyranny. Proust wished to portray "man in the universe as
endowed with the length not of his body but of his years."
Through memories the past is re-created, reinterpreted,
recast, and fused with the present. The place occupied by
man in the dimension of time is thus perpetually being augmented, according to Proust. But Chekhov presents a very
different picture of the function of memories. His characters
tend to re-create a past which appears far more concrete,
alive, and attractive than the present, dwarfing it, dimming
it, even trying to escape from it, instead of augmenting it.

Chekhov's treatment of the past is more than a Proustian artistic device for the interpretation of reality; it is also a concrete, factual theme based on observations of Russian life all around him. An outstanding example is the languid, distraught, and disoriented Ivanov, whose suicide has been previously discussed. In a long letter to Suvorin dated December 30, 1888, Chekhov gave a detailed analysis of the meaning of the play. He wanted to present a typical representative of the Russian intelligentsia, not outstanding in any way but bearing "typically Russian character traits." And one of these traits is that "like the majority of educated Russian people he considers his past as resplendent. There is hardly a member of the Russian gentry or a university graduate who does not boast about his past. The present is always inferior to the past."[6]

Great is the variety of people in Chekhov's world who cast nostalgic glances into the past. The heroine in "The Story of Miss NN" (1887) says: "I remembered my past and suddenly my shoulders began to shake. I bowed my head and burst into bitter tears." Petr Sergeich, who confessed his love for her some nine years ago, is sitting by her side and silently watching her despair. During these nine years he has grown old, ailing and resigned. He is poor and of humble origin; she is rich and well born. And nine years ago this seemed an insurmountable obstacle. "I was loved," narrates Miss NN, "happiness was so near, I lived in clover, I did not attempt to understand myself, I did not know what I was waiting for and what I expected of life and time marched on and on." Now she feels her loneliness, her empty life is moving toward "a dark and frightening horizon." She realizes that "like everybody else" she let the past slip by not appreciating that at the time it was the present, and now she sees it "so full of wonder in retrospect."

When Podgorin in "Visiting Friends" (1898) receives an urgent note inviting him to visit his old friends the Losevs on their country estate, his memories take him back ten or twelve years. He recalls long conversations, gay laughter, romances, evening walks, and a bevy of attractive young women, among them the two who had signed the invitation. "He loved them dearly but more, it appeared, in his memories than in reality. The present he knew little about, it was incomprehensible and alien." Reluctantly Podgorin accepts the invitation so as not to offend old friends. There will be no laughter, he thinks, no noise, no happy, carefree faces, no rendezvous on moonlit nights, for youth is gone. "Besides, all this is probably charming only in memories." Upon arrival he finds his misgivings more than justified and abruptly cuts his visit short, leaving hastily the very next morning.

Even remembrances of a past of want and hardship superseded by a present of affluence and comfort can, at times, evoke nostalgic longings. Twenty-five-year-old Anna Akimovna in "A Woman's Kingdom" (1894) has inherited the large industrial enterprise built from modest beginnings by her energetic father and shrewd uncle. She feels trapped by her wealth and bored by her idle existence. On Christmas Eve, driving past factory buildings and watching crowds of workmen walking home from work, she is suddenly seized with a longing for "simplicity, crudeness, and cramped living quarters." The distant past rises in her mind, the time when she was called Aniutka, when as a small girl she lay with her mother under the same blanket, listening to the sounds of laughter, swearing, children crying, an accordion playing, lathes and sewing machines humming, all drifting from next-door apartments, while she watched her father busily working near the stove. "And she longed to launder, to iron, to run to the store and to the pub, the way she used to when she lived with her mother." At the end of a tedious Christmas Day during which Anna Akimovna is surrounded by fawning guests and obsequious servants she realizes "that it was too late for her to dream about happiness, that everything was lost and that it was impossible to return to the old life when she slept with her mother under the same blanket or to devise a new, special sort of life."[7]

In "The Bishop" an unexpected visit from the Right Reverend Peter's mother, whom he has not seen for nine years, sets his mind wandering into the past. "That dear, precious, unforgettable childhood! Why, why does this time, forever lost and irretrievable, seem brighter, gayer, and richer than it was in reality?" Resting after the Palm Sunday services the bishop reflects on his years in the seminary and later in the academy: "...then life was so easy, so pleasant, and seemed endlessly long." But the entire past seemed to have disappeared somewhere, to have vanished in a fog as if it had been a dream after he became a bishop.

This evaluation of one's personal past as a regrettable, irrecoverable loss is not confined to the upper strata of Russian society. In "The Steppe" (1888) nine-year-old Egorushka is entrusted for part of his trip across the steppe to the care of the drivers of a convoy of carts and shares their rest periods and meals. Sitting around a fire, the drivers eat and chat and Egorushka listens attentively. "From this conversation Egorushka gathered that all his new acquaintances, regardless of the differences in age and character, shared one common trait: they were all people with a wonderful past and a very bad present; without exception they all spoke about their past with enthusiasm, but the present they treated almost with contempt. Russians love to reminisce but do not like the process of living (*ne liubit zhit*); Egorushka did not know this yet and before the gruel was finished he was firmly convinced that the people sitting around the cauldron had been insulted and wronged by fate."[8]

As the past, sifted through the mind of Chekhov's characters, emerges as resplendent and wonderful in contrast to a deficient and disappointing present, the sense of temporal continuity, the sense of solidarity between all moments of life, is disturbed. Obscured is the realization, so crucial to Proust, that the present is determined by the past, that the being one is has been formed by the being one formerly was. "Russians love to reminisce but do not like the process of living." They seem to love the past more than the present, to feel a gap between the two. The reminiscences of Chekhov's characters are not a source of gain, of enrichment, of growth, they do not induce corrective actions to right past mistakes and combat crippling shortcomings. They are merely wistful signs of nostalgic resignation, pensive and helpless moments of regret. They do not augment, but reduce the place held by an individual in the dimension of time. They bear tragic evidence of the tyranny of time. The most striking among Chekhov's creations exhibiting the crippling power of his heroes' memories are the old owners of *The Cherry Orchard* who are so immersed in the past that they are dwarfed and incapable of even grasping, of even seeing, the present and stand before us in their infantile chatter, sucking candy and remembering nostalgically their nursery days, reduced to the stature of two immature children.

Besides the images of a wondrous, vanished past Chekhov uses yet another device, oblivion, to stress the hold of temporal tyranny, the debilitating alienation between the characters' past and present. While many of his protagonists bemoan what has been lost forever, others are portrayed as having forgotten vital events, situations, or accomplishments which, in retrospect, could have served as a source of solace, spiritual sustenance, inducement of remorse, or further growth. Forgetting is raised to the function of a regrettable act, a failing bearing fruits as tragic as the memories that impede a forward movement in the present.

The restless and drifting Likharev in "On the Road" (1886) confesses: "I lived, but in my bemusement I did not feel the actual process of living. Believe it or not, but I do not remember a single spring. I did not observe how my wife loved me, how my children were born.... I was a scourge of all those who loved me." The stingy coffin-maker Yakov in "Rothschild's Fiddle" is utterly absorbed in his craft. "Do you remember, Yakov," asks his dying wife, looking at him joyously, "remember, fifty years ago God sent us a little girl with blond hair?" And smiling bitterly, she adds: "The little girl died." But no matter how hard Yakov strains his mind, he cannot remember. "You dreamed that up," he says. And only after his wife's funeral does the recollection of the dead child suddenly rise vividly and painfully from the depth of his consciousness.

In "In the Cart" (1897) Maria Vasilievna, a village schoolteacher for thirteen years, is returning from the local town where she regularly goes to receive her salary. Locked in the monotonous humdrum of her existence, she has forgotten almost everything about her past before she became a schoolteacher. She does not remember life in Moscow with her parents and her brother. All that is left of her former possessions is a photograph of her mother faded from the dampness in the school to such an extent that only the hair and the eyebrows are visible. The cart stops at a railroad crossing and past Maria Vasilievna flashes the sight of a woman standing on a platform of the passing train. The woman bears a striking resemblance to Maria Vasilievna's mother. A flood of memories is suddenly released and "for the first time in all these thirteen years" the forgotten past is briefly resurrected; for a short moment Maria Vasilievna, overcome by a feeling of joy and happiness, began to cry—"she did not know why."

The diocesan bishop in Chekhov's next-to-last story "The Bishop" had written a treatise on "The Freedom of the Will" in his youth, but now, immersed in bureaucratic trivialities, does not seem to remember it or to think about God anymore.

The estate manager Shamraev in *The Seagull* is asked by the writer Trigorin to stuff and preserve the dead gull which he, Trigorin, saw lying at Nina's feet and which prompted him to make a short entry in his notebook: "Theme for a short story: at the shore of a lake lived since her childhood a young girl.... She loved the lake like a gull, she was happy and free like a gull. But along came a man, saw her, and out of boredom destroyed her just like this gull." Later Trigorin comes close to destroying Nina by deserting her after the death of the child she has had by him. Yet, two years after Trigorin has asked Shamraev to stuff the gull he no longer remembers having done so. When led by Shamraev to the cupboard and shown the stuffed bird at the end of the play, he says: "I don't remember!" After a moment's thought he repeats, "I don't remember!"

Masha in *The Three Sisters* was an accomplished pianist some three or four years before. But she has now forgotten how to play. She is also painfully aware that she is beginning to forget her dead mother's face. Irina used to speak Italian, but now she cannot remember how to say "window" or "ceiling" in Italian: "I keep forgetting things, every day I forget something, and life is slipping away and will never return and we shall never, never get to Moscow." Forgetting is a painful experience for the sisters, since the radiant memories of their past life in Moscow is what they long to return to in the future. They left Moscow eleven years ago when their father was made commander of a brigade. It is early May at the opening of the play, it is warm, yet the birch trees aren't in leaf yet, says Olga. In Moscow, though, at this same time eleven years ago, she continues, everything was in bloom and flooded with sunlight: "Eleven years have gone by and yet I remember it all as though we had left yesterday." "There is no place on earth like Moscow," says Irina at the end of the third act. But Chekhov does not permit the sisters to realize their dream, to return to their lost paradise of a blooming, sunlit Moscow, to transpose the past into the future. The past should repel, and not attract.

Breaking the Hold

If Chekhov treats memories and regrettable oblivion as impediments to the growth of man's place in the dimension of time, is there then anything that could be regarded as his choice for augmenting that growth? A clue is supplied by Nikolay Stepanovich, the prominent physician in "A Dreary Story," who says in his searching self-examination: "Tell me what you want and I will tell you who you are." Desires are the key to a person's character and will, their springs reaching far beyond the bounds of rationality. In a letter to Suvorin on December 12, 1894, Chekhov clearly formulated this thought and vented his concern with the weariness, the apathy rampant among his contemporaries: "You ask in your last letter: What should a Russian wish for at the present time? Here is my answer: He should wish to wish. More than anything else he needs desires, temperament...."[9]

Desires to steer man away from the past and direct his glance toward the future, toward breaking the tyranny of time, toward gaining control over the direction of his life, toward enlarging his stature in the temporal flow.

There are a number of themes Chekhov uses to stress the need to steer away from the past and to gain control over human time. One is an insistent and repeated reference to a bleak and dreary historical past which merges unaltered with the present and stands in sharp contrast to the deceptively radiant personal recollections of his heroes. Whenever Chekhov refers to the historical past in his fiction there appears a vision of unrelieved and gloomy darkness which spills over into the present. Nothing has changed since the dawn of Russian history. In "An Attack of Nerves" (1888) the thoughts of the student Vasiliev wander even further back in time, to the dawn of Western civilization itself. Vasiliev is visiting for the first time a district of ill repute in Moscow and marvels at the brightly lit houses, the gay sounds of music everywhere, and the indifference and nonchalance displayed by waiting cabdrivers and passing pedestrians alike. He thinks that "probably in ancient times it was as gay and as noisy at the slave markets and people's faces and gait expressed the same indifference."

At the opening of "The Student" (1894) the divinity student Velikopolsky is walking home from a hunting expedition and thinks, shivering from the cold, that "the same kind of wind blew in the days of Rurik, of Ivan the Terrible, and of Peter. In those days reigned the same acute poverty and starvation; there were the same dilapidated roofs, ignorance, anguish, the same wasteland all around; darkness, a feeling of oppression—all these horrors existed then as they do now and will continue to exist; and the passing of another thousand years is not going to make life better."[10]

That the dismal backwardness of the past is not merely retained in the contemporary countryside but permeates other segments of Russia as well is twice expressed in "My Life" (1896). Misail maintains that "there is no more serfdom but capitalism is growing. And at the very height of emancipatory trends the majority continues to feed, clothe, and defend the minority, just as it did in the days of the Tartar Yoke, while it remains itself ill-fed, ill clothed, and defenseless."[11] And Doctor Blagovo says: "Cultured life has not yet begun in this country. The same uncouthness prevails, the same unrelieved boorishness, the same mediocrity as five hundred years ago."[12]

Chekhov's idea of the future is another theme he uses in his fiction as a counterpoint to the tyranny of time. The future is as bright and radiant as his idea of the historical past is somber and desolate. It is a beautiful dream set in contrast to a hideous nightmare. Long before Chekhov wrote his last play, the poetic vision of a future as a cherry orchard in bloom held a prominent place in his thoughts. Characters of different temperament, background, and age reiterate thoughts of a future luminous and full of promise, yet distant and intangible, intentionally vague in its projected state, beckoning man to dream of it, to long for it, and to work toward creating it.

There is the romantic, impractical Vershinin in *The Three Sisters*, burdened with a wife who repeatedly threatens to take her life. In the first act he joyfully exclaims: "In two hundred, three hundred years life on earth will be unimaginably beautiful and wonderful. Man has need of a life like that and if it doesn't as yet exist, he must have a foreboding of it, he must wait, dream, prepare for it...."[13] In the second act Vershinin muses that it might even be a thousand years before a new, happy life arrives, adding that the span of time is beside the point. "We will have no part in this life, of course, yet we are living for this life now, we are working for it, yes, we are suffering for it, we are creating it and this is the sole purpose of our existence and, if you want to put it that way, of our happiness."[14]

Even when thoughts about the future descend from the lofty level of a philosophical discussion to a more pedestrian plane they remain veiled and dreamlike. In "A Case from Practice" (1898) the sober, astute Doctor Korolev diagnoses the disease of a young girl, Liza, rich heiress of an industrial enterprise, as a nervous disorder. He feels that it is her wealth and idleness which cause the illness and that her recovery could be brought about if she gave up her wealth and abandoned the oppressive and cheerless milieu in which she lives. Unable to couch this thought in appropriate words, he turns to discussing the future as a therapeutic measure: "In your position as a factory owner and rich heiress you are dissatisfied, you don't believe in your rights and here you are, suffering from insomnia.... For our children or grandchildren this question—whether they are right or wrong—will already be solved. They will see more clearly than we do. Life will be good in some fifty years; too bad that we won't live long enough to see it. It would be interesting to have a glimpse."[15]

" 'But what will our children and grandchildren be doing?' asks Liza. 'I don't know.... Probably they will leave everything and go away.' 'Where will they go?' 'Where? Anywhere,' said Korolev, and burst out laughing. 'There are scores of places for a decent, clever person to go to.' "[16]

Nadia, the youthful heroine of "The Betrothed" (1903), does "go away." She leaves her small home town for Petersburg, where she will study instead of marrying a mediocre provincial man whom she does not love. And as the train starts, carrying her toward a new life, "all this past, so large and serious, shrank into a small ball and a huge, vast future unfolded, a future which had previously been barely noticeable."[17] As the story ends: "...in her mind's eye she saw a new life, vast, spacious, and this life as yet unclear and full of mysteries enchanted her and beckoned."

The thought that human life is priceless in its brevity, that time is a precious gift of freedom and not a burden of servitude, is another thought calling us to utilize human time with utmost care. The temporal movement toward death is irreversible. But despite his mortality man has the power to control the meaning and the direction of time. The urgency of this is enhanced by the fact that it is repeatedly formulated at a moment when the narrative touches upon a scene of great emotional anguish, strain, or pain.

The dying Pavel Ivanovich in "Gusev" (1890) laments over the maltreatment of human beings he has observed all around him on board a ship which was carrying soldiers home from the Far East and exclaims: "Life is given to us but once and it should be handled with care." In an outburst of disgust and despair the narrator in "An Anonymous Story" writes his former employer Orlov a long, impassioned letter before abandoning his house. He curses Orlov's cold blood and indifference, accuses him of being a cowardly animal afraid of life, of retreating behind a protective shield of irony toward everyone and everything, and ends his message with these words: "The sun does not rise twice a day and life is not given twice—so reach firmly for the remnants of your life and save them." On the day after his wife's funeral, Yakov in "Rothschild's Fiddle," despondent and at death's door himself, broods: "Why is it so arranged in this world that life, which is given to man but once passes by without use?" When Lipa in "In the Ravine," carrying her dead child home from the hospital, stops to rest on the bank of a small pond, the voices of nightingales, cuckoos, and frogs fill the air, as if "shouting and singing on purpose so that no one would sleep on that spring night, so that everyone...would cherish and enjoy every minute: life is given but once?"[18]

The brevity of life, the bleakness of the historical past, the luminosity of a nebulous distant future are all concepts intended as stimuli to the exercise of human will and desires, as means to live within the limits of time without becoming its captive. The question of desires is discussed in the story "In Exile" (1892). It is built around a dialogue between two convicts serving their sentence of exile as settlers in Siberia. They are sitting by a fire on a river bank—old Semen, nicknamed "Sensible," and a young Tartar "whose name no one knows." Both work as oarsmen with a group of ferrymen transporting passengers in a barge across the river. The young Tartar is ill, desperately homesick, longing to be near the beautiful young wife he left behind, and bemoaning the fraud instigated by his relatives and the unjust verdict that denied his innocence and that brought him to this forsaken spot. "You will get used to it," repeats Semen the Sensible in answer to the young man's complaints.

Semen boasts that he does not need anything. His is a deliberate abrogation of desires, an abrogation he is proud of. He could "sleep naked on the ground and live on grass." He has given up thinking of his wife, his home, his relatives. He can endure any kind of hardship without complaining and "may God grant everyone a life such as this," he reiterates. To illustrate his point, he tells the Tartar about a well-to-do gentleman who came to Siberia some fifteen years ago, convicted for some illegal financial transaction. Restless and defiant, he persuaded his wife to join him in Siberia. Yet his happiness was short-lived. After three years his wife left him and ran away with a lover. Hoping to win her back, the gentleman spent some eight years in vain efforts to get his case reviewed and a return to Russia granted. His hair has turned gray, his back is hunched, narrates Semen. But he did find new happiness in watching his young daughter grow. Now, though, the girl is ill. She has consumption and surely, says Semen, she will die. And that will be the end of the gentleman.

But the Tartar is not convinced. In halting and faulty Russian, groping for words, he says: "Wife, daughter...Let there be hard labor, anguish, but he did see both wife and daughter.... You say, nothing needed. But nothing—is bad! Wife lived with him three years—God gave him that. Nothing—is bad, three years—is good!" At dawn the ferry-men and their barge are summoned from the opposite bank of the river to bring a carriage across. The traveler turns out to be the gentleman Semen has been telling the Tartar about. The man tells Semen that his daughter's illness has worsened and that he now hopes to secure the help of a new doctor. Throughout the ferry ride Semen does not conceal his pleasure at the sight of the unhappy, helpless man: "Sensible's face bore an exultant expression as if he had proved something and as if he rejoiced that things turned out precisely the way he assumed they would."[19]

Semen vents his thoughts and continues to gloat after the gentleman's carriage has driven off, but the Tartar renews his ardent rejection of Semen's views, of the need to wish for nothing. Voiced in stumbling and disjointed sentences, the vehemence and meaning of his illiterate and inarticulate speech is lost on his audience. It is desires that appear "in exile." All the ferrymen burst out laughing at the Tartar's outburst and then, including Semen, go to their hut to catch some sleep, while the Tartar returns to the fire. After the men lay down a gust of wind flings the door of the hut open and a snow flurry whirls into the room. But no one bothers to get up to close the door. From the fire comes the sound of the Tartar weeping: it sounds like the howling of a dog. "He will get used to it," says Semen again, and instantly falls asleep. "And the door remained open."[20]

When old Sorin, in the fourth act of *The Sea Gull*, talks about his past, it seems as though he too had not bothered to make an effort to close a door accidentally flung open by the wind and to prevent the chilling effects of cold and snow on his life. He wants to suggest to the young writer Treplev a subject for a story: "Its title should be 'The Man Who Wished'—*L'homme qui a voulu*." And then Sorin reminisces about the unfulfilled ambitions in his life: "At one time in my youth I wanted to become a writer—and didn't. I wanted to speak eloquently—and spoke dreadfully.... I wanted to get married—and didn't; I always wanted to live in town—and here I am ending my life in the country."[21]

The argument aired in the story "In Exile" stands as an exception in Chekhov's fiction. The absence of will power, the ineffectiveness of desires, the inability to make decisions and to act on them are themes which are constantly woven into the fabric of Chekhov's narrative. And if the feeling of being a part of the stream of existence *is* experienced and expressed, it is frequently a sense of passively and helplessly merging with an uncontrollable flow of reality rather than a conscious effort to will, to give the current of life a direction, and to strive for freedom and a gradual growth of the self.

Vera, the heroine of "At Home" (1897), returns from a school in Moscow to the estate in the southern steppe region which she has just inherited after her father's death. She is repelled by the idle, carefree, and indolent life she finds, by the gluttony, by the preoccupation with games and parties, by the lack of intellectual curiosity and the cruel and despotic treatment of servants. Yet she is unable to find a way out, unable even to protest. Yielding to a feeling of helplessness and uselessness, she accepts the marriage proposal of an insignificant suitor whom she despises: "Beautiful nature, daydreams, music tell one story but real life another. Apparently, happiness and truth exist somewhere outside of life.... What one must do is not live but merge with this magnificent steppe, boundless and indifferent as eternity, with its flowers, its ancient burial mounds, and distant views, and then all will be well."[22]

Not live but merge with the boundless steppe. Chekhov's world abounds with men and women who passively surrender to the ever-moving current of existence and renounce free acts of the will. But the tyranny of time is not absolute and human will is not entirely absent. There are five works of Chekhov's which examine the existence of human will and its slow and painful struggle, showing its abortive stirrings, its groping self-assertion, searching longings, a claim to liberation, and finally a triumphant proof of victory.

In "Ionych," Chekhov shows us feeble flickers of the human will, too feeble to survive the smothering weight of a dreary and empty provincial environment. The spiritual wasteland of the local town is exposed by focusing on the trite vapidity of the Turkins, who are considered the most gifted and best-educated family in town. Mrs. Turkin writes novels "about things that never happen in real life." Her husband concentrates on word play and on forming amusing neologisms. Their daughter, Ekaterina Ivanovna, dreams of becoming a great musician. When she plays, she strikes the piano chords with such force and persistence as to evoke

images of avalanches of rocks cascading down a moun-
tainside.

The country doctor, Dmitri Ionych Startsev, becomes a
frequent guest in the Turkins' hospitable house and falls in
love with Ekaterina Ivanovna. She is not interested in his
advances and has no intention of keeping the midnight
rendezvous at the local cemetery which she teasingly suggests. "The hour cometh" reads the inscription over the
cemetery gate. Yet it is here, wandering among the tomb-
stones and crosses and waiting in vain for Ekaterina Ivanovna, that Startsev experiences a brief spell of passionate
longing and genuine desire: "He felt the urge to shout that he
wanted, that he expected love at any cost...." But the very
next day this "urge to shout" is muted and the cry muffled.
While Startsev is waiting for Ekaterina Ivanovna's appearance in order to propose to her, a small voice in the back of
his mind seems to whisper: "The dowry will probably be
considerable.... Stop while there is still time.... She is spoiled
and capricious.... Her relatives will force you to give up your
job as a country doctor and to live in town." While another
voice seems to counter: "So what? Why not live in town?
They will give a dowry, we will buy furniture...."[23]

Ekaterina Ivanovna turns Startsev down in order to go to
Moscow and pursue her artistic career. It takes him two days
to recover from the blow and to return to his routine existence. His practice grows, his income increases, and in the
evenings he counts with relish the cash collected from his
patients. Four years pass in which he steadily gains weight
and loses mobility and humanity. Ekaterina Ivanovna
returns from Moscow disillusioned in her dreams of an artistic career and now ready to marry Startsev. They meet and
for a brief moment he recalls the enchantment of that night
at the cemetery in all its minutest details. His longing seems
to return. But when Ekaterina Ivnanovna speaks with
apparent awe of his noble vocation as a doctor, he remembers
the cash he takes out of his pocket with such pleasure in the
evenings and his longing subsides.

A few more years pass. Startsev's success and wealth continue to grow, and so do his obesity, greed, and indifference. He has become irritable, impatient, and rude with his patients, pompous, and resembles, when driving around in his troika, a heathen god in his chariot. He is now a local fixture in the town and known simply as "Ionych." Slowly, the hour cometh.

At no time, even during the brief moments of volitional stirrings, did Startsev-Ionych experience any desire to escape from his environment. For Aleksey Laptev in "Three Years" the thought that escape from his stifling merchant world is the prerequisite for his salvation becomes very clear. In length and number of characters "Three Years" belongs to Chekhov's most extensive works. A wide stream of life flows by, measured and slow. The rich Moscow merchant Aleksey Laptev is in love with Iulia Belavina, daughter of a provincial doctor. He proposes and, after some hesitation, she coolly accepts in order to escape from her dreary provincial life. A child is born to them and dies of diphtheria at the age of eight months. Laptev's sister Nina slowly dies of cancer. Her two little girls, aged seven and ten, come to live with the Laptevs and greatly mature during the three years. Their father, Panaurov, who lives by the motto that "everything comes to an end in this world," leads a dissolute, aimless existence, constantly borrowing money from Laptev. Aleksey Laptev's brother Fedor contracts a fatal nervous disorder. Their eighty-year-old father, head of the Laptev enterprise, is losing his eyesight.

Aleksey Laptev looks upon the family business as a prison and his wealth as a crippling handicap. "I am rich, but what has this money so far given me, what has this power given me?... My childhood was that of a convict and money did not save me from being whipped."[24] He feels that his father's disposition is responsible for his timidity and cowardly disposition: "I have neither flexibility nor courage, nor a strong will. I am afraid of every step I take, as if I were about to be whipped.... I am afraid of janitors, of doormen, of city policemen, I am afraid of everybody because I was born of a downtrodden mother, since childhood I was oppressed and cowed."[25]

Neither has wealth contributed anything to Laptev's happiness in his adult life. When his sister Nina was ill and dying, his money did not save her. And when he married Iulia he felt that "he was buying and she was selling herself." "When I am not loved I cannot conjure up love by force, even if I spent one hundred millions." Laptev feels he is a slave, realizes that he is unable "to become master of his life." To his brother Fedor he says: "...if I had an ounce of willpower and courage, I would have long ago hurled these profits from me and gone off to earn my daily bread. But you and your warehouse, you have dehumanized me since childhood. I am yours."[26]

The impending blindness of the eldest Laptev and the fatal illness of Fedor necessitate Aleksey's moving into his father's house and taking over the management of the business. Fedor's incurable disease represents for Aleksey "a break with the past," while moving into the prison house of the family enterprise makes him feel that he has "no future either." His feeling for Iulia has changed too. He has grown resigned and indifferent. Brooding over the question of what it is that prevents him from leaving the millions, the enterprise, the house, and the yard that he has hated since childhood, Aleksey concludes that, apparently, it is "the habit of servitude, the condition of slavery."

While Iulia, matured by all the events of the three years, begins to feel a genuine affection for her husband, Aleksey feels that he has entered upon "a gray semi-life." When she embraces him trying to tell him of her love, he gently disengages himself and walks away. He ponders how much longer this life will go on—thirteen years? Thirty years? And what is still in store in the future? His resigned answer: "Time will tell—we shall see."

Aleksey Laptev clearly sees the way out, but he equally clearly realizes his inability to choose, to exert his will, and to become master of his life. Much more intense and sustained than Laptev's sense of dissatisfaction ever was is the longing experienced by the title characters of *The Three Sisters* to escape from the dreary existence in their provincial town and move back to Moscow, where they spent their childhood. This will be the beginning of a new life full of rewarding, stimulating, and useful work.

Olga, the oldest of the three, age twenty-eight when the play opens, is a schoolteacher in a local school. She is lonely and fatigued by her dreary work. Masha, married to the dull and pedantic schoolmaster Kulygin, feels trapped and unhappy in her marriage. Though both sisters regard Moscow as the symbol of a new and meaningful existence, they speak sparingly of their plans. Masha will spend every summer with them in Moscow, says Olga. It is the youngest of the three, Irina, age twenty when the play opens, who is the most articulate exponent of the sisters' dream. On her name day, a sunny fifth of May, she appears dressed in white, radiant and festive, resembling a beautiful white bird ready to spread its wings and fly into a sunlit future. By fall, she says, they will have sold their house and moved to Moscow. Their brother Andrey will become a professor at Moscow University. "When I woke up this morning," she continues, "I suddenly began to feel that everything in this world made sense and that I know how to live.... Man must work, he must toil by the sweat of his brow whoever he is—and that is the meaning and purpose of his life, his happiness, his joy...." Toward the end of the first act she goes on: "As far as we three sisters are concerned, life has not been beautiful as yet, it has been choking us like weeds.... We must work, work. The reason we are miserable and have such a gloomy outlook on life is that we don't know what work is. We were born of people who despised work."[27]

Irina speaks these words just before the appearance of the vulgar and common Natasha, who is about to become Andrey's fiancée. As his wife in the second act a year and a half later, she has begun to take over control of the house and to ease her three sisters-in-law out. She meets no resistance. Andrey has become a weak and indolent nonentity. And the sisters are incapable of defending themselves. They are painfully aware of drifting along and of moving farther and farther away from Moscow. In the third act, two years later, Irina's foreboding that they will never move to Moscow is confirmed by the news that Andrey has mortgaged the house to repay gambling debts. The money is in Natasha's hands.

The dream is dead, but not the longing. The sisters' hope to escape to Moscow, to return to the environment of their past, is gone. But the move to Moscow is not a prerequisite for a life of toil, Chekhov seems to say. A broader and deeper feeling takes the place of the dead dream—a yearning to go on living and to continue the search for a better life. This yearning is not impaired by the tragedies experienced by the sisters. Irina consented to marry Tuzenbach, but he is killed in a duel on the eve of the wedding. Masha falls deeply in love with the battery commander Vershinin, who dreams so eloquently of the distant future, but the brigade is being moved to another town and they must part. And yet, before the final curtain, the voices of the three sisters blend in a poetic melody of joyous hope and longing: "Our lives are not finished yet," says Olga, "let us live! It seems as if before too long we might find out what our lives, what our sufferings are for.... If we could only know, if we could only know!"

We leave the three sisters filled with longing and groping for an answer as to how to live. Misail Poloznev in "My Life" (1896) finds an answer. In format "My Life" resembles "Three Years." There is also a thematic connection. Misail succeeds in achieving what Laptev was incapable of doing—of breaking away from an oppressive milieu and going off to earn his daily bread. Lack of good taste distinguishes Misail's father, who is the only architect in the local town. The same aesthetic deficiency, narrates Misail, pervades his widowed father's family life. He finds his own name in as poor taste as his sister's—Cleopatra. Both have received a strict and regimented upbringing. Cleopatra, now twenty-six, is her father's submissive and cowed housekeeper. Her sickly pallor and frequent coughing speak of a serious illness which she, "for some reason," tries to conceal. Misail is twenty-five. Since he became an adult, he says, he has held and lost nine jobs. All were mechanical, clerical chores requiring neither mental effort nor creativity. Misail considers them demeaning, below physical labor. Yet his father forces him to continue, since he considers only white-collar jobs appropriate to the family's social standing and noble ancestry. He vents his wrath over Misail's dismissals by beating his son over the head and shoulders with his umbrella.

Misail's breakaway happens casually and without a hint of drama. One day he simply turns to the local contractor and painter Red'ka for a menial job and is hired as a painter. In the eyes of the townspeople he has disgraced himself, and is now frequently showered with abuse in public. His acquaintances look embarrassed when they pass him on the street. The estrangement from his father is now complete. The physical strain of the new work is at first hard to bear as well. Nevertheless, Misail feels as though he were "reborn." Time flies while he is at work. And the thought that he is free, supporting himself and a burden to no one, exhilarates him. He explains his views on the virtues of physical labor: "To eliminate oppression of the weak by the strong, of the destitute majority by the affluent minority, everybody should engage in physical work, for there is no better leveling force in society. Progress lies in acts of love, in fulfillment of moral tenets. If you oppress no one, burden no one—isn't that progress?"[28]

"Nothing passes," says Misail at the end of "My Life." "I believe that nothing passes without leaving a trace and that each step we take, be it ever so small, is significant for our present and future life...."[29] He has emerged a stronger man from the ordeal of his broken marriage. He has now succeeded in winning the respect of the town's inhabitants and is considered, next to Red'ka, the best local contractor and painter. While the title "Three Years" reflects Laptev's movement toward "a gray semi-life," the title "My Life" hints at Misail's conscious, free, volitional entry into the stream of existence. Humble as his occupation remains, he has become a useful member of society.

Misail's transition to a voluntary re-construction of his life, starting with his decision to ask Red'ka for work, is simply stated. Chekhov tells us little about the emotional deliberations leading up to that decision. In "The Betrothed," Chekhov's last completed short story, we are shown the whole process of deliberation, a dynamic series of states that permeate and strengthen one another and finally lead Nadia to the decision to leave her home and to start a new life of study and work in Petersburg. We meet her as a twenty-three-year-old girl engaged to be married two months hence. And we watch the process of her growth over a year's time.

In the beginning of the story she thinks of her fiancé as a "kind, clever man" and of her mother as "an exceptional person." The student Sasha from Moscow, a visiting friend of the family, merely bores and irritates her with his constant criticism of their idle provincial existence. Yet Sasha's words do lodge a seed of doubt in her consciousness and the seed begins to grow. At first Nadia experiences merely a vague uneasiness and apprehension over the impending wedding. When her mother fails to understand these misgivings, Nadia begins to see her in a new light and comes to the conclusion that she is an ordinary woman after all. Next the realization begins to grow that she does not love her fiancé anymore, or perhaps never did love him. Then comes the decision to follow Sasha's advice and flee from her home town with his help. A year later, after having spent the fall and winter studying in Petersburg, Nadia returns home for a visit and stops en route in Moscow to see Sasha again. She has now outgrown him too. Though as fond of him as ever, she finds him gray, provincial, and less intellectual than a year ago: "From his words, his smile, his whole figure emanated something obsolete, old-fashioned, long outlived...." Nadia's home town revisited produced a similar impression on her: "...it seemed to her that everything in the town had long since reached old age and obsolescence and was only waiting either for the end to come or for the beginning of something young and fresh."[30] At the end of her visit, vibrant and gay, she leaves the town—"as she supposed"—forever.

"The Betrothed" is Chekhov's most concentrated exposition of the dynamic process of a human consciousness arriving at independent judgments and moving on to creative decisions and a voluntary act. And in no other story of Chekhov's is the expression "for some reason" as frequently repeated. A causal determination of Nadia's feelings and thoughts is deliberately removed.

We can only speculate in what direction Chekhov's creative thoughts might have moved, had he lived longer, after the joyous ending of his last story. And what figures might have been added to the portrait gallery of the defeated Ionych, the perceptive but weak Laptev, the three sisters groping to find a meaning to their lives, the determined and practical Misail, the exuberant and vibrant Nadia. Chekhov's reflections on the life of the human will are far from revealing any heroic dimensions. But the tyranny of time can be broken. The need to wish, the value of the courage to expect and to accept grief along with happiness are voiced by the simple-minded, inarticulate, and illiterate Tartar convict in "In Exile" who is pitted against the "sensible" Semen, who has abrogated all claims to desires. And the two protagonists who are successful in their volitional efforts to mold their own lives, to reach for temporal control, could hardly be more modest: Misail, who becomes a respected contractor, and the young, inexperienced Nadia, who embarks upon an independent life of her own. These are achievements which could be emulated by anyone—a message particularly arresting since it was formulated at a time when our contemporary "age of the disordered will" had hardly begun, an age when "people go to the therapist to find substitutes for their lost will."[31]

Notes

1 V, 15.
2 L., III, 132.
3 XIII, 162.
4 IX, 56.
5 X, 31.
6 L., III, 109.
7 VIII, 296.
8 VII, 64.
9 L., V, 345.
10 VIII, 306.
11 IX, 222.
12 IX, 230.
13 XIII, 131.
14 XIII, 146.
15 X, 34-5.
16 Ibid.
17 X, 215.
18 X, 173.
19 VIII, 49.
20 VIII, 50.
21 XIII, 48.
22 IX, 324.
23 X, 32-3.
24 IX, 57.
25 IX, 80.
26 IX, 81.
27 XIII, 135.
28 IX, 220.
29 IX, 279.
30 X, 219.
31 Rollo May, *Love and Will*. New York: Dell Publishing Co., 1969, p. 15.

V

The Paralysis of Human Isolation

Dostoevsky's exploration of human isolation was conducted on the lofty level of spiritual reality and closely bound to the question of freedom. The freedom of his godless heroes is based on their deliberate ascent above ordinary human beings. Their elevation is vertiginous, nurtured by a belief in the prodigious strength of their own free will and in the power proffered to them by intellect and by money. But the fallacy of seeking freedom along this road of willful isolation is experienced by all of Dostoevsky's protagonists who rule out God. Only those who arrive at or approach apprehending the redeeming freedom in human communion offered by Christian humility are spared annihilation.

Chekhov's examination of human isolation is brought down from the lofty heights of spiritual reality to the pedestrian level of everyday existence. It lacks any attributes of

147

exclusiveness, intent, or power. It is not a function of freedom sought. An infinite gradation of involuntary impulses
and unpremeditated acts creates a fine web of helpless indifference, inertia, and impediments to human rapport. The
forces held instrumental by Dostoevsky's atheists in propel-
ling them upward in their dizzy ascent lose their momentum.
Human will is weak, seldom capable of gaining control over
one's personal destiny and throwing off the tyranny of time.
Reason appears merely as a component part of human consciousness. And money does not function as a fount of
power; it turns instead into an additional impediment to free
acts of the will.

Dostoevsky's heroes speak of their chosen seclusion in
terms of dramatic, haughty omnipotence. Stavrogin regards
his strength as boundless and the scope of his desires as
limitless, deriving equal pleasure from doing good and doing
evil. Ivan Karamazov admits that his love for men in particular diminishes in proportion to the increase of his rational
love of mankind in general. Raskolnikov wishes to write his
own Napoleonic law of conduct and test his right to murder.
Arkady Dolgoruky aims, by amassing a fortune, to reach a
position of awesome and solitary power and strength. All are
feverishly active, plotting and executing acts exhibiting
their willful freedom or immersed in intense intellectual
speculations in support of their behavior.

With one notable exception to be discussed presently,
Chekhov's heroes seldom speak of their own isolation; most
are not even aware of it. A lack of "action" is a characteristic
feature of the plots. But there are few topics that hold their
creator's attention more assiduously and persistently than
the solitude of human beings. Isolation is not a matter of life
and death, it is not the central topic of the drama enacted in
the towering reaches of Dostoevsky's art, in the chiaroscuro
of the great abyss of nothingness lit by the beacons of rebirth
in Christian freedom. Rather it is a gray shadow, a fog, a
malaise with many debilitating symptoms afflicting all
parts of the social body. And the Christian concept of freedom in human solidarity ceases to be the bright beacon

flashing in the darkness of Dostoevsky's world. Rather it becomes a faint glow, a light diffused, visible here and there for brief passing moments only, when Chekhov observes men reaching out to touch one another in search of contact and rapport.

The degree of impediment and paralysis one experiences by being locked within oneself, by not establishing, not maintaining, or not even understanding the need of meaningful contacts with one's fellow beings is a central concern of Chekhov's. There is hardly a story, or a play, where this theme is absent. This was not a systematic, chronological progression. Chekhov's artistic eye roamed at large and observed at random thousands of variations on this topic. But if we survey his life work as a whole, setting its chronological sequence aside (Chekhov himself was, at times, prone to ignore the precise order in which he had completed his stories), we discover that he has left us a rich gamut, a graded scale of observations that descend deeper and deeper into the chilling, paralyzing reaches of human isolation.

At the top of the scale stands what has come to be regarded by critics as Chekhov's dominant theme—the lack of verbal understanding. People talk at cross-purposes, not really listening to each other. In the second act of *The Three Sisters* Chebutykin and Solenyi argue about the meaning of what they think is the same word, while they are actually using two different words which happen to have the same first syllable, *che*, and the same ending, *a*. Chebutykin speaks of *chekhartma*, which, he says, is a Caucasian roast of lamb, while Solenyi replies that *cheremsha* is not a roast but a plant related to the onion.[1] This absurd argument stands as the epitome of countless verbal misunderstandings and inattentive replies which occur so frequently between Chekhov's characters and which may even degenerate into a complete absence of response.

An early story, "The Mail" (1887) takes us a step further down the scale, to a complete refusal to communicate. It is a letter-carrier himself, a conduit of written messages, whom Chekhov chooses to present as an utterly surly and taciturn individual who steadfastly and inexplicably refuses to engage in conversation with a friendly young co-traveler. Only when the horses, suddenly frightened, bolt and the mail carrier falls off the troika, does he display a startlingly voluble capacity for expression. Though he has escaped injury, he vents his rage at the driver of the carriage—and then, after this wrathful outburst, again retreats into his dour and morose silence.

Pitiful gestures filled with longing for reciprocity are described in "Heartache" (1886). The cabdriver Iona has lost his son a few days ago. In vain he tries to share his grief with the various passengers he picks up in the twilight hour of a snowy, frigid evening. Like a funereal cloth the large wet flakes settle on Iona's shoulders and on his horse's back. Clumsily and laboriously he turns his whole body again and again toward his successive passengers in the hope of a word of comfort, only to receive an indifferent or even rude response. To each of them, Iona is nothing but a tool, a vehicle carrying them toward their destination. The plot does not focus on the death of Iona's son, but on the fact that no one will listen to Iona's tragedy. It ends with Iona back at the stables, pouring out his grief to his little mare, who listens "munching and breathing on her master's hands."

At times, people can be not only deaf but blind as well when it comes to a plea for reciprocity. The prostitute Vanda in "A Male Acquaintance" (1886), just dismissed from a hospital and penniless, visits her one-time client, the dentist Finkel, hoping to get some financial assistance. But he fails to recognize her in her present shabby attire. In this incomparable blend of tragedy and comedy, Chekhov has Vanda feign a toothache and submit to an extraction to cover up her embarrassment and shame. How frequently Chekhov resorts to a blend of tears and laughter in depicting human intercourse, in contrast to Dostoevsky's blend of light and shadow, or rather of evil's vast darkness pierced by rare shafts of the brilliant light of goodness.

In another early story, "The Privy Counselor" (1886) the dapper general from St. Petersburg spends the summer at his sister's provincial country home. Flighty, absent minded, egocentric, and utterly absorbed in selfish pursuits, he fails altogether to take notice of his young nephew throughout his visit, though the boy is utterly fascinated by the presence of such a high-ranking military figure and distinguished relative. It is the boy who makes a final, futile attempt to bridge the chasm, to pierce the curtain that shrouds him from the sight of this awesome figure. Getting into the carriage, ready to leave at the end of his visit, the general repeats, for the nth time, "And who is this boy?" Feeling a sudden upsurge of pity the boy impulsively embraces and enchants this empty, frivolous man with the query "Uncle, have you ever been in a real battle?"

The absurd argument about *chekhartma* and *cheremsha* between Chebutykin and Solenyi lies at the tip of the iceberg of human alienation. The aborted attempts at a friendly chat in "The Mail," Iona's rejected plea for a word of compassion or comfort, Finkel's failure to recognize Vanda, the general's inability to enter into a spontaneous contact with his young nephew—are all but random samples from a vast score of encounters among Chekhov's protagonists who are indifferent to verbal exchanges and, beyond that, do not care to become aware of the human beings who happen to cross their path. The deepest, ultimate layer of the iceberg of human isolation is exposed in "A Dreary Story." Chekhov's brilliant professor Nikolay Stepanovich, representative of the world of science, formulates at death's door his diagnosis of the deadly disease spawned by the sovereignty of reason and intellect: indifference, a paralysis of the soul, premature death.

The story has been frequently compared with Tolstoy's *Death of Ivan Il'ich*, which is also a retrospective review of a dying old man's life. Ivan Il'ich led an easy, pleasant, "decorous" existence. Pursuing one of his favorite themes, the indictment of the mores of modern society, Tolstoy shows how "decorum" has replaced human sincerity and warmth in Ivan Il'ich's life. He begins to feel his isolation when he falls ill. Longing for genuine compassion and comfort when he gets progressively worse, he meets with feigned and hypocritical concern instead. It is flickers of warmth, the artless kindness of his servant Gerasim and a kiss from his son, these touches of love and therefore of eternity, that ease his final agony, his passage through the terrifying "dark sack, the black hole" of death, and permit him to die peacefully, to merge with the divine realm of good and love.

Chekhov has no comparable relief for Nikolay Stepanovich. His tragedy is not the indifference of others toward him, as is the case with Ivan Il'ich, but the revelation of his own indifference toward the professional and personal contacts formed during his successful life as a physician, scholar, husband, father, and guardian. His intellectual capabilities, his powers of reasoning, are unimpaired and his physical decline but a side issue. It is his soul that he himself diagnoses as paralyzed. His emotional responses, not just his ability to hear and to see but his *desire* to do so, his wish to answer calls for help from others, have withered, have induced his isolation, and brought him to death's door. But in contrast to Dostoevsky's godless heroes, intoxicated by their imagined superiority, he experiences his isolation and the absence of nonrational impulses and stimuli in helpless misery as a confining trap, instead of seeing his solitude as a mark of distinction, strength, and freedom.

The division of mankind into strong and weak beings, into an elite of power-hungry, self-willed individuals and the mass of obedient, submissive humanity that lies at the core of the drama of Dostoevsky's atheists, is examined by Chekhov in the novella "The Duel" (1891). It is set in the summery atmosphere of a Black Sea resort, of tourist pavilions, boardwalks, beaches, magnificent vistas of mountains and sea. Its ideological core concerns a contest between the zoologist Von Koren and the young civil servant Laevsky. In primitive societies, claims Von Koren, elimination of the weak was carried out by environmental conditions, by the struggle for life. In our modern society the annihilation of the unfit must be executed by man himself, by the strong. Von Koren stresses that he believes in Christ and in the

Christian ideal of brotherly love, but "in his own way," that is to say, "reasonably and intelligently."[3] Love of mankind should stem from the mind and not from the heart. To love every passerby indiscriminately would amount to repudiation of common sense, of justice toward people. Love means a victory of the strong over the weak. Von Koren's design of rationally enforced improvement of the human race, his deliberate distortion of the Christian ideal of brotherly love, is a prosaic counterpart to the grandiose ideas of Dostoevsky's Grand Inquisitor, a down-to-earth project to substitute terrestrial improvements for spiritual freedom.

Von Koren's adversary, Laevsky, complains of being a superfluous man, a victim of civilization, is bored with life, does not work, and schemes, while borrowing money from his friends, how to escape from the woman he is living with. In spite of his inadequacy Laevsky gives a shrewd analysis of Von Koren's character. He is "a despot first and a zoologist second....his ideals are despotic.... When ordinary mortals work for the common good, they have their neighbor in mind, people like me, like you, in a word—man. But Von Koren looks upon people as if they were puppies and nonentities. He works...not in the name of brotherly love, but in the name of such abstractions as mankind, future generations, ideal species of men. He is concerned about improving the species of men and in this respect we are to him only slaves, cannon fodder.... And what is this human species? An illusion, a mirage. Despots have always been phantom-chasers."[4]

Antagonism between the two men mounts and culminates in Von Koren challenging Laevsky to a duel. Though Von Koren is determined to exterminate his adversary as a useless, weak, and therefore harmful specimen of humanity, his shot proves abortive and the aftermath of the duel points away from radical and violent solutions to human conflicts. The two enemies bury the hatchet before Von Koren has to leave the resort, and the idea of dividing humanity into superior and inferior beings appears defeated by the "duel." A remarkable change takes place in Laevsky. He marries his mistress and takes up serious work. His conversion may

seem too sudden and radical to be psychologically convincing. But who could begrudge Chekhov that flush of hope
formulated in the finale of the story, though it lacks the
dramatic impact of the silent kiss bestowed by Christ on the
withered lips of the Grand Inquisitor at the end of the latter's
monologue? Watching Von Koren's dinghy move toward the
steamship, bobbing up and down in a stormy sea, Laevsky
ponders: "No one knows the real truth...the dinghy...moves
two steps forward and one step back.... The same in life....
Searching for truth people take two steps forward, one step
back. Sufferings, mistakes, and the boredom of life throw
them back, but the yearning for truth and an obstinate willpower drive them onward again and again, and who knows?
Perhaps they will reach the shores of real truth."[5]

The acquisitive greed that consumes so many of Dostoevsky's protagonists with burning passion, helping to
propel them to positions of power, is absent in Chekhov's
world. The rich feel ill-at-ease in their affluent surroundings.
The millionaire Aleksey Laptev in "Three Years" regards
his wealth as a ponderous and murky force that suffocates
his creative energies. He feels trapped in the oppressive prison of the family warehouses and offices. Liza Lialikova in
"A Case from Practice," rich heiress of a large industrial
enterprise, suffers from insomnia and spells of nervous anxiety induced by her lonely life in the confines of the drab
industrial compound. The advice that Doctor Korolev, summoned to her bedside, would have liked to give is that she
should relinquish her wealth. But he does not know how to
say it: "It is embarrassing to ask a condemned person why
he has been sentenced; and it is equally awkward to ask very
rich people why they should have so much money, why they
manage their wealth so badly, why they do not abandon it,
even when they know that it is the source of their unhappiness."[6] The millionairess Anna Akimovna in "A Woman's
Kingdom" dislikes her realm, built from modest beginnings
by her deceased father. In the first chapter of the story she
has just received the sum of fifteen hundred rubles won in a
law suit by her manager. The sight of the money fills her

with unease and embarrassment. Only after she decides to use the money for a charitable purpose does her despondency momentarily clear. Even the lavish generosities of the princess in the story of the same title, so scathingly criticized by Doctor Mikhail Ivanovich, are condemned as the frivolous, capricious efforts of a spoiled, rich woman to fill her idleness with amusing recreation, to play "a game of brotherly love," rather than as a vainglorious display of her power.

By the time Chekhov began to write, the social and economic milieu from which Dostoevsky drew his irreligious and freedom-seeking protagonists, held spellbound by the metaphysical power of money, had perceptibly changed. In the last two decades of the nineteenth century industrialization advanced at a rapid and accelerating pace and the machine rose to an even more prominent role in the life of the country than in Dostoevsky's lifetime, vying with capital in importance. Chekhov's astute, sober mind, schooled in medical training and practice, welcomed these advances of material civilization. In his letters and conversations he frequently voiced his approval of technological progress and his eager anticipation of further industrial and technical advances to come. But in his fiction the machine is far from functioning as an instrument of power, far from elevating the owners to a position of proud and lofty superiority over the mass of humanity; instead it contributes to the sense of entrapment generated by money and voiced by the rich. Both money and machines are misused in a way that hampers human progress instead of promoting it.

On the pages of Chekhov's stories the machine appears as a new, powerful, mysterious force in human life, alien both to men and to nature, a diabolical monster, a force humans have not yet learned how to manage and to control properly since they are unable to bring it in accord with concepts basic to Christian civilization. Anna Akimovna in "A Woman's Kingdom" thinks of the engine room in her factory as "an inferno." "It seemed to her as though the wheels, levers, and hot, hissing cylinders attempted to break away from their couplings in order to destroy the people, and the people, their faces preoccupied and *their ears deaf to one another* [italics mine], ran and hustled around the machines trying to stop their terrible motion."[7]

These impressions are corroborated and extended by the sober observations of Doctor Korolev in "A Case from Practice." He had been told that the workers in the Lialikov enterprise are loyal to the firm and pleased with recent improvements in their living conditions. But as a physician he assesses these improvements as a palliative treatment comparable to a drug administered in the case of an incurable disease. He thinks of the thousands of workers toiling away in unhealthy surroundings, on a starvation diet, finding the only release from this nightmare in the pub; he thinks of the hundreds of workers' supervisors who spend their time distributing penalties and fines, dispensing injustices and abuse; and he thinks of the handful of idle and hapless owners caught in this incomprehensible web of human relationships. It seems to him that there is a mysterious and diabolical power that has created these relations between the strong and the weak, "this terrible and now irreparable mistake. It is a law of nature that the strong make life miserable for the weak, but in human life it is an absurd paradox when the strong as well as the weak fall victim to their mutual relations, submitting involuntarily to some governing force which is mysterious, extrinsic to life, and alien to man."[8]

This dehumanizing regression in men's relations with their fellow men brought about by the advent of the machine age reveals itself to Doctor Korolev in its full sinister implications during a nocturnal stroll through the Lialikov factory grounds. Everything looks different from the way it appears in daylight. He completely forgets that inside these buildings there are steam engines, electricity, telephones. Instead he is insistently reminded of "pile dwellings and the Stone Age" and feels the presence of a rough, inanimate power. His hearing is jarred by sharp, dissonant, metalic beats announcing the hour. A rough, rude voice "like a prison guard's" accosts him at the gate. Sporadic flames mingling with smoke leap from the chimney of a smelting oven. Two windows are lit and the building looks like "a huge diabolical monster with crimson eyes who ruled here over the masters as well as over the workers and deceived them all."[9]

In "The Duel" the division of mankind into the strong and the weak is repudiated on ideological grounds as violating the basic Christian concept of the equal worth of every single individual. In "A Case from Practice," and wherever Chekhov examined the contemporary industrial and pecuniary milieu, the concept of that division itself appears fallacious and unreal, yielding to the "absurd paradox" of the masters of machines and of capital as well as their servants being trapped and held in bondage by the powerful, inanimate forces of technological and economic progress. There is no victory of the strong over the weak. The spectral mirages of pile dwellings and of people sinking to the level of savages of the Stone Age that haunt the imagination of the astute Doctor Korolev illustrate the predicament of modern men as Chekhov saw it, lost in solitude and helpless separation, their sight clouded, their hearing dulled, their voices so frequently unheeded, and their actions falling short of realizing man's generous potentialities.

If arrogant pride is the dominant emotion that intoxicates Dostoevsky's atheistic protagonists in their upward climb to a chilly summit of isolation, the helplessness and inertia in which Chekhov's solitary characters exist, lost in the maze of their contemporary environment, frequently mount to the intensity of fear, fear as an overpowering emotion that grips them and holds them in its vise. The high-ranking civil servant Orlov in "An Anonymous Story" (1893) displays an ironic approach to all aspects of existence. Irony has become an ingrained habit of his, an involuntary reflex, for "he is afraid of life" and holds irony "always in readiness as a savage holds his shield."[10] Orlov is far from a conspicuous exception in Chekhov's world. The millionaire Aleksey Laptev in "Three Years," trapped by his wealth, speaks of his timidity, of the fact that he is "afraid of everybody,"[11] even of janitors, doormen, and policemen. In the story "Fear," (1892) the landowner Dimitri Petrovich finds life, particularly the commonplaces of life, "terrifying, infinitely more terrifying than phantoms and apparitions. I do not understand people and I am afraid of them."[12]

Belikov, in "The Man in a Case" (1898) is the ultimate embodiment, the culminating symbol of fear and of isolation caused by fear. Perhaps he can be classified as an exception in the thronging, multifaceted variety of Chekhov's characters, each one individualized, each drawn as a unique, inimitable being. For the concentration on the attributes of a cowardly withdrawal from life, of self-incarceration, is so intense as to make Belikov a worthy successor to Gogol's brilliant gallery of misfits, each exemplifying a single human failing or defect. Fear assumes monstrous proportions in Belikov's life. It engulfs him, it cripples him, it immures him, it becomes a compelling motivation for conformity, for obeying rules and regulations, it dominates at all times his thoughts, his behavior, his surroundings, even his attire. Anticipating inclement weather even when the sun is shining, he never leaves the house without wearing a warm coat and rubbers and carrying an umbrella. Afraid of being burglarized or murdered during the night, he goes to bed drawing the blanket over his head. His sleep is constantly troubled by anxious dreams and nightmares. His small, stuffy bedroom with the curtained bed resembles a shuttered, bolted box. Being a teacher of Greek and Latin at the local school, Belikov turns even his profession into a shield from reality. His aversion for the present is evident in his perpetual praise of the distant past, of the beauty of the ancient world. What irony that Chekhov has this crazed cripple choose the word *Anthropos*—man—to exemplify the melodiousness of the Greek language!

For Chekhov the word Man shone in its numinous connotations. As a counterpoint to the protagonists gripped by fear in their solitary abandonment there stand Chekhov's priests, Father Christopher in "The Steppe" and Deacon

Pobedov in "The Duel," radiant in their serenity and humaneness. Even Father Yakov stands as a luminous image in the finale of "The Nightmare," dispensing loving attention to his parishioners though spattered with all the mud that obstructs his daily path. The idea of man as the reflection of the Divine Being may be frequently forgotten by Chekhov's protagonists, but it is seldom challenged the way it is persistently questioned by Dostoevsky's godless heroes. And repeatedly Chekhov gives the idea of man as the image of God a decisive formulation.

The reason for Vasiliev's attack of nerves in the story with that title is the shock of coming face to face with the abject degradation of the prostitutes he meets, their "human dignity, personality, image and likeness of God, defiled down to its very foundations."[13] In his farewell letter to Orlov in "An Anonymous Story" the narrator asks: "...why is it that, before having had a chance to begin life, you hastened to throw off the divine image and likeness and turned into a cowardly animal which barks and frightens others with this bark because he himself is afraid?"[14] The chief protagonist in "The Story of the Senior Gardener" (1894) is Mikhail Karlovich, a venerable, clever, kind, and generally respected old man. The three customers who have come to purchase flowers listen to his stories, which all center on his humanitarian beliefs. He welcomes verdicts of not guilty in court, even if there is doubt that the defendant was guiltless: "If the judges and the jury believe in *man* more than in damaging circumstances, material evidence, and speeches, isn't this faith in man in itself worth more than all worldly considerations?"[15] The gardener concludes his discourse with the assertion that God rejoices when men remember that they are his image and likeness and grieves when human dignity is forgotten and people are judged as inferior to dogs. "Faith in man...generates noble impulses and always prompts us to love and respect every single person. Every single one! And that is important."[16]

There are moments in Chekhov's world when man, lost in the fog of isolation, seems to shed his paralysis and amnesia, and remembering his otherworldly ties, turns in quest of contact and rapport toward another human being. Those are luminous moments of reaching out, of spontaneous gestures seeking freedom in human communion. When speaking of such moments Chekhov seems curiously to anticipate by some thirty or forty years the thoughts of the religious philosopher Martin Buber, author of the much acclaimed book *I and Thou*. The fundamental fact of human existence is man with man; all real living is meeting, writes Buber. "Something takes place between one being and another the like of which can be found nowhere in nature." Only man, among all the creatures on earth, is able to say "Thou." And it is only in saying "Thou" that a man becomes an "I," becomes aware of God's presence manifest in himself, in those he addresses, and in all parts of creation. "There is no place where God could not be found."[17]

The moments of human encounters that Chekhov shows us are far less numerous than the incidence of inattentiveness, neglect, and withdrawal, but they too occur on a scale of varying intensity that matches the gamut of indifference and retreat. Some of these moments do not even entail a dialogue. There may be only a voice heard or a silent response to an emotion displayed. But there is always that "something" Buber spoke of that can take place only between one human being and another, that something indefinable and ineffable, but indispensable for the divine image to shine through. There is always reciprocity, the whole being of the participants is involved in the address and in the response as well, even if mute. It is an exchange that reaches beyond verbal intercourse.

The monk Nikolay in "On Easter Night" would get up in the middle of the night when his friend, the novice Ieronim, was on duty operating the rope ferry and shout a word of greeting and encouragement across the water of the river to dispel Ieronim's sense of loneliness and abandonment. Gratefully Ieronim recalls these incidents and recounts them to the narrator of the story after Nikolay's death. On the eve of Palm Sunday Bishop Peter in "The Bishop," ill, lonely, and weighed down by the burden of his rank, weeps quietly during the service. Suddenly the congregation responds, spontaneously and inexplicably, to these tears by crying too and mutely sharing a pain sensed but not comprehended. In "A Nightmare" Kunin observes from his window how Father Iakov blesses with warm affection the coachman and the boy who eagerly run up to greet him. And then there is the melodious finale of *Uncle Vania*, Sonia's consoling words of infinite compassion for Uncle Vania, words that move him to shed tears, calling him to endure his joyless life to the end, conjuring the vision of a starlit sky and the sounds of angels' voices at the final advent of rest, evil and suffering drowned in mercy and universal peace.

The story "The Student" (1894) ranked among Chekhov's favorites and contains one of the most numinous of all the human encounters in his works. At its core stands a brief, spontaneous, luminous moment of human contact that draws on a biblical subject. On a cold, raw spring evening two peasant women are tending a bonfire on their garden plot. The divinity student Ivan Velikopolsky, on his way home from a hunting expedition, stops to greet them. He is in a gloomy mood as he stretches his hands toward the dancing flames, stiff and chilled by the penetrating, harsh wind. It is Good Friday and his mind dwells on Holy Week. He speaks of the events in the Garden of Gethsemane nineteen centuries ago and of the Apostle Peter thrice denying Jesus. His words are casual and simple, in no way calculated to influence the women's reactions and he is overwhelmed by the intensity of their attention and the emotionally charged response. He feels that the two women are not merely listening to his simple narrative but are actually reliving the events, participating in the agony and remorse endured by the Apostle Peter. He sees tears rolling down the older woman's cheeks, while the younger one struggles to control a spasm of pain on her face. All three are sharing a moment of living relation, communicating in a sphere of numinous portent spanning nineteen centuries. As Ivan continues on his way, his gloom dispelled and his heart singularly warmed, "Life seemed to him enchanting, miraculous and full of lofty meaning"[18]— a vivid illustration of Buber's words that "real living is meeting."

In "On Official Business" (1899) Chekhov resorts to a dream to draw a perspective of human rapport more revealing and more vivid than the reality experienced by the protagonists. The magistrate Lyzhin has been summoned to the village of Syrnia to attend an autopsy. The local insurance agent, Lesnitsky, has committed suicide under such bizarre circumstances, in the midst of preparing for a meal, that murder is suspected and an inquest in order. While waiting for a violent blizzard to subside and the inquest witnesses to appear, Lyzhin listens to the guileless prattle of the local policeman, Loshadin, a white-haired, stooped, and frail old man who tells him about the vagaries of his thirty years of service. His is the lowest rank of rural police. His duties have kept him ceaselessly tramping the road delivering all sorts of official papers and documents from one administrative office to another. He is used to being treated with contempt and received with insults and abuse. He has suffered robberies and endured beatings from convicts whom he was convoying and who tried to escape; he has lost his way in snowstorms and come close to drowning in swollen streams.

It turns out that Loshadin knew the suicide Lesnitsky well. Lesnitsky's father, Loshadin recounts, was a landowner who had died leaving crushing debts. Penniless and unable to make his way in the world, the young Lesnitsky subsisted miserably on the meager earnings of an insurance agent. Loshadin does not doubt that his death was indeed a suicide. The magistrate Lyzhin suddenly remembers having briefly met Lesnitsky once. He recalls his dark eyes, black hair, and pale, thin face: "He had an unpleasant look in his eyes, such as one sees in people who have slept too long after dinner, and it marred his delicate, intelligent profile; and the high boots he was wearing did not suit him either, they looked clumsy."[19]

The autopsy is delayed by the unabating snowstorm and Lyzhin is forced to spend the night near the scene of the tragedy. As he dozes off, the policeman and the suicide appear before his eyes, walking side by side in a snow-covered field, supporting each other in the swirling drifts and chanting: "We go on, we go on, we go on.... It is warm and light and cozy where you are, but we go on in freezing weather, in a blizzard, in deep snow.... We know no rest, we know no joy.... We carry the whole burden of life, of ours as well as yours.... Hoooo... We go on, we go on, we go on...."[20]

Lyzhin awakens from this strange and unpleasant dream with an oppressive feeling of puzzlement and unease. Why had the suicide and the policeman appeared together in his dream? Perhaps their lives had indeed something in common. "Didn't they go through life side by side, holding on to one another? There does exist some kind of tie, invisible yet significant and essential, between these two, even between them...and all human beings?"[21] Twice more Lyzhin dozes off and twice more the insistent dream returns. The dead insurance agent and the downtrodden policeman tramp and chant, "we go on, we go on, we go on," lamenting the cruel chasm between the bitter burden of their lot and the ease and security in which people like Lyzhin live.

In "On the Road" (1886) an incident of encounter dominates the entire plot. It also brings us close to one of the most important aspects of human relations, one capable of breaching isolation—the bonds between a man and a woman. Two travelers, the young woman Ilovaiskaia and the dissolute, middle-aged Likharev, detained by a raging snowstorm, meet accidentally in a wayside tavern. From their conversation springs a momentary, fragile bond of genuine mutual awareness. The young woman Ilovaiskaia listens attentively as Likharev pours out to her the sad story of his restless and chaotic life. She is deeply moved by the tale of his mistakes and misfortunes, and seems on the verge of offering some helpful suggestion as she prepares to continue her journey on the following morning. Her sleigh has already started to move when she casts a parting glance at Likharev "as if she wanted to say something." He eagerly runs up to her. He is aware that his imagination might have deceived him, "but it suddenly seemed to him that with another touch or two this girl would have forgiven him his failures, his age, his misfortunes and would have followed him, without questions or arguments."[22] But the sleigh continues on its way and Likharev is left standing, his eyes still searching the whirling clouds of snow. Soon the tracks of the sleigh are obliterated and the lonely figure, snowflakes settling thickly on his shoulders, assumes the appearance of "a white rock." The paralysis of isolation has returned. Ilovaiskaya failed to speak the final "Thou."

Notes

[1]   XIII, 151.
[2]   V, 142.
[3]   VII, 432-3.
[4]   VII, 399.
[5]   VII, 455.
[6]   X, 84.
[7]   VIII, 260.
[8]   X, 82.
[9]   Ibid.
[10]   VIII, 140.
[11]   IX, 80.
[12]   VIII, 131.
[13]   VII, 212.
[14]   VIII, 189.
[15]   VIII, 346.
[16]   Ibid.
[17]   Martin Buber, *I And Thou*, trans. Walter Kaufman, Charles Scribner's Sons, New York, 1970, p.128.
[18]   VIII, 309.
[19]   X, 93.
[20]   X, 99.
[21]   Ibid.
[22]   V, 477.

VI

Love Trapped

When Aleksey Laptev in "Three Years" comes to realize that he is hopelessly in love with Iulia Belavina, his mind goes back to long conversations in Moscow in which he participated only a short while before—saying that it is possible to live without love, that passionate love is a psychosis, or that there is no such thing as love, there is only physical attraction between the sexes, and so on and so forth; "he remembered it all and thought sadly that now he would be at a loss for an answer if anybody asked him what love was."[1] Only as long as he himself was not involved did he seem clearly to understand what this phenomenon is.

Alekhin in "About Love" also speaks of human affection as a great, inexplicable mystery before embarking upon the story of his romance with Anna Alekseevna. Each case must be discussed separately, he says, without attempts at generalizations: "As the doctors say, each case should be individualized."[2]

It is the mystical aspect of love, the intensely individual, inner urge to stretch and reach out and upward toward another being of the opposite sex in search of fulfillment and the complement of one's own being and destiny, that Chekhov perceived and that led him to lift this experience above the realm of cognition, to remove it from accessibility to verbal concepts and definitions.

Chekhov's keen awareness of the bounds of human discourse, of the fragmentation that speech necessarily entails, is singularly evident in his frequent recourse to silence when speaking of the interior climate of human consciousness. This is particularly true when he refers to love: "A sentence, no matter how beautiful and profound, affects only those who are indifferent and cannot always satisfy those who are happy or unhappy; this is why silence is, more often than not, the highest expression of happiness or unhappiness; lovers understand each other best when they are silent."[3]

Perhaps the most striking feature of Chekhov's treatment of love—this highest, verbally illusive manifestation of individual life, the supreme expression of breaching human isolation—is that he consistently and emphatically divorces it from marriage. Here lies perhaps one of the most arresting contrasts between him and Tolstoy the novelist. There is hardly a happy marriage among Chekhov's stories and plays. There are no counterparts to Natasha and Pierre in *War and Peace* or Kitty and Levin in *Anna Karenina*.

The malfunction of love begins within the confines of marriage. To a degree, Chekhov approaches Dostoevsky's views on this subject, though he does not go as far as to speak of the "chaotic state" of family life among Russia's upper class. There is none of the plethora of illegitimate children, illegal liaisons, and dissolute fathers lacking moral principles which we find in Dostoevsky's novels. Marital discord is lowered to a pedestrian but no less portentous level. In the early years stories abound about disenchantment, ennui, and lack of respect between husband and wife. Or tyranny in

marital life is the subject. Mercenary marriages and pecuniary considerations are frequently treated with vaudevil-
lian overtones by the young Chekhov.

In his mature period Chekhov relates matrimonial diffi-
culties to loneliness and "chronic irritation" rooted in the
discord between present and past, that fatal rift that Chekhov observes in the temporal progression of so many of his
protagonists, unable to reach for the potentialities offered by
the future. When Vsevolod Meyerhold, while preparing to
play Johannes in Gerhard Hauptmann's *Lonely People*,
asked Chekhov to help him interpret the role, Chekhov an-
swered: "Portray a lonely man and show irritability only as
far as it is indicated by the text. Do not treat this irritability
as an individual trait; remember that in our times almost
every educated person, even the healthiest one, experiences
the highest degree of irritation in his own home, in his own
family, for it is in the family that the discord between present
and past is felt most acutely. It is a chronic irritation...a
domestic, an intimate irritation, so to speak."[4]

"Teacher of Literature" (1894) holds a place of paramount
importance in Chekhov's exploration of this phenomenon of
inner attrition and lonely stagnation within the confines of
a marriage lacking an upward urge toward the future, lacking mutual stimulation and shared desires to encourage
human potentialities. The story does not spotlight already
existing frictions and discord, but rather traces the evolution
of a young couple deeply in love at the beginning of the story
who get married, settle into an environment of material
plenty, and yet rapidly come to an impasse of alienation.
Twenty-six-year-old Nikitin is a teacher of literature in the
local school of a provincial town. He is madly in love with
eighteen-year-old Maniusia, daughter of the well-to-do and
socially prominent widower Shelestov. Nikitin senses that
Maniusia is also in love with him. They ride side by side
during an excursion on horseback to the outskirts of the
town, and Nikitin is so overcome with happiness that he
thinks his horse is riding on air and about to climb into the
crimson sky. That evening the seed of future trouble is

planted by a casual, haphazard remark. During a supper party at the Shelestovs' one of the guests, Shebaldin, asks Nikitin whether he has read Lessing's *Hamburgische Dramaturgie*. Nikitin shamefacedly confesses that he has not read it and makes a mental note to fill this gap, for, he feels, this is a serious flaw in the erudition of a teacher of literature. That night Nikitin's erotic dreams about Maniusia are interrupted by a vision of Shebaldin shouting at him: "You have not read Lessing!"

A month later Nikitin proposes to Maniusia and they become engaged. Before falling asleep that night Nikitin, worn out with excitement and happiness, suddenly remembers that he has not yet read Lessing: "I should read him," he thinks, "though why should I read him? To heck with him." The seed of trouble has sprouted.

Nikitin was an orphan. He had known poverty and want in his childhood and early youth. This leads him to regard his present happiness—the wooing of Maniusia, the lovely wedding, the dowry of twenty thousand rubles, the gift of a new house from his father-in-law—as personal achievements and just rewards for past hardships. Life becomes an effortless cycle of domestic bliss and monotonous hours of teaching school. Maniusia acquires three cows and starts a veritable dairy farm. The cellar is full of pitchers of milk and pots of sour cream, all about to be made into butter. Before a year passes, Nikitin begins to feel restless and depressed and to see his happiness as a gratuitous gift for which he did not work; it is "a luxury, like medicine for a healthy person." If he were fighting for his existence, if he came home with his body aching from hard work, then the cozy rooms, the family happiness would be a reward, an adornment of his life. As it is, he experiences a growing desire to escape into a world of creative toil and struggle, where he would forget his own affairs and become indifferent toward personal happiness, "the sensations of which are so monotonous." And suddenly in his mind's eye appears the vivid image of a horrified Shebaldin shouting at him: "You haven't even read Lessing! How backward you are! My God, how low you have sunk!"

While beset by these troublesome thoughts Nikitin watches Maniusia, who is in bed. She sleepily reaches for a glass of water, drinks greedily, and remarks, "I ate too much marmelade." The sight of her neck, her plump shoulders, and ample bosom fill him with disgust and anger. The story ends with an entry in Nikitin's diary, a cry for liberation. He wants to flee before he loses his mind, to flee from these boring, worthless people, from the pitchers of milk and the pots of sour cream.

The recurring motif of Shebaldin, who reappears in Nikitin's mind with mounting and accusing urgency, has blossomed forth into a symbol of intellectual stagnation, of a meaningless vegetating in the temporal confines of the present. The marriage founders on this rock. Though physically and legally united, Nikitin and Maniusia lack a common urge toward inner growth, toward sharing a life of the spirit. While Nikitin ponders about "reading Lessing," longing to escape from a pedestrian egoism à deux, Maniusia is engrossed in churning butter.

The vicissitudes of an older couple are explored in "My Wife" (1892). This dissonance concerns the husband's retreat into the past and refusal to share his wife's concern for the present. The narrator, the forty-six-year-old engineer Asorin, and his twenty-seven-year-old wife, Natalia Gavrilovna, have been married for seven years. Asorin uses the words "family happiness" in quotation marks, for after a brief initial phase of "passionate but restless love" his married life has been marked by recurrent outbursts of bitter arguments, recriminations, and mutual hatred. At the time the narrative opens, though, relations with Natalia Gavrilovna have assumed a less violent pattern. They live on separate floors of the same house—Asorin on the second, where he is working on "A History of Railroads," his wife on the first. A famine is raging in the province and Natalia Gavrilovna is organizing financial help for the starving peasants. She finds a new purpose for her life in this activity and gains a measure of happiness and satisfaction from it. It is at this point that a new outburst of marital hostility occurs and that the reasons for their recurrence are disclosed. Asorin cannot endure the thought of his wife's independent endeavors. He comes down to the first floor to tell her that he wants to help her and protect her from making mistakes in the management of large financial sums—mistakes which, he thinks, are inevitable due to her inexperience. Natalia Gavrilovna is quick to perceive that the motivating force behind this offer is Asorin's vanity and despotic disposition rather than concern for the starving peasants. She flings bitter accusations at her husband about his egoism, his indifference, and inability to feel compassion: "During your entire life you have not done a single good deed, everybody hates you, you have quarreled with everybody.... I have wasted my youth fighting you."[5]

The story has a curious ending. Asorin claims to understand at last his own shortcomings and to have turned a new leaf. He gives Natalia Gavrilovna his entire fortune for distribution among the starving peasants and begs her to make him her servant. He is fully aware that the past, when they lived as man and wife, is irretrievably lost. But he is now at peace with himself and able to return to his book on the history of the railroads. Thoughts of starving peasants no longer disturb his nightly rest or his preoccupation with his personal affairs. Though he claims that Natalia Gavrilovna is the only human being that matters in his life, his withdrawal into a new form of egoism precludes any speculations that the marriage might be salvaged after all.

Love withers in the confines of marital bonds as portrayed by Chekhov. Perhaps the least corrosive among Chekhov's stories on marriage is "Name Day Party" (1888), Chekhov's "Tolstoyan" indictment of the hypocrisy rampant among Russian society, a hypocrisy that creates a serious strain in the marital relations of the two chief protagonists. All day long the pregnant hostess, Olga Mikhailovna, feigns pleasure and interest in her guests, who have come to celebrate the name day of her husband, Petr Dmitrich. It seems to her that Petr Dmitrich too is acting unnaturally and hypocritically, showing off and basking in his role of amiable host.

She comes to feel genuine hatred for his gait, his insincere laugh, his voice. In an irrational outburst of temper after the guests' departure she accuses him of being a hypocrite and of hating her because she has more money than he does. His expression of disbelief, pain, and humiliation brings her to her senses and she suddenly remembers their deep mutual devotion. At this moment she is seized with the first pangs of a premature childbirth. A stillborn infant is delivered. Husband and wife are drawn together by this catastrophe, remorseful at having lived by the false standards of social status and prestige, and neglecting the most important thing in their lives—the expected child. Yet the reader is left with the impression that this reconciliation may well be a passing moment of penitence and regret and that before long both will revert to their old ways of pretense and worldly involvement.

With all the attention Chekhov devotes to the imperfections of married life, he relegates jealousy to a minor role in relations between men and women. An early treatment of this topic, "The Avenger" (1887), is pure satire. A betrayed husband walks into a store to buy a revolver. The words of the salesman praising the excellence of various brands of weapons alternate with the wavering thoughts of the husband: "I will kill her first, and her lover, then myself.... I will kill him and myself and leave her to live and suffer.... I will kill him, go to his funeral—but I will be arrested—then I shall expose her baseness during the trial.... If I am convicted, I will only give her an opportunity to marry again.... So, I shall neither kill her, nor him, nor myself. I must think of something more rational. I shall brand them with contempt and start a scandalous divorce suit."[6] The husband leaves the store after purchasing a net to catch quail.

In two major works of Chekhov's mature period, "The Duel" and "The Grasshopper" (1892), infidelity fails to arouse even a trace of jealousy. When Dymov, the dedicated and scholarly doctor in "The Grasshopper," begins to realize that his wife is having a love affair with the artist Riabovsky, he behaves as if it is he who has a guilty conscience:

"He could no longer look his wife straight in the eyes, nor did he smile happily when they met. So as to be alone with her as little as possible, he frequently brought his friend Korostelev home for dinner...."[7] During dinner they talk about medical problems as though to give Dymov's wife an opportunity to remain silent, "that is to say, not to lie." Later Dymov is ready to forgive and forget everything if only his wife is willing to share his triumph at having successfully defended his dissertation and his joy at the possibility of being offered a teaching position at the university. Dymov's tragic and sudden demise after catching diptheria from a young patient of his raises the image of this modest, warm-hearted, and all-forgiving man to an even higher and more noble stature.

In "The Duel," when Laevsky surprises his mistress in the arms of another man, he is moved to thoughts about his own part in her moral decline. What he just witnessed, he thinks, is only the continuation of what he himself has started. When he confronts her again, he impetuously and ardently embraces her, realizing that "this wretched, wanton woman was the only close, dear, and irreplaceable person in his life."[8] When "The Duel" was first published, some contemporaries interpreted Laevsky's behavior toward his mistress as Chekhov's artistic rebuttal of Tolstoy's *Kreutzer Sonata* in which the jealous Pozdnyshev brutally murders his wife, whom he suspects of having a love affair with the violinist who accompanied her playing the piano. References to *The Kreutzer Sonata* in Chekhov's correspondence seem to support this conjecture. In December 1890 he wrote to Suvorin: "Before my trip to Sakhalin *The Kreutzer Sonata* appeared to me to be an event, but now it seems ludicrous and muddled—either I have matured from the trip or else lost my mind."[9]

Can the treatment of jealousy be interpreted as springing from Chekhov's continually exhibited display of tolerance for human weakness and follies? Or should perhaps the impact of Christian precepts, the admonition not to judge, be brought to mind? Or did Chekhov regard jealousy as a debasing impulse violating another person's freedom of choice and emotional involvement, the freedom of an individual to follow the dictates of his own free will?

How much importance Chekhov assigned to love as an absolute value, to love free of social compulsion, of any impediments—or stimulation—from the outside, nurtured exclusively by the inner springs of the self, is attested by the prominent place held by unrequited affection in his works. It is a recurring motif in all of his plays, and some of the most lyrical pages in his stories are devoted to it. "In "Verochka" (1887), for instance, the heroine confesses her passionate love for Ognev—who remains unresponsive—against the background of a beautiful late summer night. The scent of flowers hangs heavy in the air and wisps of a light, transparent fog bathed in moonlight float like ghosts among the trees and bushes.

All the vigor, intensity, and vitality that love seems to lose once it is entrapped in the marriage bonds of Chekhov's works, it retains and radiates when it is free and not reciprocated. *The Seagull* is a particularly telling example. For, as Chekhov himself remarked, the play contains "five tons of love." There are six attachments not returned in kind, each evolving along different lines which cross and recross along a tortuous path of anguish, suffering, and faltering. Yet in the end the path leads to a pinnacle of victorious human endeavor. Here again Chekhov resorts to the device of scale and gradation. The motivations, the intensity of the emotions, and the behavior of the various protagonists are subjected to a careful critical scrutiny, leading toward the triumph at the top.

At the lowest level of the route we meet the middle-aged Polina Shamraeva, who is in love with the fifty-five-year-old Doctor Dorn. With comic alarm she is concerned for his health and physical well-being. She admonishes him to put on his rubbers because the evening air is getting damp and damp air is bad for him. When he takes off his hat, she urges him to put it on again lest he catch cold. Her frank and desperate appeal in the second act to let her come to live with him because "our time is running out, we are no longer young," brings his curt reply that "it is too late to change one's life." Polina believes that there are other women in his life, though she understands that, being a doctor, he "cannot avoid women." In the last act resignation sets in. Polina still loves Dorn but comes to believe that "a friendly glance" is all a woman needs.

The next level of the scale is less innocuous. It is more dramatic, even melodramatic, and bears tragic consequences. Polina's twenty-two-year-old daughter, Masha, is in love with the young writer Treplev. She knows that there is no hope, wears black as a symbol of her sorrow, snuffs tobacco, and drinks vodka. In the third act she decides to marry the dull and pedestrian teacher Medvedenko, who has wooed her for a long time. She hopes that this marriage will make her forget Treplev. In the fourth act, two years later, she has a child by Medvedenko, but her love for Treplev is undiminished. Though she still hopes to tear it "with its roots" from her heart, it has now crushed her. She despises her husband, is rude to him, and shows no maternal interest in her child.

Would Medvedenko's love for Masha have fared better if she had not married him? His loneliness, his self-effacement, and humble unhappiness are expressed in the last act by his "apologetic gait" as he leaves for home to look after their neglected child, having vainly tried to persuade Masha to accompany him. She wants to stay a little longer where she can feast her eyes on Treplev.

Treplev's mother, Irina Nikolaevna Arkadina, is an actress. Self-centered, conceited, and engrossed in her theatrical successes, she anxiously clings to the self-image of a youthful and gifted star. Her liaison with the much younger but already famous writer Trigorin fits well into her egotistic life pattern. She dominates him and controls his every move. "You are mine! You are completely mine!" she exclaims in a violent outburst of emotion when she discovers his interest in a young girl, Nina Zarechnaia.

Treplev is in love with this girl. He has written an avant-garde play in which Nina is to have the leading role. Her monologue opening the performance of this play in the first act of *The Seagull* is repeatedly interrupted by Arkadina's derisive comments, and the performance is called off by her enraged son. Nina's interest in Treplev begins to wane after the flop of his play, causing him acute and deepening anguish. In the second act he lays a dead seagull, "which he was mean enough to kill this morning," at her feet adding that soon he will end his life in the same manner. In the third act this threat is followed by Treplev's abortive attempt to kill himself. In the two years which pass between the third and fourth acts he anxiously follows the course of Nina's personal life and career as an actress, though she consistently refuses to see him. Treplev himself has gained a measure of literary success, but the final confrontation with Nina in the fourth act convinces him how hopeless his love for her is. He sees how far she has outgrown him and matured, while he is still floundering in the chaos of dreams and images. He now finds his life without direction and without meaning, and we watch him tearing up all his manuscripts. The play ends with his suicide.

None of the unrequited attachments in *The Seagull* wither or abate though all we have mentioned thus far fail to bring personal enrichment or rewards. Polina Shamraeva grows resigned, Masha becomes harsh and embittered, Medvedenko retreats into silent resignation, Arkadina remains steeped in self-adulation, and Treplev takes his love to the grave. But all provide a foil for Nina the Seagull. It is Nina who strikes a triumphant note at the end of the play. She had fallen in love with Trigorin, Arkadina's lover, and had a child by him. After the child's death Trigorin left her and returned to Arkadina. But Nina is not crushed. She perseveres in her efforts to become an actress. As yet she is far from famous, but she believes in her strength, in her vocation, in her future. In the fourth act she revisits the place of her youthful debut in Treplev's play and tells him of her inner victory: "I am now a real actress, I revel, I am in ecstasy when I play, I become intoxicated on the stage and I feel that I am beautiful.... I feel that every day my emotional powers are growing." Though she knows that Trigorin has returned to Arkadina, she confesses that she still loves him: "I love him even more deeply than before.... I love him passionately, desperately."[10]

Nina is suffering and life is rough, yet there is no trace of rancor, jealousy, or complaint in her words about Trigorin. Her love has given her an ennobling enrichment. It has given her strength to reach out for self-perfection and to construct her future. She will never become another egocentric Arkadina. For she now knows that "the most important thing is not fame, not glory...but the ability to endure...and to have faith."[11] "I am not afraid of life," she exclaims toward the end of her momentous monologue as if echoing Alesha Karamazov's admonition to the children at Iliusha's funeral "to set forth on your separate paths and not to be afraid of whatever lies ahead." Treplev was unable to draw strength from his unhappy love for Nina, unable to use it as a generating force in his literary endeavors. And we associate him with the image of the dead seagull, while Nina soars like a vibrant, white bird toward her future, alive with an inner glow of strength and freedom.

But what about love reciprocated or fulfilled? To begin with, there are three stories which stand out as crucial among Chekhov's observations on this aspect of love: "The Darling" (1898), "Ariadna" (1895), and "About Love" (1898). The protagonist of "The Darling" is Olenka, "a quiet, good-natured, and softhearted young woman with meek, gentle eyes and very good health" who could not live without loving someone. "Darling" becomes her second name because everybody spontaneously calls her that, attracted by her naive and artless kindness. Olenka falls in love and marries the manager of an open-air theater, Kukin. She becomes totally absorbed in her husband's business and shares his every worry. His thoughts and views of the world become her own. The theater, she repeats to everybody, is the most remarkable and important thing in the world and the public is contemptible in its ignorance and indifference to art. Three months after Kukin's sudden death Olenka marries the sedate timber merchant Pustovalov, and becomes immersed in the problems and intricacies of her husband's trade. The theater has lost all value in her eyes. "We are working people," she says, "we have no time for trifles."[12] The marriage lasts six years. After Pustovalov's death Olenka enters into a liaison with the veterinarian Smirnin, who is married but separated from his wife. Sanitary questions and cattle epidemics now absorb Olenka's mind. After all, she says, the health of domestic animals is as important as the health of humans.

When Smirnin leaves the town, Olenka withers and loses all interest in life: "Worst of all she now has no opinions whatsoever.... And how terrible it is to have no opinions!... Living with Kukin, with Pustovalov, and later with the veterinarian, Olenka could explain everything and would have expressed her opinion about anything at all, but now there was the same emptiness in her head and in her heart and in her courtyard."[13] Olenka comes to life again when, years later, Smirnin unexpectedly knocks at her door. He departs again after a brief stay leaving his ten-year-old-son Sasha with her so that the boy may attend the local school. Olenka comes to treat Sasha as if he were her own child: "Oh, how she loved him! Not one of her former attachments had been so deep, never before had her soul surrendered so wholeheartedly, so selflessly, and with such joy as now when her maternal instinct was developing by leaps and bounds."[14] Olenka feeds and tends the boy and helps him with his homework. "An island," reads Sasha in his textbook, "is a body of land, surrounded on all sides by water." "An island is a body of land...," repeats Olenka, and... "This was the first opinion which she expressed with confidence after so many years of silence and mental inanity."[15] School problems, textbooks, teachers, classes now occupy Olenka's mind and her views are those of Sasha.

Tolstoy placed "The Darling" among Chekhov's best stories and treated it as one of his favorites. He read and reread it aloud, laughing and weeping as he went along, and in 1905 wrote an afterword to it. Chekhov himself labeled "The Darling" a "humoristic story," but Tolstoy interpreted it differently, for he saw in it a confirmation of his own views on love and on women. To him, Olenka, in her selfless, humble, and artless devotion, was a model of what a woman should be like in order to be happy herself and to make those happy who shared her life. Tolstoy thought he detected a discrepancy between Chekhov's intention and its artistic execution: "...having begun to write 'The Darling' he wanted to show what a woman should not be like...but having begun to speak the poet blessed what he set out to curse."[16]

An illuminating commentary on this story of Chekhov's is provided by Renato Poggioli in his book *The Phoenix and the Spider*. He reminds us that the Russian title of "The Darling" is *Dushechka*, a term of endearment and a diminutive of *dusha*, the Russian word for "soul." *Dushechka* is the Russian equivalent of the Greek Psyche, who was named after a word meaning soul and who was the wife of the god Eros. Professor Poggioli sees Chekhov's story as a reinterpretation of the ancient legend which carries the message that love is blind. For Psyche remained happy only as long as she abided by Eros' pleas not to try to see his face in daylight: "And there is no greater miracle than to have changed into a new Psyche, with no other sorcery but that of a single word, this heroine of the commonplace, this thrice-married little woman, neither clever nor beautiful, and no longer young."[17]

Olenka's self-effacing devotions were blind indeed, but did Chekhov the artist really "bless" her as Tolstoy claimed? If we examine the evolution of Olenka's unquestionably embraced opinions, there emerges a downward trend, a decline of mental concepts which the creator of "The Darling" could not have meant to be overlooked. Olenka begins by speaking of the significance of the theater and the low cultural level of the public. She then turns to the mercenary concepts of the timber trade, later to equating health problems of animals with those of humans, and ends up by adopting the mentality of a ten-year-old. Moreover, Chekhov is careful to show us Sasha's lack of affection or respect for her. Toward the end of the story we see Olenka as she escorts the boy to school. He is embarrassed to be followed by a tall, stout woman," tells her to go home and to leave him to his own devices, addressing her all the while with the formal "you" rather than the familiar, warm form of the word.

If egoism is self-destructive and incompatible with genuine love so is self-effacement. "Selfishness is only a vice if it means an undue regard for self; unselfishness is only a virtue if it is countered by self-respect. The two loves, therefore, so far from being opposites, appear to require the presence of each other."[18] As Olenka's absorption in the lives of the persons she loves increases, her self-esteem, her awareness of herself as a person, as a steward of her own being, diminishes, as reflected in the satirically presented decline of her mental process and borrowed opinions. Poggioli's comment on Olenka's love should be carried a step further. Her devotions were not only blind but self-destructive as well.

The Psyche motif is used obliquely in "The Darling," the Ariadne motif is indicated in the title of the story "Ariadna."[19] In the Greek legend Ariadna gave Theseus a ball of thread to help him find his way out of the Labyrinth, the place of confinement of the monstrous Minotaur, who had previously devoured many a young Athenian. Chekhov's Ariadna is a young, extremely slender, graceful, dark-haired beauty with highly noble features whom "the rare and beautiful name suits very well." Yet her appearance belies her character and behavior, Shamokhin, Ariadna's present and disillusioned lover, tells the narrator. She is highly sensuous, though cold at heart, and longs for power over people and for personal success. To be admired is the goal of her life. She had a love affair with the ordinary, flighty Lubkov and traveled to Italy with him, reveling in extravagant expenditures and gorging on elaborate meals. When the affair broke off, she implored Shamokhin, who had been in love with her for a long time, to come and save her. After a month of enraptured bliss living with her, Shamokhin began to understand her true nature and his passion waned. He found that her basic trait was "an astounding craftiness." She was never natural but constantly acted cunningly and deviously with the sole purpose of impressing, pleasing and appearing attractive and desirable to everyone she met.

Shamokhin is far from regarding Ariadna as an exceptional character he had the misfortune to meet. He considers her as a telling product of an educational system which teaches a woman to regard a man as a prey to be attracted physically and then conquered and subdued. Modern woman, he asserts, thinks of a man only in terms of his sex. She does not think of him as a human being, as an equal to herself. This mentality represents a return to the outlook of a primeval female and has already adversely affected human progress. "This backwardness of the educated woman presents a serious threat to culture. In her retrograde movement woman tries to drag man along with her. She slows down his forward movement. This is beyond doubt."[20]

Adriadna's ball of thread which saved Theseus from the Minotaur thus turns, in Chekhov's story, into a mesh stultifying and stifling human growth and endangering man's progress. In his own fashion, Chekhov used both the Psyche motif and the Ariadne motif to lead the reader to reflect about what love should not be. Love should not be blind and self-effacing. But neither should it aim at conquest and domination. Love requires equality between the lovers. Equality is the prerequisite of a real communion between a man and a woman. "One must love an equal" is an entry we repeatedly encounter in Chekhov's notebooks.[21]

Chekhov's innermost sanctuary, his "holy of holies," was the image of an individual vibrantly alive, conscious of his worth and dignity, straining to develop, in "absolute freedom," the unique personal potentialities every single man is born with, reaching toward the ideal formulated by Doctor Astrov in *Uncle Vania*: "Everything must be beautiful in a human being, his face, his clothes, his soul, his thoughts."[22] Chekhov rejected the egalitarian summons sounded by Tolstoy, since social equality could only obstruct the road toward the blossoming of individual, personal endowment. But Chekhov did not entirely reject the idea of equality. He transferred it from a social to a personal level, to the relations between a man and woman, to a sphere where mutual give-and-take of love offers the sublime exit from human isolation.

The idea of give-and-take between two equals is touched upon in "About Love," the third story dealing with flaws in the relations between the sexes. The attachment discussed is neither self-effacing nor possessive. When the narrator, the landowner Alekhin, meets the charming young Anna Alekseevna, wife of Luganovich, the assistant president of the circuit court, he experiences the feeling that he has known her for a long time: "As though I had seen this face, these friendly, intelligent eyes long ago, in my childhood, in an album which lay on my mother's bureau."[23] Spring and summer months of intensive work on his estate prevent Alekhin from revisiting the urban residence of the Luganoviches, yet "the memory of the slendor, fair-haired woman stayed with me at all times; I did not think of her, but it was as though her shadow lay lightly on my soul."[24]

That Anna Alekseevna went through a similar experience is revealed when she and Alekhin meet again at a theatrical performance in the late fall. She says that, for some reason, she frequently thought about him during the summer and, while getting ready for the theater, had a feeling that she would see him again that night. A delicate communion of consciousness is established between the two. Alekhin becomes a frequent guest at the Luganoviches and is befriended by the entire household. If Anna Alekseevna is not at home when he arrives, he waits, plays with her child or talks to its nurse or lies on the couch in the study and reads a newspaper. On Anna Alekseevna's return he narrates: "I would meet her in the hall, take all her parcels from her, and for some reason, I would carry these parcels every time so lovingly and so solemnly as if I were a little boy."[25]

Alekhin is increasingly aware that something new, extraordinary, and important has come into his life. He loves Anna Alekseevna deeply and tenderly. They spend many hours together, talking or sharing long silences but never speaking of their mutual devotion, concealing it timidly and jealously. "We feared everything that might reveal our secret to ourselves." Alekhin is beset by fears and doubts. How could he break up a home where he is trusted and liked by all? Would he be able to make Anna Alekseevna happy? What if he fell ill? Or died? Or if they stopped loving each other? And apparently Anna Alekseevna too is troubled by similar misgivings. It is as though the give-and-take between them is restricted to the parcels Alekhin takes so lovingly from her hands when she returns from a shopping expedition and which he carries with the pride of a small child entrusted with an important mission.

Years go by, Anna Alekseevna now has two children, old enough to shout with joy when Alekhin appears. She has grown irritable, nervous, and depressed, conscious of her ruined life. And then her husband is transferred to another province and the moment of parting from Alekhin is at hand. The doctors are sending her to the Crimea for a cure prior to joining her husband and Alekhin sees her off at the railroad station. At the last minute before the train starts, he rushes into her compartment and takes her in his arms. Her face and hands are wet with tears. He covers them with kisses and confesses his love for her: "...with a burning pain in my heart I realized how needless, how petty and how misleading was all that had prevented us from loving each other..... I kissed her for the last time, pressed her hand, and we parted—forever."[26] Too late Alekhin realizes that love has an absolute value of its own, not bound to considerations about happiness or unhappiness, not fettered by tenets of sin or virtue "in the common sense of the words." Love is mutual giving and taking, and neither Alekhin nor Anna Alekseevna had mustered the will and the courage required to shed their inertia, to overcome their misgivings, and to come to a decision, a decision that would be an act of their whole being.

"The Lady with the Dog" (1899) is the crowning masterpiece, the pinnacle of Chekhov's reflections about love. At the opening of the narrative the protagonist, middle-aged Dmitri Gurov, seems less likely to form a serious attachment to a woman than any other character in Chekhov's stories or plays. When very young he married a woman considerably older than himself and has no affection for his wife. He delights in frequent amorous adventures and refers to the female sex as "the inferior race." His affair with the young married woman Anna Sergeevna at the seaside resort of Yalta starts out as another fleeting liaison. When they part, both assume that they will never meet again.

Back in Moscow, Gurov is eager to return to the routine of his bank job, his social engagements, his children's demands. Yet over a month goes by and the memories of Anna Sergeeva grow in vividness and intensity, as if they had parted only the day before: "He did not dream of Anna Sergeevna, but she followed him everywhere like a shadow and watched him. Closing his eyes, he would see her as though she were there herself, and she seemed lovelier, younger, tenderer than she had been; and it seemed to him that he too was a better man than he had been back there, in Yalta."[27]

On an impulse Gurov takes a train to the provincial town where Anna Sergeevna lives and locates her house. He watches the little dog he remembers so well from Yalta being taken for a walk by an elderly attendant but he does not dare to ring the doorbell. That night, on the hunch that Anna Sergeevna probably attends opening nights at the theater, he buys a ticket for a performance he saw advertised at the railroad station, and his intuition proves to be correct. Gurov sees her entering the theater and taking a seat. And suddenly "...he clearly understood that there was no human being in the whole world so close, so precious, and so important to him."[28] When he comes up to Anna Sergeevna during the first intermission, she is overcome with surprise, fright, and emotion. They wander aimlessly along the corridors and staircases of the theater. She confides that she too was unable to forget their Yalta experience. Not caring whether they are being observed or not, Gurov takes her in his arms and covers her face and hands with kisses. She implores him to leave and promises to come to Moscow to see him.

And then, once every two or three months, Anna Sergeevna leaves her hometown, telling her husband that she is going to Moscow to consult a doctor, and she and Gurov meet at a hotel formerly agreed upon. Anna Sergeevna grows more and more deeply attached to him ("she worshipped him") and Gurov gives up his views of women as "the inferior race." "Only now, when his hair had turned gray, he had truly, really fallen in love—for the first time in his life."[29] And both feel that their love has transformed and ennobled them: "...it seemed to them that fate itself had meant them for each other and it was incomprehensible why he had a wife and she a husband; they were like two migratory birds, a male and female, caught and forced to live in separate cages."[30]

We leave them on the threshold of the crucial step toward a permanent union: "How to escape the need to hide, to deceive, to live in different towns, to be separated for lengthy periods of time? How? And it seemed as though in a little while the solution would be found and then a new and beautiful life would begin; and both clearly saw that the end was still very far off and that the most complicated and difficult part was only just beginning."[31] A series of unanswered questions end the story. But the two trapped "migratory birds" are poised for an escape, ready to soar like Nina the seagull. The poetic reality of an ideal union which is to be the final consummation of Gurov and Anna Sergeevna's love is removed into a distant and nebulous future. If the ideal of "a new and beautiful life" could be imagined as attained or described, it would cease to be an ideal. Silence is Chekhov's artistic device to imply that the possibility of approaching an ideal is infinite.

Notes

1   IX.
2   X, 66.
3   VI, 35.
4   L.VIII, 274-5.
5   VII, 483.
6   VI, 332-3.
7   VIII, 21.
8   VII, 439.
9   L.IV, 147.
10 XIII, 59.
11 XIII, 58.
12 X, 107.
13 X, 109-10.
14 X, 112.
15 X, 111.
16 L.N. Tolstoy, *Sobranie sochinenii*, in 20 Vols., Moscow 1960-65, Vol. 15, p. 349.
17 Renato Poggioli, *The Phoenix and The Spider*, Cambridge, MA: Harvard Univ. Press, 1957, p.130.
18 D.C. D'Arcy, *The Mind and Heart of Love*, New York: Holt, 1947, p. 308.
19 Soviet critics relate Chekhov's choice of the name to the fact that the attractive and flirtatious wife of the teacher of Latin in the Taganrog school attended by Chekhov, V.D. Starov, was named Ariadna.
20 IX, 130.
21 XVII, 20, 41, 154.
22 XIII, 83.
23 X, 69.
24 Ibid.
25 X, 71.
26 X, 74.
27 X, 136.
28 X, 139.
29 X, 143.
30 Ibid.

VII

The Stifled Voice of Conscience

Would it be an exaggeration to say that the atmosphere in nineteenth-century Russia was surcharged with emotions, in a country rent by divisiveness, fraught with turmoil, laden with social blight and economic imbalances? There were high hopes and deep despair, there was frustration, fear, resignation, rebellious rage. But above all, there was the pain of a guilty conscience. The educated class was experiencing a mounting sense of guilt and responsibility for the depressed living conditions of the vast majority of the Russian people, a sentiment forcefully channeled into literature under the existing conditions. A guilty conscience was the underground spring that nurtured the literary masterpieces, their moral outcries and indictments so powerful and gripping as to arrest attention the world over. But there was also the Government, the State, that had for centuries shaped the destiny of the country and the structure of society and that still controlled important aspects of people's lives. The power of the bureaucracy, of censorship, the official grip on public habits and opinions fostered the development of a phenomenon destined to make vast gains in the industrialized world of the twentieth century and to become known as the authoritarian conscience.

Chekhov directed his attention to this phenomenon early in his career, though the power of collective authorities to manipulate an individual's thoughts and behavior was as yet, even in Russia, incomparably weaker than that of today's anonymous institutions. An individual's lack of courage to act on his own and to bear personal responsibility in the face of authoritarian standards and commands drew Chekhov's thoughts even before he began to speak of the positive power of personal conscience to act as a guide of human conduct, before examining whether personal conscience was capable, in the world he saw around him, of activating human will, of promoting the freedom of independent judgment and actions, of establishing a balance between the human mind and heart, between reason and intuition, between regard for right and wrong, good and evil.

In four early stories we are confronted with individuals who grovel with servility before their superiors, who have accepted obedience to authority as the greatest virtue, and who tremble in fear of punishment or reprisal if disrespect or disobedience should be detected in their behavior. All four protagonists have lost a sense of personal integrity. Three of them have names, and the names reflect the low quality of their character: Cherviakov—the Worm, Ochumelov—Off His Head; Sergeant Prishibeev—the Repressive Bully. Their speech, halting and muddled, tending toward servile effusiveness or grotesque eulogy of rank, law, and order, is true to the inner essence of their nature.

Chekhov pours laughter and satire mingled with tragedy into the tale of "The Death of a Civil Servant" (July 1883). The clerk Cherviakov, while attending a theatrical performance, sneezes violently on the bald head of a spectator who is sitting in the row ahead of him. Recognizing a high-ranking official, a general no less, in this man, Cherviakov feels an urgent need to apologize for his misdemeanor. This need mounts as each humbly and haltingly worded excuse is carelessly brushed off by the general, who considers the sneeze as a trifle not worthy of his attention. First Cherviakov leans forward in his seat and whispers his apology; then he proffers his regrets during an intermission. The next day he goes to the general's office during reception hours. When even here he fails to be rewarded with an appreciative acknowledgement, he waits for the last petitioner to depart and steps into the general's path as he prepares to leave his office. At this fourth approach the general shows signs of annoyance and suggests that Cherviakov must be laughing at him. Horror-striken by such a suspicion of disrespect, Cherviakov returns on the following day to prove his innocence: "How would I dare to laugh? If we laughed, then there would be no respect left...respect for important people...."[1] The mentality of Dostoevsky's hapless Devushkin comes here to mind. The general flares up in sudden anger and exasperation. Shaking with rage, he orders Cherviakov to get out. The blow proves fatal to the little man. Terror-stricken, he stumbles home, collapses on his sofa, and dies.

The last names of the two protagonists in the next story, "Fat and Thin" (October 1883), are not given. The bare outlines of their physical dimensions are given to stress the central issue, the dehumanizing effects of abject infatuation with rank. Fat and Thin are old friends and former schoolmates who accidentally meet at a railroad station. Fat, his lips glossy after a good meal, smells of sherry and cologne; Thin, burdened with suitcases, bundles, and cartons, smells of ham and coffee grounds. Fat is alone, Thin is accompanied by his spindly wife and a rangy schoolboy, his son. Both friends are genuinely delighted to see each other and exchange warm greetings. Thin bubbles over with reminiscences of their school days and speaks cheerfully of his modest rank and income—until he hears that Fat has attained the prominent position of privy counselor. The of friendship is abruptly severed by the chasm in rank. Thin turns pale, huddles, stoops, and shrinks—and with him his entire entourage. His suitcases, bundles, and cartons seem to huddle, stoop, and shrink. His wife's long chin grows longer, his son comes to attention. Thin now addresses Fat as "Your Excellency" and insists on formally reintroducing his wife and son to such a prominent acquaintance "whose gracious attention...is comparable to life-giving moisture."[2]

In "The Chameleon" (1884), Police Inspector Ochumelov, accompanied by an assistant, shoulders his way through a crowd that has gathered around a small dog trembling with fright and a man who is waving his finger bitten by the dog. Ochumelov's handling of the situation is entirely dependent on the question of who might be the owner of the dog. He starts out by ordering the owner found and fined and the dog destroyed. When a voice from the crowd suggests that the dog looks like General Zhigalov's, he reverses his stand, for this suggestion fills him with dismay. He turns against the injured man and accuses him of having trumped up his charges—a dog so small could not possibly have bitten him. Twice more the general's ownership of the dog is doubted and subsequently affirmed and twice more Ochumelov's opinions shift accordingly. When it is finally established that the dog belongs to the general's brother, in town for a visit, Ochumelov voices deep concern for the dog's well being and safe return to its owner and threatens the man with the bitten finger that he "will get him yet."

Sergeant Prishibeev, hero of the story which in 1885 appeared under the title "The Slanderer," is the embodiment of total subservience to authority. His face is wrinkled and prickly, his voice hoarse, and he rasps out each word as if issuing commands. Law and order are his favorite words in an amorphous flow of diatribes which fail to camouflage his lack of wit and sensitivity. He has taken upon himself, now that he is retired, to police his home village. He is harshly unsympathetic toward anything that is not specifically permitted by the law. He particularly dislikes crowds, which he invariably addresses with a bellowed order. "Break it up!"

since there is no law allowing people to congregate. He orders the peasants not to burn lights and not to sing songs, for there is no law that says people should sing songs.

Keeping the censor in mind, Chekhov presents Prishibeev as an anachronism, as a relic from pre-Emancipation times. We meet him in court. He is charged with assault and battery committed while trying to disperse a crowd that had gathered on a river bank around the body of a drowned man. He is sentenced to a month in jail. As we leave him, he is bewildered and confused, unable to understand the reason for his conviction, sensing only "that the world has changed and that it is now quite impossible to go on living."[3] Leaving the courthouse and seeing a group of loitering peasants, Prishibeev cannot refrain from drawing to attention and shouting in a hoarse and angry voice: "Hey there, break it up! No loitering! Go home!"[4] In spite of Prishibeev's portrayal as an anachronism the Moscow Censorship Committee twice rejected the story, and it appeared as "The Slanderer," instead of the original title, "A Superfluous Guardian," in the Petersburg Gazette.

In Chekhov's lifetime the moral uneasiness of the educated segment of Russian society steadily increased in the face of the failure of the Emancipation to bring about any appreciable betterment of living conditions for the majority of the population. There was Tolstoy, feeling guilty for belonging to the class of the affluent and educated while all around him he saw masses of people living in bondage to poverty and ignorance; Tolstoy, driven by his conscience to repudiate his literary masterpieces and to devote decades of his later years to didactic tracts and sermons. There was the Populist movement that produced a whole generation of tormented moralists devoting their lives—frequently shortened by alcoholism, insanity, or suicide—to combat starvation, epidemic, and illiteracy throughout the countryside.

Chekhov's conscience was no less sensitive than Tolstoy's, though he did not experience any sense of social guilt, being the grandson of a former serf and the son of a grocer who went bankrupt in his later years. Neither was his medical training conducive to stimulating abstract philosophical investigation. Chekhov's versatile and unrelenting humanitarian activities and ventures bore witnesss that his selfless concern for his fellow men certainly equalled that of the Populists. But as a thinker and as an artist the egalitarian theories and the political activities of the Populists were as alien to his temperament and talent as any other quest demanding the submission of individuals. And if we venture to speculate about the crucial decisions most likely to have been shaped by Chekhov's conscience and instrumental in the evolution of his art, then the trip to Sakhalin must be recognized as of the highest priority, a trip that stands as a line of demarcation setting off the mature period of his creativity.

Individual conscience as a guide of human conduct was first examined by Chekhov in the story "The Lights," written two years before his departure for Sakhalin. And there is a reference to that island in the story that points to a connection between its central theme and Chekhov's train of thought and action immediately preceding the trip. The construction engineer Ananiev, reminiscing about a youthful aberration, bemoans his former rationalistic pessimism which gave rise to the mistaken conviction that "the life of convicts on the island of Sakhalin was in no way different from life in [the resort town of] Nice."[5]

Ananiev is working on the construction of a railroad and plays host to the narrator, a stranger in the area who loses his way in the dark and stumbles upon the half-finished embankment, the scattered pieces of equipment, and the workers' barracks illuminated by a long string of lights. Ananiev offers the narrator overnight shelter and proceeds to entertain him with a story out of his past, intended to illustrate the fallacy of rationalism and pessimism so popular among contemporary Russian youth and apparently firmly embraced by Ananiev's young skeptical assistant, the engineering student Von Stenberg. In the late 1870s Ananiev too, at the age of twenty-six, had been convinced that life was senseless and aimless, that everything was a sham, an illusion, death being inevitable and final, and that there was no reason to differentiate between a convict's penal servitude and a tourist's lavish indulgences. It was in this frame of mind that Ananiev, revisiting his home town of N. seduced, easily and unscrupulously, a young, unhappily married woman, Kisochka, whom he had been madly in love with as a schoolboy. Although Kisochka was ecstatic and immediately suggested breaking up her marriage, Ananiev left town the very next morning without a word of warning or explanation.

Sitting in the train that carried him away from N. he experienced a strange feeling of growing uneasiness. He tried to convince himself that nothing mattered since both he and Kisochka would some day die and Kisochka's grief was nothing compared to death. Yet Ananiev felt more and more deeply troubled by his conscience. Finally the realization dawns on him that he had committed a crime "tantamount to murder." He came to understand that this was the first time in his life that he was really thinking, that even "the technique of thinking" was an unfamiliar process to him, that up to this moment he had had neither convictions nor a definite moral code, nor a heart, nor a mind. "My normal thinking began, as it seems to me now," said Ananiev to finish his story, "only from the moment when I started with the alphabet, that is, when my conscience drove me back to N. and I confessed to Kisochka without sophistry, imploring her like a little boy to forgive me, and after we had cried together."[6]

Ananiev's assistant, Von Stenberg, appears unmoved by the story and his face continues to express "mental apathy"—as it has from the beginning. Before retiring, the narrator and Ananiev step outside, and the long string of lights along the railroad embankment is compared by Ananiev to human thoughts, which, he says, also strive to pierce darkness yet fail to illuminate anything. This metaphor sets the tone for the confusion experienced by the narrator on the following morning. He is awakened by the harsh and angry voice of Ananiev refusing assistance to an exhausted peasant who is unable to find the proper place to deliver some railroad equipment. His horses have been without food for two days. This strange contrast between Ananiev's heart-less behavior and last night's story leaves the narrator puzzled and confused. As he takes his leave he feels lost in speculation, unable to comprehend Ananiev's contradictory behavior. Did Chekhov intend to hint at how difficult it was for conscience to maintain a constant, unrelenting vigil over human conduct? Or had he perhaps begun to move toward an understanding of the deterioration in human relations brought about by the advent of the machine—a deterioration which he returned to examine some ten years later in stories such as "A Case from Practice"? Was perhaps Ananiev's youthful discovery of conscience now lost to the middle-aged engineer, too busy with the construction of the railroad to show concern for the exhausted peasant and his horses?

Before his experience with Kisochka, Ananiev had con-fessed to total indifference toward the life of convicts on the island of Sakhalin. But Sakhalin was precisely the place that increasingly attracted Chekhov's attention soon after finishing "The Lights." Close to half a century was yet to pass before the full emergence of the vast and sprawling network of Soviet prisons and forced-labor camps, Solzhe-nitsyn's "Gulag Archipelago." In Chekhov's lifetime it was Sakhalin that appeared as the ninth circle, the ultimate boundary of human misery and unfreedom, though in com-parison to any island in the "Archipelago" it would rank as an El Dorado of leniency and humaneness.

The reasons for Chekhov's decision to visit Sakhalin not only puzzled his friends but later commentators as well. The Soviet writer and literary critic Korney Chukovsky gives the following explanation for Chekhov's restlessness and resolve to take the trip: "This renunciation from serving art, this abdication of an artist from his craft is, it seems, a peculiar-ity of Russian talents, especially of great ones. Nowhere else, it seems, has it ever happened that people of such titanic strength as Gogol and Tolstoy would suddenly, at the zenith of their fame, begin to despise the great things they have created and, beliving that their art was a useless occupation, force themselves to withdraw from art in the name of a more fruitful service to mankind.

"Now the same thing, but fortunately not for long, happened with Chekhov. Only, Gogol's and Tolstoy's renunciation of art was demonstrative and loud, resounded all over Russia, all over the world, whereas Chekhov, accustomed with his Chekhovian reticence not to show anybody his feelings, moved away from fiction writing silently, without any declarations or sermons."[7]

It is significant that Chukovksy omits the role of conscience in his analysis and speaks of the great Russian artists' withdrawal from art as motivated by a desire to perform "a more fruitful service to mankind." In her book *Hope Against Hope* Nadezhda Mandel'stam, widow of the great poet Osip Mandel'stam, who perished in 1938 in a concentration camp, makes an arresting comment helpful in examining Chukovsky's omission: "Since the 1920s a number of terms such as 'honor' and 'conscience' went out of use in the Soviet Union. The measure of social structure is man, but there are eras in which this is lost sight of, when people say they have no time for man and that he is to be used like bricks or cement, as something to be built from, not for."[8]

But to Russia's great writers of the nineteenth century man was the central pivot around which revolved their creativity, imagination, and concern. The authoritarian conscience had not yet emerged in its full power and portent. And Gogol's epistolary sermons and Tolstoy's reformatory endeavors sprang from individual tormenting urges prodding contemporaries to change their course, addressing men and not an abstract mirage of mankind shrouded in the folds of the future. But Chekhov's trip to Sakhalin cannot be mentioned in the same breath as Gogol's and Tolstoy's renunciation of art. It was not even a temporary renunciation. It proved a fount of the most vibrant, concentrated artistic inspiration, a fount so enormous, so powerful, that Chekhov, when he returned, spoke of the difficulty to find words, to decide where to begin when he wanted to speak of it.

Against the desolate and gloomy environment of damp chill and cloudy skies, rainfall so abundant that sunny days were a rarity, there stood in Chekhov's memory the nightmare of the thousands of human beings imprisoned on the island, moving about listlessly like shadows, in tattered garb soaked by rain and caked with mud, their bodies wasting, their faces gray from malnutrition and fatigue. What sounds must have haunted Chekhov after his return? The clanking shackles? The wind howling and moaning? The raindrops falling on the corrugated iron roofs? The waves breaking on bleak, rocky beaches? Or the voices of the sickly, pale, constantly hungry children talking casually about cohabitation, flogging? Or the voices of the women speaking of living "by their bodies"? Or that voice he thought he heard once in the middle of the night, repeating over and over again in whispered despair: "Oh my God, Oh my God!" None of these found their way into Chekhov's fiction. All were meticulously locked and sealed in his documentary *The Island of Sakhalin*. But it was the gruesome spectacle of finding freedom, this highest good in human life, dead, dismembered, hideously defiled, and so desperately needed on the island that fired Chekhov's creativity after Sakhalin. And with it, the theme of conscience advanced to a new position of crucial importance in his fiction.

It is the same dual theme Chekhov had begun to explore in "The Lights"—conscience as a powerful, active agent discovered by Ananiev in his youth and conscience as a voice silenced and suppressed in Ananiev's middle years. Conscience misunderstood or intentionally deceived appears and reappears in a number of post-Sakhalin stories. There are none of the intoxicating extremes etched by Dostoevsky's godless protagonists, who claim to have deliberately stilled their conscience, to have risen to vertiginous heights of intellectual supremacy above remorse, above concern for other human beings, indifferent to suffering they have inflicted on others, recounting hideous crimes "with the irrepressible, childlike, merry laughter" of the inmates of *The House of the Dead* or with the icy, remorseless detachment of a Stavrogin. Many of Chekhov's protagonists experience only dim moral stirrings, gropingly indulge in self-deception, or hear ineffectual admonitions.

In "My Wife" (1892), the selfish and self-centered Pavel Andreevich is beset by vague feelings of his own shortcomings: "I did not understand the promptings of my conscience but my wife, acting like an interpreter, explained to me, in her feminine way, but clearly, the reason for my anxiety ...my not being what I should be."[9] In "An Anonymous Story" the narrator speaks in his accusatory letter of Orlov's shameless attitude toward women and of his contempt for them: "...in order to deceive your conscience you started to assure yourself loudly that it was not you who were at fault but women, that they were as debased as your relations with them."[10] In "At Home," the young girl Vera, who has returned from Moscow to her estate in the southern steppe region, speculates about hypocrisy of the local officials and landowners. They talk of the need for education while keeping teachers on a starvation salary of fifteen rubles a month: "The schools and talks about ignorance—it all served the only purpose of silencing one's conscience because one is ashamed to own five or ten thousand acres and to be indifferent to the lot of the people."[10] In "In the Ravine" old Tsybukin approves of his wife's generous charities and attentions to the poor for they help him forget his own illicit affairs—the rotten meat and the bad vodka he is selling in his shop: "...when sin seemed to close in like a thick fog it was a relief to think that up there, at the house, there was a gentle, neatly dressed woman who had nothing to do with the meat or the vodka; during those oppressive, murky days her charities had the effect of a safety valve in a machine."[12]

From the earliest stories onward, though, Chekhov had linked the life of the mind with the role of conscience, in contrast to the deliberate divorce made by Dostoevsky's atheistic characters who denied, from the summit of their rationalistic pride, the existence of conscience. Inarticulate speech and muddled thinking were distinctive features of Chekhov's Cherviakov, of Thin, of Ochumelov, of Prishibeev, their conscience withered under authoritarian pressures. In "The Lights" Ananiev discovers that even "the technique of thinking" is directly dependent on the existence and exercise of moral precepts, while "an expression of mental apathy" on the face of Von Stenberg reflects the blasé pessimism of the young engineering student.

But it is in "Ward No. 6" (1892), that Chekhov reaches a pinnacle and unfolds his most dramatic confrontation between mind and heart, reflection and feeling, cognition and intuition, and presents conscience as the supreme arbiter, the link between the two worlds, the temporal and the eternal, inhabited by man. The setting in "Ward No. 6" is grimly confining. In unrelieved gloom dilapidated houses line unpaved, muddy streets, rotting fences surround dirty backyards overgrown with weeds, and, central to it all, stands the filthy, prison-like communal cell of Ward No. 6, a hospital wing reserved for the mentally ill in a small provincial town of Russia.

Andrey Efimovich Ragin is the doctor in charge. According to rumor he had been forced by his father to choose the medical profession instead of following his own inclination and becoming a priest. In any event, he himself frequently mentions that he never felt a calling for medicine. He was, however, at first disturbed by conditions in the local hospital, which he found highly objectionable and harmful to the health of the local population. Soon, though, he resigned himself to what he came to regard as inevitable—the zoo-like stench, the bedbugs, the smelly hospital gowns, and particularly the brutal guard in Ward No. 6, Nikita, with his enormous fists which he freely used to uphold "order," beating the inmates savagely and indiscriminately in the face, chest, or back.

To justify his toleration of these conditions Ragin built a protective wall of rationalization around himself. Intelligence is what elevates man above animal, what even compensates, to a certain extent, for immortality—which does not exist. Thought, mental activity, is the highest gift in life. Man should strive for a rational comprehension of life, he should rise above his surroundings, he should rise above suffering, for which he should cultivate indifference.

Thus does Ragin try to convince himself that he is not to blame for his ineffectualness as a doctor. He is a product of his times. Had he been born two hundred years later, he might have become a different person. Living up to his theory, Ragin becomes an avid reader and retreats into a world of books. But he also becomes interested in Ivan Dmitrich Gromov, an educated and highly articulate inmate of Ward No. 6 who suffers from a persecution complex. After outlining the origin and progress of Gromov's illness with clinical precision, Chekhov writes of his irresistible urge to talk: "His speech is disorderly, feverish, like delirium, impetuous, and not always intelligible, but at the same time something terribly good rings in his words and in his voice. When he speaks you realize that he is a madman and a human being."[13]

Gromov greets Ragin's first visit with peals of mad laughter and a burst of wild anger: "The doctor is here! At last! Gentlemen," he says, turning to his fellow inmates, "I congratulate you, the doctor is honoring us with a visit! Damned cur!" he then yells and stamps his foot with a frenzy never yet exhibited in the ward. "Kill the cur! No, it's not enough to kill him! Drown him in the latrine!"[14]

Ragin gradually succeeds in calming Gromov and in gaining his ear. He spends increasingly lengthy hours in Ward No. 6 enjoying Gromov's flashes of brilliance and trying to convert him to his philosophy of life, trying to persuade him to rise above the sordidness of the ward milieu, to embrace a life of the mind, to accept the view that intelligence is the only source of enjoyment in life.

But Ragin suffers ardent rebuttals from Gromov. Not intelligence but feeling is what matters: "To pain I react with a cry and with tears, to meanness with indignation, to abomination with disgust. This, I think, is what is known as life.

And how about Christ? Christ reacted to reality by weeping, smiling, grieving, being angry, even by pining; he did not advance toward suffering with a smile and he did not disdain death, but prayed in the garden of Gethsemane that this cup might pass from him."[15] Gromov brands indifference toward suffering as "the most convenient philosophy for all Russian do-nothings" and vaunts his own superiority over Ragin: "You have never suffered, you have fed like a leech on the sufferings of others, but I have suffered incessantly, from the day I was born to this day. Therefore I say frankly: I consider myself superior to you and more competent than you in every respect. It is not up to you to teach me."[16] Gromov pays no attention to Ragin's attempts at establishing a rapport between them, and to the doctor's sadly spoken words: "The point is not that you have suffered and I have not.... The point is that we both think...this establishes our solidarity."[17]

Ragin's frequent visits to Ward No. 6 and his prolonged discussions with an inmate are being closely watched by his assistant, Evgenii Fedorych Khobotov (*khobot* is an elephant's trunk), who seizes this opportunity to advance his own career. It does not take long for Khobotov to convince the authorities that Ragin should be replaced, that he is insane and should be locked up. Under pretext of a "consultation" Ragin is lured to Ward No. 6, where the guard Nikita is waiting to strip him of his clothes and presents him with a hospital gown which reeks of smoked fish. When Ragin, aided by Gromov, attempts to break out by force he is brutally beaten by Nikita. As he collapses, his mouth filling with the salty taste of blood, the thought flashes through his mind that the pain he is presently experiencing has been endured by his patients for years, day in and day out. And his conscience, "as intractable and rough as Nikita," makes him turn cold from head to toe. He dies of a stroke toward the following evening, his conscience reactivated too late. Reason had not figured in Ragin's thoughts as an instrument of attaining power. He considered the life of the mind merely as the best tool to derive maximum enjoyment from human existence. But neither did Chekhov grant him the experience of living with a reactivated conscience, of reaching humility through remorse, the humility which placed Dostoevsky's Father Zossima on the threshold to another world.

There are other stories in which Chekhov speaks of the active impact of conscience on the human psyche and every time the impact is likened to the effects of a physical blow. One, "The Princess," predates the trip to Sakhalin by one year. When the doctor meets the princess in the monastery garden he briefly lifts his hat as a gesture of greeting. When he begins to fling his bitter accusations at her, he removes his hat and swings it in his agitation. And the princess "began to experience the feeling that the gesticulating doctor was beating her over the head with his hat."[18] He showers her with examples of her heartless and contemptuous treatment of people. And though she considers him a rough, uncouth, vicious and ungrateful person and does not understand what he is talking about, the illusion of being beaten over the head with his hat persists throughout his harangue; " 'Go away,' she said with tears in her voice, raising her arms to protect her head from the doctor's hat, 'go away!' "[19]

The doctor's efforts to arouse in the princess feelings of remorse for the egocentric mode of living do not succeed beyond forcing her to experience a passing feeling of physical discomfort. On the following day, embarrassed by the vehemence of his outburst, the doctor asks the princess to forgive him. And she leaves the monastery, her sense of well-being and of her importance restored and the doctor's accusations all but forgotten.

The recurrent dream about the dead insurance agent and the destitute rural policeman which harass the magistrate Lyzhin in "On Official Business" lead him to realize "that this suicide and the peasant's destitution lay on his conscience."[20] He comes to understand the injustice, the selfishness of dreaming about success, ease, and leisure for himself while simultaneously accepting as inevitable the harsh terms life imposed on these helpless, resigned, and so vulnerable people. And as Lyzhin recalls the insistent chant of the two figures in his dreams, "We go on, we go on, we go on..." he feels "as though someone were knocking with a hammer on his temples."[21] In Russian, the rhythmic beat of this chant is much more pronounced: "My idém, my idém, my idém..." Yet it seems that these blows too fail to leave a lasting imprint. On the following morning the blizzard has passed and Lyzhin prepares to be driven to the autopsy. As he is getting into the carriage the policeman Loshadin approaches him with a friendly, humble greeting. But Lyzhin does not answer and drives off.

Ragin's conscience awakens at the very last moment of his life. In the princess it is reduced to a fleeting experience of physical discomfort. In Lyzhin it stirs and subsides again. In Nikolay Ivanovich, protagonist in "Gooseberries," it seems to be absent altogether. Upon reaching middle age he has finally succeeded in realizing the ambition of his life and has acquired a small country estate. Immersed in the petty enjoyments of his life as an idle country squire he has turned into an obese, contented, and conceited bore. It is the narrator, Nikolay Ivanovich's brother, who is "seized by an oppressive feeling bordering on despair" when he visits the estate for the first time. Chekhov describes the scene in terms of the grotesque, and we are again, as in the case of Belikov epitomizing fear, reminded of Gogol's hyperboles. The dog who greets the narrator is fat as a pig and too lazy to bark. The cook looks like a pig too. And Nikolay Ivanovich, who is resting in bed after a copious dinner, has grown older, stouter, and flabby: "His cheeks, his nose, his lips jutted out as though at any minute he might grunt like a pig into his blanket."[22] The home-grown gooseberries, which he consumes with the relish of a child hugging a long-wanted toy, are actually hard and sour, but they symbolize the self-deception which permits Nikolay Ivanovich to feel happy in the narrow confines of his attained dream and to speak with insolent conceit of education for the masses as "premature" and corporal punishment as "in some cases useful."

The narrator's thoughts swell into a mounting dirge lamenting the large number of people who lead similar lives of material well-being, smugly oblivious of the sufferings of their fellow men, ignoring the messages of "mute statistics" which record that so and so many people are reported insane, so and so many gallons of vodka have been consumed, so and so many children have died from malnutrition. "Behind the door of every contented, happy man," concludes the narrator, "there ought to be someone standing with a little hammer and continually reminding him with a knock that there are unhappy people.... But there is no man with a hammer."[23]

Yet, in Chekhov's world the man with the hammer is present. The sway of authoritarian conscience and the human condition of inertia, apathy, and indifference have combined to stifle but not to silence this supreme arbiter of human conduct. Chekov's world reverberates with the knocks of "the little hammer," with the blows of Nikita's enormous fists, with the slaps of the hat of the gesticulating doctor, with the rhythmic beat of the two phantoms' feet disturbing Lyzhin's sleep. These sounds are loud notes in Chekhov's melody of freedom, a counterpoint to the monologue of Dostoevsky's Grand Inquisitor aiming at silencing human conscience. And at the end of Chekhov's career the blows of the ax felling the trees of the cherry orchard join the orchestration, for the terrain where human conscience is active extends far beyond the realm of human life. It includes the existence of nature as well, the destiny of the entire terrestrial globe.

Notes

[1]   II, 166.
[2]   II, 251.
[3]   IV, 125.
[4]   Ibid.
[5]   VII, 114.
[6]   VII, 136.

[7] Korney Chukovsky, "O Chekhove" [On Chekhov], Moscow, 1967, pp. 41-42.

[8] Nadezhda Mandel'stam, *Hope Against Hope*, New York, Atheneum, 1970, p. 165.

[9] VII, 484.

[10] VIII, 190.

[11] IX, 320.

[12] X, 146.

[13] VIII, 75.

[14] VIII, 94.

[15] VIII, 102.

[16] VIII, 105.

[17] Ibid.

[18] VII, 241.

[19] VII, 244.

[20] X, 100.

[21] Ibid.

[22] X, 60.

[23] X, 62.

VIII

Man and Nature[1]

The relationship between man and nature is presented by Chekhov in a manner all his own, far different from the approaches used by the two great bards of nature preceding him in nineteenth-century Russian literature, Turgenev and Tolstoy.

In a letter to Suvorin on February 23, 1893, Chekhov wrote: "his [Turgenev's] descriptions of nature are good...but I feel that we are moving away (*otvykaem*) from descriptions of this sort, we need something different."[2] Turgenev painted his nature scenes with infinite poetic care, blending colors, sounds, lights, and shadows into compositions which highlight and reflect or contrast the emotions and experiences of his heroes. Turgenev knew the botanical names of every tree, bush, and grass; the species and characteristics of every bird and animal are observed and registered. Yet there is a gulf

impassable to man, a precipice which dooms man to eternal
loneliness and isolation from nature. "You are no concern of
mine," says nature to man in *"A Trip To the Woodland"*. "I
reign supreme and you see to it that you don't die."[3] Turgenev believed that nature's healthy equilibrium and serenity were inaccessible to man. Coldly and indifferently nature
gazes at man, who is doomed by death the day he is born—
frail, insignificant, and fortuitous. "No matter how much
you knock at nature's door, you will not receive an intelligible word in response, because nature is mute," says Shubin
in *On the Eve*.[4]

Turgenev believed in man's innate powerlessness to bridge
the precipice that separated him from nature. Tolstoy saw
the abyss formed by modern civilization and called man to
return to the healing folds of a pristine environment. Without nature man cannot be happy nor can he hope for human
dignity. "Majestically beautiful" is the simple girl Mariana
in *The Cossacks*, while Olenin experiences the most vivid
moments of happiness when he thinks of himself as "another
mosquito, pheasant, or deer" rather than as a member of the
nobility. Magnificent, valiant, proud, and tenacious is the
Caucasian rebel Khadzhi Murat in his unspoiled, primitive
environment.

Against a background of nature in its pristine majesty,
grandeur, and nobility, Tolstoy paints a vast panorama of
human folly, weakness and aberration. In the famous scene
of the Battle of Austerlitz in *War and Peace*, when the
wounded Prince Andrey gazes at the "immeasurable high
sky" above, he muses how quietly, calmly, and solemnly the
gray clouds float by—a movement so different from the running, shouting, and fighting of the men below. The noble
death of the tree in *"Three Deaths"* is an indictment of
human pettiness. The dying peasant Fedor gives his boots to
young Serega in return for a promise to erect a stone on his,
Fedor's, grave. But Serega fails to fulfill this promise. Driven
by remorse, though still unwilling to go to any expense to
buy a stone, he cuts down the young tree to make a cross over
Fedor's grave. The simultaneously majestic and pitiful old

age of the horse Kholstomer in the story of the same title contrasts with the reprehensible moral deterioration and ugly physical decline of his former owner, Serpukhovskoy. After Kholstomer's death every bit of his body re-enters the eternal cycle of life. His hide is worked into leather, his flesh is eaten by a pack of young wolves, and his bones are gathered by a peasant to be ground up. The "eating and drinking dead body of Serpukhovskoy," on the other hand, "walked this earth for quite a while longer." When he was finally buried, "neither his skin, nor his flesh, nor his bones were of any use whatsoever."[5]

The different treatment of a similar theme by Chekhov introduces us to the originality of his approach. "Gusev" is one of the few stories in which the author's attention to his hero continues beyond the point of death. The soldier Gusev, returning after five years of service in the Far East, dies of tuberculosis on board ship. His body is sewn into a canvas and now "resembles a carrot or a horse-radish: wide at the top and narrow at the feet."[6] The body is lowered into the sea. A shark approaches the sinking and drifting shape. It "lazily opens its jaws with two rows of teeth." After playing around with its find, the shark cautiously touches the shape with its teeth and "the canvas rips from head to toe."[7] Like that of the horse Kholstomer, the body of Gusev will re-enter the eternal cycle of life.

Neither Turgenev's notion of the innate separation between man and nature nor Tolstoy's indictment of a divide brought about by civilization is accepted by Chekhov. Man and nature are one, they form a cosmic unity. Trees, grass, flowers, birds, clouds, each particle, large and small, of life on this earth leads its own individual existence and at the same time is integrated into the universal process of life. Nature is a being in its own right, an enormous whole pulsing with sensations, animated by experiences, changing moods, and conditions which Chekhov brings brilliantly and reverently before our eyes with images taken from the realm of human life. In "The Witch" (1886), the humanization of nature turns a snowstorm into a warlike contest between feuding enemies: "Outside, in the field, a genuine war was going on. It was difficult to tell who was murderously inclined and whose destruction this turmoil in nature aimed at. But judging by the unrelenting sinister roaring, someone was in great trouble."[8] The winning force was storming in the forest, raging on the rooftop, hammering "its fists" angrily against the window. The "pitiful weeping" that floated from window to roof to stove "was not a cry for help, but a hopeless wail that it was too late." A thaw had settled on the field, but since the night was dark, "the sky did not see that" and, "using all its strength," dumped new snow on the ground. The wind, "reeling like a drunk," did not give the new snow a chance to lie down and whirled it wantonly in the dark.

The snowstorm in "On Official Business" is punctuated by violent crashing sounds of objects splitting and pounding outside. When the storm subsides, the naked willows, their branches drooping helplessly, stand motionless and there is a great stillness "as if nature were now ashamed of her debauch, of her wild nights and passions unleashed with such abandon."[9]

In "The Steppe" natural phenomena explicated in human terms relate to the hot month of July. At sunrise the steppe "smiles and sparkles with dew" and "feels betrayed" when the moisture evaporates. But "the woes of the day are forgotten" and "all is forgiven" as "the steppe takes deep breaths" in the cool of the night. Nature seems on the alert, afraid to move, afraid to lose a single moment of life. In the darkness the parched grass "does not see its senility" and fills with gay, youthful chirpings, buzzings, and whistlings. All the nocturnal sights and sounds combine to express the steppe's loneliness and "passionate desire to live," the feeling that her wealth and inspiration are ignored and forsaken by all. Above the happy humming of the insects rises "her wistful, hopeless, insistent pleading for a bard."[10] Before the violent thunderstorm erupts on the third night of the trip, nature appears to experience "a langorous foreboding"; the moon is a dark crimson and gloomy, "as if indisposed." When pale streaks of lightning pulse on the darkened horizon, "they blink like eyelids." Large clouds hanging like black rags in disarray on the edges of the advancing storm give it "a drunken, mischievous appearance." And when the dark sky "opened its mouth," it "breathed a blinding fire of lightning."[11]

Frequently Chekhov conjures "humanized" images to point to the rapport between two elements of nature. In "Champagne" (1887) two small clouds had moved away from the moon and stood at some distance "with a mien as if they were whispering about something the moon should not know about."[12] After the scorchingly hot day on the first evening described in "The Steppe," the land, the hills, and the air rally in a concerted effort to throw off the stifling, oppressive heat. When an ash-gray curly cloud suddenly appeared from behind the hills, "it exchanged a glance with the steppe, saying, 'I am ready,' and glowered."[13] In "Grasshopper" an autumnal atmosphere envelops the vistas of the Volga the artist Riabovky and Olga Ivanovna intended to paint. It seemed as if nature had removed all that was luxurious and festive from the river and "stored it in trunks until next spring," while "crows were flying about the Volga teasing it: 'You are naked! You are bare!' "[14] In "In the Ravine" the setting sun "took cover under a crimson golden brocade, while long red and purple clouds stretched across the sky guarding its rest."[15]

Guided by a sense of universal solidarity and interdependence Chekhov refrains from contrasting nature to man's actions. Frequently nature shares in human experiences. Chekhov rarely uses epigraphs, but there is one in the early story "Heartache," words taken from a psalm: "To whom shall I tell my sorrow?" It is to his horse that the cabdriver Iona finally turns in his grief. He pours out his suffering over the loss of his son to the little mare who had shared with her master a wet and snowy evening, transporting callous, impatient, and indifferent passengers who refused to listen to Iona's woes.

In "Enemies" (1887) Doctor Kirillov had lost his only son to diphtheria that very evening. Overcoming his own despair he gives in to the urgent pleas of Abogin and consents to visit Abogin's sick wife. As the carriage passes through a dark, wooded portion of the road, "crows awakened by the noise of the carriage wheels began to stir in the foliage and raised an anxious, plaintive clamor as if they knew that the doctor's son had died and that Abogin's wife was sick."[16]

In "Happiness" (1887) fanciful tales of treasures buried in the steppe lead the protagonists to muse about the nature of human happiness. The large flock of sheep guarded by the two herdsmen not only provides a framework for the story but is drawn into the reflective process of thought as well. The narrative begins at an early hour of dawn. Not all of the sheep are asleep. Some are standing, their heads lowered, "thinking about something. Their thoughts, lengthy and slow, brought on by hypnotic notions of the broad expanse of steppe and sky, of days and nights, probably stunned and depressed them to the point of unconsciousness."[17] At the close of the narrative, "the first, broad, still-cold shafts of sunlight begin to fall upon the earth, bathing in the dewy grass and stretching gaily as if wanting to show their enjoyment," while the two herdsmen are still puzzling about happiness, that mysterious, elusive, hidden treasure. The story ends with these words: "The sheep too were thinking."[18]

In "An Unpleasantness" (1887) the windows of Doctor Ovchinnikov's reception room are open. Outside, a group of starlings is hopping along a path. When disturbed by a noise from the window, the starlings turn their foolish noses[19] to investigate and to decide: Should they get frightened or not? "And, deciding to get frightened, they rush off one by one toward the tops of the birch trees, shouting gaily as if mocking the doctor, who does not know how to fly."[20]

Before dying from the fatal stroke Doctor Ragin in "Ward No. 6" has a fleeting thought about immortality. But it is quickly replaced by a nature scene: "...he did not want immortality and he only thought about it for an instant." Instead, "the vision of a herd of uncommonly beautiful and graceful deer he had been reading about the day before passed through his mind...."[21]

In "Three Years" Laptev, who feels trapped by his wealth and commercial enterprise, sees a black dog lying in the middle of the yard. Thinking of his own powerlessness to escape, Laptev "felt annoyed at himself and at this black dog, who lay around on the stones instead of running to the fields or woods.... Apparently what prevented him and this dog from escaping was one and the same thing: habit of captivity, of slavery."[22]

In "The Peasants" young Sasha has been delegated by the grandmother to watch the geese, who like to invade the vegetable garden. The little girl neglects her assignment and the geese do invade the garden. After expelling the geese, the grandmother whips Sasha. While Sasha is crying from pain and fright, "the gander came up to the old woman and hissed something; when he returned to his flock, all the geese greeted him with an approving 'go-go-go'."[23]

In "A Case From Practice" a crowd of workers is walking home from the factory on a Saturday evening, and "it seemed that together with the workers on the eve of this holiday the fields, the forest, the sun too were getting ready to rest—to rest and perhaps to pray."[24]

Even trees and plants participate, at times, in human experiences. Kovrin's first hallucinatory visions in "The Black Monk" (1894) occur in the midst of a thriving compound of orchards, nurseries, and gardens. He is visiting his former guardian, the horticulturist Pesotsky, who tends his enterprise with a care and proficiency that have earned him a nationwide reputation. But when Kovrin returns a year later to recuperate from his nervous disorder, he has no rapport with the natural environment. "He paid no attention to the magnificent flowers in the garden," and when he goes down to the river "the gloomy pine trees with the shaggy roots which, a year ago, saw him here so young, so happy, and so cheerful now did not whisper and stood motionless and mute, as if they did not recognize him."[25]

In "The Teacher of Literature," after Nikitin tells Maniusia of his love for her, they run out to the garden: "A half moon shone above the garden and on the ground, out of the shadows of the grass, feebly lit by this half moon, sleepy tulips and irises reached out as if they too were begging for a declaration of love."[26]

In his mature period Chekhov increasingly uses attitudes and behavior toward nature as a measure of the character and moral stature of individuals and groups. Indifference or thoughtlessness or cruelty to nature is seen as evidence of character and moral deficiency. Of Lubkov, the flighty, dissolute, irresponsible, forever laughing character in "Ariadna," Chekhov says: "Lubkov loved nature but regarded it as something long familiar and moreover actually infinitely inferior to himself, something created only for his pleasure. He would stop before a magnificent panoramic view and say: 'Wouldn't it be nice to have a tea party here?'"[27] Later, preparing to seduce the beautiful, cold Ariadna, Lubkov says: "I respect women....but I think that certain relationships are compatible with lyricism. Lyricism is one thing, and a lover is another thing. The same as in farming: beauty of nature is one thing, and the income from forests and fields is another thing."[28]

In the story "Pecheneg" (1897) the old cossack Zhmukhin has been dubbed Pecheneg by his neighbors, for his life style resembles that of the tenth-century nomadic steppe tribe, the Pechenegs. Untutored and uncouth, he keeps his wife in pitiful subjection and his two illiterate teenage sons in total neglect. "To tell the truth I do not consider a woman to be a human being."[29] Zhmukhin invites a chance acquaintance, a middle-aged attorney whom he meets on a train ride, to spend the night at his house. As Zhmukhin and his guest arrive at the house, they see the two boys: "The younger one threw a chicken into the air, which flew in an arc, cackling; the older one, holding a rifle, fired and the chicken, killed, hit the ground. 'Those are my sons, learning to shoot on the wing,' said Zhmukhin."[30]

Misail, the hero of "My Life," speaks of his provincial town as inhabited by lazy, stupid, dishonest people. And as he looks back upon "a long, long row of suppressed, agonizingly slow sufferings he has incessantly observed in this town since his childhood," he thinks of "the tortured dogs that went mad, the sparrows plucked bare while alive by boys and then thrown into the water..."[31]

Conversely, in "The Black Monk" Pesotsky, a straightforward, kind, and ebullient, though irascible man, is portayed as the loving and efficient guardian of his huge and profitable fruit orchards and flower gardens. Another Chekhov character devoted to the care of the things of nature—"clever, very kind, and universally respected"—is the hero of "A Story of the Head Gardener."

Chekhov's humanized images of nature as a living being capable of experiencing rage, passion, disappointment, longing, capable of sharing human emotions, his images of birds teasing a river, mocking a man or sensing his pain, of flowers reaching for affection, of trees mutely rejecting a maniacal madman, all point to his fundamental concept of man's role in his natural environment as the guardian of this vast, intricate, powerful, and awesome living being. While Turgenev saw man as a frail and lonely figure lost in an indifferent universe and cast in a passive role when faced with nature, and Tolstoy looked at nature as the savior of man, Chekhov wanted man to become the guardian and savior of nature.

Chekhov came to speak with increasing insistence of man's active role toward nature, of man's responsibility toward the preservation of natural harmony and balance. The sour berries in the story "Gooseberries" symbolize a dream too trivial and too small to be worthy of standing for man's aspirations in the world. Neither the unsavory green fruit nor the "six feet of ground" needed to inter a corpse, nor flight and hiding from life's struggles and turmoil, is what man needs. He needs "the whole terrestrial globe," he needs the whole realm of nature. There, unfettered, he can unfold all the qualities and drives of his free spirit, says Ivan Ivanovich before launching on the doleful tale of his brother's voluntary incarceration in his petty dream turned to reality, blissfully immersed in a sea of trivialities and self-deceptions, savoring his home-grown, unpalatable gooseberries.

At an early stage in his artistic development Chekhov

began to voice his concern for the state of health of man's natural environment. In the story "The Reed Pipe" (1887) we hear the lament of an old shepherd: "The sun and the skies and the forests and the rivers and the creatures—all this is created, adapted, adjusted to each other. Each is at work and knows its place. And all this is doomed to perish."[32] He bewails the declining abundance of game, of animals, of bees, of fish. Rivers are drying up, forests are cut down or burnt, plant life is diminishing. At least people are getting more intelligent, the shepherd's listener, the bailiff Meliton, interjects, trying to introduce a more cheerful note into the conversation. This may be so, the shepherd agrees, but "what use is intelligence to a hunter if there is no game? I am of a mind that God has given man intelligence but has taken away his strength. People have grown weak, extremely weak...."[33] The name of the old shepherd is revealed only toward the end of the story as if to stress the significance of a heretofore anonymous lament: Luka Bedny—Lucas the Poor.

Chekhov adhered to this basic view of the unity of all living things and of a disturbed harmony in nature to the end of his life. The lament of Luka Bedny sounds like a prelude to the marvelously musical opening words of Treplev's play in the first act of *The Seagull* —a melodiousness that can be only inadequately conveyed in translation: "People, lions, eagles, and partridges, antlered deer, geese, spiders, silent fish living in water, star fish, and stars invisible to the eye—in short, all lives, all lives, all lives, having completed their doleful cycle, are extinct...."[34] In "The Reed Pipe" Luka Bedny plays a simple, melancholy melody on his crude instrument, a melody which consists of only five or six notes, the highest note sounding like human weeping. The opening words of Treplev's play sound, in Russian, like a poetic transcript of Luka's plaintive motif.

It is when Chekhov turns his attention to human activities which ravage the face of the earth or result in widespread natural disturbances that the question of man's responsibilities toward nature comes most forcefully to the fore. And it is then that the idea of unity and solidarity between man and his environment is most vividly and insistently expressed. The heartless Iakov in "Rothschild's Fiddle" goes for a stroll along the river after his wife's funeral and sees an old, spreading willow tree with a huge hollow and with crows' nests in its branches, and suddenly realizes that this is the tree his wife had spoken of on her death bed: "Yes, this is that very same willow tree—green, quiet, sad...how it has aged, the poor thing!"[35] Iakov sits down and memories crowd upon him. Where he now sees water meadow, there used to be a large birch forest. The bare hills on the horizon used to be covered by an old pine forest. Remorse about his own past life merges with apprehension of the changes he observes around him. Why did they cut down the birch trees and the pines? Why did he, all his life, scold, growl, brandish his fists, mistreat his wife? "The results are such losses, such terrible losses!"[36]

Deforestation is the most reprehensible intrusion of man upon nature discussed by Chekhov. The physician Khrushchev in *Leshy* (*The Wood Demon*, 1889) has earned a nickname, the title of the play. His energies are divided between tending the sick and caring for trees. Survival of trees is tied to survival of people. He sees human destiny closely bound to the success or failure of his foresting. "When I hear the rustling of my young forest planted with these very hands, I realize that climate is a little bit in my power and if in a thousand years man will be happy, in some small measure the responsibility will be mine."[37] Besides cultivating tree nurseries, Khrushchev cuts peat to reduce the burning of wood logs and to counteract the depletion of forests. His monologue in the first act is a forceful variation on Luka Bedny's lament in "The Reed Pipe": "All Russian forests crumble under the blows of axes, billions of trees perish, the abodes of animals and birds are ravaged, rivers grow shallow and dry up, wonderful landscapes vanish irrevocably, and all this because lazy man does not have enough sense to stoop and to pick up fuel available on the ground."[38]

It is Khrushchev's conservatory ardor that has led to his reputation of being strange, as strange and remote from ordinary people as the mythical spirit of Russian folklore he is nicknamed after, a spirit that dwells in the forest, forever ready to frighten humans with his mindless pranks. The heavy dual burden of medical practice and conservatory work leads Khrushchev to confess to Sonia, whom he is in love with, that he "suffers unbearably at times in the midst of his unending toil and continuous struggle against people who do not understand him."[39]

Khrushchev is disturbed by the fact that Sonia too, like everybody else, finds him strange and tries to put a tag on his personality, to assign him to a category of people clearly identifiable by a label. He is not well born like herself, she ponders. Does that mean that he is a populist? Or a democrat? Or perhaps he is a phrasemonger with all that eloquent talk about trees? Or a psychopath? Khrushchev feels suffocated by the narrow—mindedness around him and beseeches Sonia, "Try, above all else, to look for the human being in me."

The parallel between human destiny and nature is expressed even more forcefully by the beautiful and unhappy Elena Andreevna, faithless wife of Professor Serebriakov. "There, as the 'Wood Demon' has just said, you all recklessly destroy forests, and soon nothing will be left on earth; in the same way you recklessly destroy humans, and soon, thanks to you, there will be neither faithfulness, nor purity, nor ability for self-sacrifice left on earth.... You have pity neither for forests, nor for birds, nor for women nor for each other."[40]

The theme of the wood demon is expanded by Khrushchev himself in the fourth act, before Sonia overcomes her doubt, gives him the answer he pleaded for, and tells him that she does love him. In his view, the characteristic traits of *leshy*, the forest sprite, include far more than peculiarity. A wood demon is petty, blind, and insensitive to human needs. "You call me a wood demon," he says to the assembled entourage of Professor Serebriakov, "but I am not the only one. That demon sits in all of you. All of you wander in a dark forest and live with unseeing eyes. We all have only enough intelligence, knowledge and heart to spoil our own and other people's lives...."[41] His lament that there are no genuine heroes, no talents, no true eagles, no people who would show the way out of the dark forest and repair what is being ruined, is preceded by the spread of the glow of a conflagration on the horizon. The sounds of a fire alarm help Khrushchev to overcome his despondence and to burst forth with an outcry of sudden vigor and new hope before he rushes off to the rescue of the burning forest and before Sonia tells him of her love for him. "I may not be a hero but I shall become one. I shall grow the wings of an eagle and neither the glow of this conflagration nor the devil himself will frighten me. Let the trees burn—I shall plant new ones. Let my love be rejected—I shall love another woman."[42]

By 1896 Chekhov had reworked *The Wood Demon* into *Uncle Vania*. The number of characters was reduced, the action partly changed and concentrated in one place. The transformation of Khrushchev into Doctor Astrov, who is no longer the central figure, was among the crucial changes. The parallel between trees and people was retained, but the survival of both is less closely interrelated. The theme of the wood demon was removed and the stigma of being peculiar was lifted from Doctor Astrov, whose name hints, in Russian as it does in English, at an affinity with the stars. Yet the doctor's personality is now shaded by resignation, hopelessness, and alienation, which he attempts to drown in alcohol. Astrov deliberately shuns people. He does not reciprocate Sonia's love for him. He does not plead for recognition as a human being anymore the way Khrushchev did. He does not rush to put down a conflagration which is destroying trees, he does not burst forth with a surge of enthusiasm and hope. But the monologue of the Wood Demon is repeated, with minor changes, by Astrov in the first act of *Uncle Vania*, and graphically enlarged upon in the third. Astrov, like Khrushchev before him, has prepared a map of the local districts and now explains its meaning at length. Different colors are used in the map to show the distribution of flora and fauna as it was fifty years ago, twenty-five years ago, and as it is today. The picture is one of the continuing depletion of forested areas, a drastic decline in some animal and bird aspects and a complete disappearance of others; elk, swans, and grouse are gone: "A picture of gradual and indubitable degeneration," remarks Astrov, "...if in place of these destroyed forests we would see highways, railroads, plants, factories, schools—people would be healthier, richer, more intelligent, but there is nothing of the sort here. We have in the district the same swamps, mosquitoes, lack of roads, poverty, typhus, diptheria, fires...."[43]

This meticulous analysis of the state of health of the natural environment and the diagnosis of a continuing decline in the last fifty years by a member of the medical profession places Doctor Astrov on an equal level with profesor Nikolay Stepanovich's diagnosis in "A Dreary Story." The professor assessed the lack of genuine concern for other people as the virus destroying the fiber of contemporary society. By denying Astrov the central position which Khrushchev held in *The Wood Demon* Chekhov strengthened and underscored the symbolic image of trees and people progressing on a parallel downward path. The survival of trees and the survival of sensitive, self-effacing, humble people like Uncle Vania, crushed by Serebriakov's indifference and self-centered, callous behavior, is threatened by the same force of senseless, mindless destruction.

Chekhov also observes the beginnings of water pollution. In the humorous skit "Fish Love" (1892) a carp, sole inhabitant of a large pond situated near a foundry, falls madly in love with a young girl who daily comes to swim in the pond. "Due to proximity to the foundry...the water in the pond has long since turned brown, but nevertheless the carp could see everything."[44] In "Gooseberries" the estate bought by Nikolay Ivanovich in fulfillment of his life's dream is situated near a river, "but the water in it was the color of coffee because on one side of the estate stood a brick factory and on the other a bone-processing plant."[45] In "In the Ravine" a leather factory lay on the outskirts of Ukleevo. This factory is responsible for a good deal of pollution. "The water in the stream often turned malodorous; the factory's waste matter contaminated the meadow, the peasants' cattle suffered from anthrax, and the factory was ordered closed. It was considered closed, but operated secretly with the knowledge of the district's police officer and doctor, who each received ten rubles a month from the owner."[46]

Chekhov has amply demonstrated in his works that the human capacity for folly has never been matched by any other species of living things on earth. But he was also among the first writers to speak of man's role as the sole responsible guardian of life on the planet. While the animal and plant world lives immersed in its environment, powerless to change reality, man can detach himself from his environment; he can destroy it, to be sure, but he can also rise above it in the freedom of his will. Man's spirit is the only living force on earth capable of voluntary and emotional acts, capable of creative achievements. An example of such a detachment, such a rise, is shown by Chekhov in "Rothschild's Fiddle." To alleviate his remorse over a cheerless, wasted life and his anguish at surveying a ravaged environment, Iakov reaches for his fiddle. "Thinking about a lost, unprofitable life, he began to play he did not himself know what, but it came out plaintive and touching and tears began to stream down his cheeks. And the deeper he thought, the sadder sang the fiddle."[47] A member of the Jewish orchestra Iakov belongs to, with the nickname of Rothschild, listens, enraptured, to the sad and beautiful melody. Iakov has always been mean to Rothschild but now, at death's door, decides to give him his fiddle. Played by Rothschild, Iakov's melody lives on after his death, moving the local inhabitants again and again to tears. It is as if the song of the fiddle were an answer to nature's pleading, plaintive cry "for a bard" in "The Steppe."

"A Letter," begun a year or so before Chekhov's death, was left unfinished. In it, Chekhov extolls the proud potentialities of the human spirit, saying through the author of the letter that "The most beautiful and the most rational, powerful, invincible part of nature is the part created by the genius of man, independently from nature's will."[48] The genius of man, to Chekhov, is not only the ability of outstanding, gifted individuals to create works of art and excellence; he includes the spiritual potentialities, the divine spark, to be found in every single man as well. In "A House with a Mezzanine, a Story of an Artist" (1896) the plight of the peasantry is discussed and the artist says: "the whole horror of their situation is that they have no time to think about their soul, no time to remember their own image and likeness; hunger, cold, blind fear, and mountains of labor have blocked, like avalanches, all roads to spiritual activity, to the very thing which distinguishes man from animal and constitutes the only thing that makes life worth living."[49]

None of Chekhov's protagonists who speak of man's place in the world, of man's responsibilities and unique attributes, are endowed with exceptional abilities or achievements. In no way do they rise above the mass of simple, inconspicuous people whom Chekhov liked to focus on. They are as ordinary and humble as the heroes who extolled the value of desires and the virtue of exerting one's own free will. Khrushchev in *The Wood Demon* says that every day he is gaining in stupidity and pettiness and losing in talent. Astrov in *Uncle Vania* feels sucked in by the surrounding provincialism and has taken to drink. Nikolay Ivanovich's brother in "Gooseberries," a veterinarian, is old, "unfit to struggle"—as he puts it, and bemoans the fact that he is no longer young. The coffin-maker Iakov in "Rothschild's Fiddle" is morose and engrossed in his petty business. The author of the unfinished "Letter" is an invalid and former seminary student who left the academy without finishing his studies. And the artist in "A House with a Mezzanine" confesses to total idleness and to endless hours of aimless dreaming and roaming the countryside.

Yet every one of these characters who express Chekhov's views on man and nature experiences or is aware of something that belongs to the realm of the spirit, the realm of freedom accessible only to man. In the last act of *The Wood Demon* Khruschev experiences a great upsurge of will and determination. Astrov's spiritual experience in *Uncle Vania*, aside from his love for his trees, is esthetic. He is temporarily drawn to the beautiful Elena Andreevna, yet neither in lust nor in love. It is beauty that attracts him: "I do not love anyone and I will not fall in love either. What still captivates me is beauty. I am drawn to it."[50] The sight of the vegetating Nikolay Ivanovich in "Gooseberries" leads his brother to an acute outburst of despair and indignation over people who sink into the stupor of material contentment to the exclusion of higher goals and interests. Out of Iakov's remorse and sadness in "Rothschild's Fiddle" springs the beautiful melody that lived on after his death. The author of "A Letter" writes to Maria Sergeevna of the sense of wonder, reverence, and ecstasy he felt while reading the book he is sending her, and the idling artist in "A House with a Mezzanine" dreams of "genuine sciences and art which would be oriented toward eternal and lofty goals rather than be concerned with passing needs and current problems of the day."[51]

The spark of the sublime is there in every one of them. Resignation and enthusiasm, despondency and esthetic transport, pettiness and creative inspiration, physical deficiency and mental ecstasy, inertia and artistic insight—they are all there side by side in man. Chekhov's ultimate vision of life on this earth was one of a cherry orchard in bloom, rooted deeply in nature, be it fifty, one hundred, two hundred, or perhaps even one thousand years away.

The choice of recurrent literary symbols in Chekhov's fiction is closely linked to his view of man's role on earth.

Notes

[1] This chapter is based on my article, "Nature in Chekhov's Fiction," *The Russian Review*, April 1974, pp. 153-66.

[2] L., V, 175.

[3] I.S. Turgenev, *Sobranie sochinenii*, 10 Vols., Moscow, 1962, VI, 150.

[4] Ibid., III, 10.

[5] L.N. Tolstoy, *Sobranie sochinenii*, 20 Vols., Moscow, 1960-65, Vol. XII, 44.

[6] Chekhov, VII, 338.
[7] VII, 339.
[8] IV, 375.
[9] X, 101.
[10] VII, 46.
[11] VII, 85.
[12] VI, 16.
[13] VII, 28.
[14] VIII, 17.
[15] X, 172.
[16] VI, 36.
[17] VI, 210.
[18] VI, 218.
[19] Chekhov uses the word *nosy* ("noses") and not *kliuvy* ("beaks") as rendered by some translators.
[20] VII, 147.
[21] VIII, 126.
[22] IX, 90.
[23] IX, 292.
[24] X, 75.
[25] VIII, 250.
[26] VIII, 322.
[27] IX, 114.
[28] Ibid.
[29] IX, 332.
[30] IX, 326.
[31] IX, 269.
[32] VI, 323.
[33] VI, 325.
[34] XIII, 13.
[35] VIII, 303.
[36] Ibid.
[37] XII, 141.
[38] XII, 140.
[39] XII, 156.
[40] XII, 144.
[41] XII, 194.
[42] XII, 197.
[43] XIII, 95.
[44] VIII, 51.
[45] X, 60.

[46]   X, 144.
[47]   VIII, 304.
[48]   VII, 512.
[49]   IX, 184.
[50]   XIII, 85.
[51]   IX, 186.

IX

Recurrent Symbolic Images:
The House, The Road, The Light

The symbolic use of objects by Chekhov is well known and has been widely discussed. The host of trivial objects figuring in his plots anchor the protagonists firmly in the flow of human time and form a bridge between the palpable and visible outer world and the realm of the characters' consciousness. The pots of milk and cream that fill the newlyweds' cellar in "A Teacher of Literature" illustrate the vapid mode of domestic bliss Nikitin decides to flee from. The umbrella in "Three Years" left behind by Iulia is reverently held by Laptev and spreads an aura of happiness all around him, but is discarded and tucked away in a drawer "for useless things" once his ardor wanes. Belikov, "The Man in a Case," retreats from reality into an encasement fashioned of rubbers, gloves, dark glasses, and a host of similar protective paraphernalia. The plate of hard and sour gooseberries

223

consumed with such relish by Nikolay Ivanovich stands for the self-deception generated by the attainment of a petty and selfish dream. The brilliant ties worn by Uncle Vania hint at his yearning to escape from a colorless and meaningless existence. The trite painting of the naked woman and the purple vase with the broken handle in "The Betrothed," decorating the house made ready to receive the bride and groom, plays its role in Nadia's decision to refrain from marrying a worthless and boring man and to flee from her stifling provincial environment.

Chekhov uses these and similar trivial items to reiterate in a thousand different connections the symbolic link of objects with man's progression on this earth and his inner self. But there is a number of images that run through his works with such insistence and recurrence that they reveal themes crucial for his overall vision of reality, themes conceived early in his career and retained and elaborated upon in a large number of variants to the end of his mature period. One of these is the image of a house. Images of enclosures can suggest refuge, they can be centers of harmony, concentration, and creativity, or they can imply retreat from the world, isolation, imprisonment. It is with this second function that the house appears and reappears in Chekhov's fiction.

In an early story, "The Dowry" (1883), the confining attributes of a house are already clearly sketched. On a deserted street in Moscow, never traveled by carriage and seldom traversed by pedestrians, stands a very small, one-storied house with three windows facing the street. It is plastered white, equipped with a tile roof topped by a dilapidated chimney. It looks very much "like a little hunchbacked old woman in a lace cap." The house is submerged in the foliage of mulberry trees, acacias and poplars planted by the grandfathers and great-grandfathers of the present owners. A multitude of gay and lively birds nest in their branches and creates, together with all the greenery, "an earthly paradise" right under the windows of the house. But the shutters are always closed and the windows never opened. The walls shut out the real world and the sky. It is dark and stiflingly hot inside in summer and winter, for the inhabitants wish neither light nor fresh air nor bird songs. They are not interested in nature or in human contacts.

The narrator discovers the reason for this voluntary seclusion of the middle-aged woman who lives in the house with her brother-in-law and her young daughter. The woman's husband, Petr Semenovich, is away on business and the narrator enters the house for the first time bringing greetings from the absent breadwinner. The sole interest in the lives of the two women is the accumulation of a dowry, although no suitor has as yet presented himself to the daughter. She nervously exclaims that she will never, never marry though the word "marry" brings a wild gleam to her eyes. The dowry fills five trunks and numerous suitcases and boxes. But there will be more. For the women purchase fabrics and notions at an annual fair and spend the subsequent twelve months sewing.

The futility and the empty, helpless rhythm of life in the little house become even more apparent to the narrator on two subsequent visits. He is now witnessing the relentless flow of time that cannot be stopped, the advance of change that a retreat cannot stem, the impossibility of reversing the atrophy of life within the walls of voluntary isolation. Seven years separate the second visit from the first. The narrator hears that the husband, Petr Semenovich, is dead and that his brother, a heavy drinker, now finances his alcoholic needs by stealing from his niece's dowry and selling or pawning the items. Both women appear greatly aged. "I will never, never marry," says the daughter again, looking up at the ceiling and apparently not believing her own words. On his third visit a few years later the narrator is greeted by the mother mourning the death of her daughter. Her brother-in-law is still drinking and stealing from the dowry accumulated over so many years.

Years later, in "My Life" (1896), Chekhov expanded this aspect of the house symbolism to a theme of spiritual void and dreariness enveloping an entire community. The architecture of Misail's home town suggests a society that has lost contact with moral impulses and civilized activities. Misail's father, a mediocre man lacking artistic abilities but convinced of his distinctive talents, is the only architect in town. Says Misail, "During the last fifteen or twenty years not a single decent house has been built in our town, as far as I can remember."[1] The muddled, stunted, and unclear thinking of the architect is reflected in his customary layout of the rooms, each with two or even three doors too many, "which invariably turned them into corridors." Little staircases would lead to nooks with ceilings too low to permit a person to stand upright and three huge steps instead of a floor, "like the shelves in a Russian bathhouse." The facades of these houses—which all look alike—bear a stubborn, indifferent expression, their lines stiff and timid. Yet, as time went on, says Misail, "people became accustomed to father's mediocrity; it took roots and became the local style."[2] Was Chekhov here perhaps influenced by the parallels Dostoevsky drew between the rooms, apartments, and houses of his protagonists and their characters and destiny? The coffin-like room of the brooding, seclusive Raskolnikov? The neat, spiderweb appearance of the old money-lender's apartment with its soulless tidiness and petty vulgarity? Or the gloomy, cold, and inhospitable facade of the house owned by the wealthy merchant Rogozhin, consumed by thirst for power and sexual passion?

There is no park, no theater, no decent orchestra in Misail's home town. The well-to-do inhabitants sleep in stuffy bedrooms on bug-infested beds. Children are kept in "revolting dirty rooms called nurseries" while servants sleep on the kitchen floor covering themselves with rags. After Misail leaves his father's house and becomes a plain laborer he experiences the indignity of being treated with contempt, rudeness, or, at best, indifference by those in a superior station of life. Shops invariably cheated him and his fellow workmen selling them rotten meat, mildewed flour, and used tea leaves. Everybody accepted bribes and "there was not a single honest man in the whole town."

As Misail enters his father's study for a final confrontation he feels an upsurge of pity and affection for the old man. But he sees that his father is sketching the plan of a villa "with Gothic windows and a thick turret like the watchtower of a fire house, something extremely stiff and tasteless." And the sight of this villa dissipates Misail's warm and conciliatory feelings and drives him to fling bitter accusations at the old man: "...why is your life...so boring, so mediocre? You have been building these houses now for thirty years...and not a single honest man is living in them. These houses of yours are cursed nests where mothers and daughters are driven toward death, children are being tortured.... A man must dull his wits with vodka, cards, and gossip, be mean, play the hypocrite, or go on drawing sketches for decades on end, if he is to overlook the horrors lurking in these houses."[3]

Misail's home town is a large panorama of thick walls, closed doors, shuttered windows, and forbidding fences looming as barriers and obstructions, containing and fostering stagnation and isolation. In miniature form they were already present in "The Dowry." But it is Ward No. 6 in the story of that title, the hospital annex reserved for the mentally ill, that rises as the epitome of imprisonment, as the ultimate symbol of confinement which reaches far beyond its dilapidated walls, crumbling chimney, and rotting porch steps. Not only the five inmates but their guardian as well, the rough and insensitive Nikita with the huge fists which he uses so freely to keep his charges in submission, are all captives of the same confining walls, a miniature Sakhalin. When Doctor Ragin is forced against his will to join the imprisoned group, he gazes through the window bars at the nearby tall, white building surrounded by a stone wall. It is the prison. " 'So this is reality,' he thinks, and fear grips his heart. "[4]

The walls of the ward witness violent gestures of futile protest and reverberate from some of Chekhov's most dramatic, poignant exchanges and cries of human agony and despair. In panic Ragin grips the window bars with both hands and tries to shake them, using all his strength. "But the solid bars did not yield." Before Ragin receives the fatal blows from Nikita, Gromov, the highly intelligent inmate whom Ragin came so frequently to converse with during his days of freedom, voices a violent protest before hurling himself against the door and threatening to smash his skull: "The law, I think, clearly states that no one may be deprived of his liberty without a court order. This is an outrage! Tyranny!"[5] But his outcry too is silenced by Nikita's fists. And the moonlight that filters through the windows throws the shadows of the prison bars in sharp relief.

There are further aspects of life suggested by the symbol of a house besides constriction and restraint. The failure to relate, the breakdown of communication with one's fellow men—so crucial to Chekhov's vision of reality, is also amply reflected in house symbolism. Frequently a house mirrors the alienation among its inhabitants through the distribution of its space. In "My Wife" (1892) husband and wife live on separate floors of their large and empty country house. The egotistic Pavel Andreevich, who cares little for the plight of others, is estranged from his wife, Natalia Gavrilovna, who is deeply interested in organizing help for the starving peasantry during a famine. Pavel Andreevich occupies the second floor while Natalia Gavrilovna "dined, slept, and received her guests on her own lower floor caring little how I [her husband] dined, slept and whom I received."[6]

Misius, the sensitive, naive, and docile heroine in "A House with a Mezzanine," is dominated by her stern and imperious older sister Lida. Misius lives in the mezzanine. And it is here that her fate is sealed when she tells her mother and the disapproving Lida of her love for the artist, the narrator of the story. It is night and the artist, filled with tender emotions after parting with Misius, lingers in the garden to have one more look at "the house where she lived, the dear, naive old house which seemed to be looking at me with the windows of its mezzanine which were like eyes and understood everything."[7] The artist saw the bright light of a lamp in the mezzanine changing to a subdued green as the lamp was covered with a shade. He saw shadows move and he thought he heard voices. An hour later the green light went out and the shadows vanished. The next day he learned the full meaning of the light extinguished in the mezzanine: Misius had gone on a trip with her mother and would spend the winter abroad, an abrupt departure arranged by Lida. The artist never saw Misius again.

Even more suggestive of human conflict is Professor Serebriakov's house in *Uncle Vania*. The house was already described in the first draft of the play, *The Wood Demon*. "I do not like this house," says Serebriakov in the third act before announcing his proposal to sell the estate and leave Uncle Vania and Sonia homeless, "it's like a labyrinth. Twenty-six enormous rooms with people wandering off in all directions so you can never find anyone."[8] In the second act the nature of the labyrinth is analyzed by Serebriakov's wife, Elena Andreevna, addressing Uncle Vania: "Things are not right in this house. Your mother hates everything except her pamphlets and the professor is irritated, does not trust me, is afraid of you; Sonia is annoyed with her father, is annoyed with me. She has not spoken to me for two weeks now; you hate my husband and openly despise your mother; my nerves are on edge and today I started to cry twenty times.... Things are not right in this house."[9]

From alienation among people living under the same roof, "The New Country House" (1899) moves to a broader spatial and temporal arena. The new house stands on the crossroad between past and present, between old rural Russia and the advent of industrialization. While supervising the construction of a large railroad bridge across a river, the engineer Kucherov discovered a picturesque spot in the vicinity of the high bank of the river with a magnificent view of the valley, its villages, churches, and pastures. He and his wife decide to build a country house on this spot. The new house is a beautiful two-storied structure with a terrace, balconies, and steepled tower, and is surrounded by elaborate plantings and new gardens. But the affluence of the newcomers—the well-fed horses and the handsome carriage driven by an arrogant coachman, the sailboat gliding on the river—all arouse envy and animosity among the poverty-stricken inhabitants of the neighboring villages. The peasants oppose change and regard the new house and the construction of the railroad bridge as an undesirable and unnecessary intrusion.

The new owner too fails to establish a "bridge" of good will and mutual trust with his rural neighbors in spite of his initial, sincere endeavors. An engineer by profession, no longer a member of the old landowning gentry, he is unable to understand the peasants' mentality, the blend of resentment mixed with a residue of paternalistic expectations among a class so recently and so incompletely extricated from the legal bond of serfdom. Repeated thefts of equipment and endless petty annoyances drive the Kucherovs to the decision to sell their new house and to move away. The new owner is a minor government employee who arrives with his family on holidays only to spend a few hours in the country and then returns to the city in the evening. "He speaks and clears his throat like a very important official and when the peasants greet him he does not answer."[10] On their way home from work on a spring evening a group of villagers passes the silent and deserted new house and one of them mutters: "We lived without a bridge and we didn't ask for it.... We don't need it."[11] This comment of the peasant's runs like a refrain throughout the story.

Shadows and dim lights are characteristic features of Chekhov's symbolic houses. The tavern of the Jew Moses in "The Steppe" is a particularly striking example: that "large, one-storied house with a rusty iron roof was dark inside as well as outside. The walls were gray, the ceiling and the cornice were black with smoke, and it seemed that even if one hung ten lamps in the room, it would still be dark."[12] There is a feature of this tavern, however, very succinctly stated, that could serve as an epilogue to the use of the house image as a symbol of human alienation and lack of rapport in Chekhov's writing though "The Steppe" belongs to his earlier works: There is an engraving on one of the walls with the inscription "The Indifference of Men." "But it was impossible to tell what men were indifferent toward, since the engraving was very much darkened with age and liberally spotted by flies."[13]

The first act of *The Three Sisters* seems to disprove the assertion that gloom and shadows prevail in Chekhov's houses. The home of the Prozorovs is bathed in spring sunshine and steeped in an atmosphere of joyous celebration and eager anticipation of a happy future. But Chekhov uses the house to reflect the collapse of the sisters' dream. To escape, to move toward a new life, the sisters are forced to abandon the house. The more the vulgar Natasha succeeds in infiltrating the house, the further the sisters drift away from a fulfillment of their dream to return to Moscow, the dimmer grow the lights, and the more the shadows lengthen.

It is eight o'clock in the evening at the opening of the second act. The scene is the same as in the first, but Chekhov's directions state that "the stage is dark." We see Natasha enter carrying a candle, anxious to ascertain that no lights be left burning anywhere in the house, intent on dampening merriment and gaiety around her. It is carnival time and a group of mummers is expected, but Natasha orders that they be sent away and tells Chebutykin and Tuzenbach, the two devoted friends of the Prozorov family, to go home. There will be no party. Under the pretext that her son Bobik needs a sunnier room, Natasha schemes to get Irina to double up with Olga. She wants to move the child into Irina's room.

It is in the room shared by Olga and Irina two years later that the climactic third act takes place, the triumphant advance of Natasha. It is past two o'clock in the morning. Outside a fire that devastated the neighboring town block is subsiding. And inside the sisters lose their last hold over their home against the lurid glow of the abating conflagration. Natasha stages an ugly scene over the presence of the old and faithful family retainer Anfisa, whom she wants moved to the country. "I like to see a house run properly," she says, "there should be no room for useless people in this house." The sisters join this category of "useless people" after Andrey's confession that he has mortgaged the house to pay his crushing gambling debts. Natasha holds the money.

The scene of the fourth act is no longer the house where Natasha now reigns supreme, but the Prozorovs' garden. Twice during the act Masha repeats that she is not going inside the house any more. She cannot bear to do so. It is here, in the garden, that all farewells are exchanged. Toasts of champagne to the officers of the departing battery have been drunk on the terrace. A brief cry of longing for liberation is voiced by Andrey who is momentarily overcome with revulsion for his present life: "How wonderful it feels when I think about the future! Everything becomes so easy, so spacious; far ahead dawn will break; I see freedom, I see myself and my children becoming free from idleness, from this despicable living like parasites...."[14] A pitiful and unconvincing cry this, in view of Natasha's strong hold over her husband. Andrey's voice is silenced by her angry harangue delivered through an open window, from the house, her vulgarity spiked with affected faulty French phrases, admonishing Andrey not to speak so loudly. He is disturbing their daughter's sleep. And it is here, in the garden, that the sisters voice their determination to go on living in spite of life's vicissitudes, to go on searching for a meaningful existence, though Moscow is no longer the destination of their flight.

The theme of escape from the dreariness and desolation embodied in a house is supplemented by the motif of doom and demolition sketched in an early story, "The Old House" (1887), and brought to brilliant fruition in Chekhov's last and crowning work, *The Cherry Orchard*. "The Old House" pictures a dwelling in Petersburg slated for demolition to make room for a new building. The narrator, owner of the old structure, escorts the architect of the new one through the empty rooms. Against the background of windows dimmed by grime, torn wallpaper and stoves darkened by soot, images of former tenants are evoked in kaleidoscopic fashion by the narrator. Death ushers the procession in. An open coffin was once carried down the stairs by drunken pall bearers. They stumbled, fell, and were bruised while "the corpse remained very serious as if nothing had happened, his head swaying as he was picked up and put back in the coffin."[15] A group of prostitutes used to occupy one of the apartments; an obscure musician was the tenant of another. Again, it seems as if the shadow of Dostoevsky were leaning over Chekhov's shoulder, conjuring thoughts of destitute humanity huddled in the garrets and cellars of Petersburg's slums.

The negative features associated with a house throughout Chekhov's works are here couched in mysterious, eerie and macabre tones. The narrator's kaleidoscope dwells in particular detail on the three-room apartment "saturated with microbes and viruses. Something is wrong here. Many tenants have lost their lives here."[16] The narrator is convinced that at some point a curse was placed on the apartment and that "someone invisible always lived in it along with the tenants."[17] He proceeds to describe the misfortunes that befell the sober and hard-working clerk Putokhin. His wife fell ill and died; he lost his job, took to drink, pawning whatever he could lay his hands on, beating up his mother and getting into fights with Egorych, the sedate locksmith to whom he subletted one room. Soon Egorych too stopped working and joined Putokhin in drinking bouts. One day Putokhin left and never came back. His mother took to drink too, fell ill, and was taken to a hospital, while three of his four children went to live with some relatives. The oldest boy, Vasia, stayed for a while doing odd jobs in the house and running errands for the prostitutes. What finally happened to him the narrator does not know.

The theme of demolition is central to *The Cherry Orchard*. In *The Three Sisters* the garden provided the setting for the escape, the flight from the house, the stepping stone toward a new future, but in Chekhov's last play the cherry orchard is itself included in the death sentence. That Ranevskaia's house is doomed to be torn down is expressed by Chekhov in one of his comments on the play: "The house is old, large, and grand. At one time people lived in it on a large scale and the furniture must reflect this. Rich and cozy...Summer people do not rent such houses. Houses of this sort are usually torn down and the material is used for the construction of summer cottages."[18]

But this socio-economic comment touches only on the fringes of the tragic destiny of the house. There is a deeper reason for its demise. The mysterious invisible being in the early story "The Old House," heaping adversities on the inhabitants of the apartment, grows to formidable proportions in *The Cherry Orchard*, though the eeriness is masqued by poetry. It is time itself that all three characters most intimately connected with the estate are vainly attempting to escape, to deny, to arrest, to stop in its destructive advance. All three—Mrs. Ranevskaia, owner of the estate; her brother Gaev; and Firs, the faithful family retainer—substitute the distant past for the present. All three are deaf and blind to temporal reality and the flow of time. Entering the room "which is still known as the nursery" in the first act Mrs. Ranevskaia exclaims: "The nursery, my dear, wonderful room...I slept here when I was a little girl.... And now I feel like a little girl."[19] Her brother Gaev, forever playing imaginary billiard games, sucking candies and making senseless speeches, remembers the days when he too slept in this room. And Firs thinks of Gaev as a reckless young man and speaks of the days of serfdom as the time of stability and prosperity. The emancipation of the serfs, he says, was "the calamity."

All three—Ranevskaia, Gaev, and Firs—see the cherry orchard as an appendix to the house, firmly rooted in the past. To them it is not the radiant symbol of a new and beckoning future, as Trofinov and Ania see it, when "all Russia will be a blooming orchard." Neither is it the symbol of a lucrative present, which is Lopakhin's view as he starts cutting down the trees to parcel out the land and make room for summer cottages even before the old owners have left. Gaev sees the worth of the cherry orchard in the fact that it is mentioned in the Encyclopedia Dictionary as among the notable sights of the region. Ranevskaya momentarily conjures an image of her dead mother, dressed in white, strolling in the blooming orchard. And Firs reminisces about the quality and abundance of the cherries that used to be harvested some forty or fifty years ago, dried, pickled, marinated, made into jam and sold at great profits. But now no one remembers the methods used.

Dimly Mrs. Ranevskaia does sense the approaching disaster of losing the estate. In the second act she expresses a vague anticipation that the house is about to collapse about their ears. In the third she complains, "I seem to have lost my eyesight, I do not see anything." She seems to regain her eyesight in the fourth act just before her final exit from the now-empty "nursery": "I'll sit down just for a minute. I feel as though I'd never before seen what the walls of this house were like, the ceilings, and now I look at them avidly, with such tender affection."[20] But a realistic view of time still eludes Ranevskaia. Neither Ania's plans for the future nor Lopakhin's triumph as the new owner of the estate interest her. There is no temporal perspective in her thinking. She does not link the demise of her house to causal forces and the march of time but sees it merging with the eternally revolving cycle of the seasons: "Goodbye, dear house, old granddad. Winter will pass, spring will come, and you will no longer be here, you will have been torn down. How much these walls have seen!"[21]

For Gaev and Firs too, images of the past drift forward to obscure the present before the final curtain. Gaev's last flash of recollection before his farewell embrace of Ranevskaia takes him back to his childhood: "I remember when I was six years old, on Whitsunday, I was sitting on this window sill watching my father going to church."[22] And Firs, while sharing the final chord of death and doom with the house, also retreats into the past. Ill and feeble, locked up and forgotten in the abandoned house, he moans that he did not "keep an eye" on Gaev, who probably left wearing a light wrap instead of his fur coat. "When they are young they're green," he mumbles.

Next to the house the road is the most insistent image in

Chekhov's fiction, though frequently it is not clearly deli-
neated. His writing is continually shifting back and forth
between the confinement, immobility, stagnation, and isolation perpetrated within the walls of darkened, airless houses
and the realm of release, motion, the feeling of space, of open
vistas, and moments of enchantment, and fascination with
nature's world experienced on a road traveled or a path
walked. There is little of the conventional use of the road by
Chekhov to convey the image of life as a voyage and of men
as travelers on a set course toward a charted destination and
the end-station of death. Above all, the function of the road is
that of an open door, a moving away from confining enclosures, the way the trip to Sakhalin signaled in Chekhov's
personal life a breaking away from a humdrum routine and
heralded a quest for new horizons.

It is arresting that one of the most insistent calls to escape
is sounded in his fiction by the spectral Doctor Chebutykin
in *The Three Sisters*, himself a lifeless phantom, stripped of
human drives and urges, yet summoning the insight to give
Andrey, who is well on the way of following in Chebutykin's
footsteps, a significant piece of advice. The advice comes in
the fourth act, in response to Andrey's confession of loneliness and confusion over his relations to his vulgar wife
Natasha. "I, my friend, am leaving tomorrow and maybe we
shall never see each other again; so here is my advice to you.
Put on your hat, grab a cane, and leave...leave and keep on
going without looking back. The further away you will get,
the better."[23] It is just flight, escape, that Chebutykin suggests; neither goal, destination, nor the dangers of new
entrapments are mentioned.

A distinct restlessness in the Russian people observed by
Chekhov, the keen diagnostician, has no doubt contributed
to this treatment of the road symbol. "Tumbleweed" (1887) is
the title of a story devoted to this condition, set among the
thousands of pilgrims and drifters who crowd the court and
the hostelry building of the monastery of the Holy Mount on
the bank of the River Donets, celebrating the feasts of St.
John the Divine and of Nikolay the Wonder-worker. "If it

were possible to scan with one glance the Russian land in its entire expanse, what a multitude of such tumbleweeds would appear before one's eyes, all looking for a better life, marching along big and small roads or dozing and waiting for dawn in inns, taverns, and hostels or on the grass in the open."[24] In the earlier story "On Easter Night" Chekhov had already touched upon the restless "searching for something" the meandering crowds displayed during the midnight service in the monastery church.

"The Steppe, the Story of a Trip" (1888) ranks among the more extensive of Chekhov's masterpieces. It is far more than the account of a journey or the mapping of a road. It is Chekhov's first major exploration of open spaces versus restrictive enclosures. It begins with an explosive release from confinement. On a hot July morning a carriage, drawn by two lively horses, carrying the boy Egorushka, his uncle Ivan Ivanovich Kuzmichev, and Father Christopher, flies exuberantly past locales associated with confinement and death—the prison, the smithy, the cemetery, and finally the brick factory on the outskirts of the travelers' home town. Egorushka's widowed mother is sending her son to enroll in the distant city's school, for she wants him to receive a better education than what is available in their small home town. The boy's red shirt billows like a balloon on his back, and like a small float tossed into the sea Egorushka enters the vast and open spaces of the steppe stretching ahead.

The panorama, the people encountered on the way, the major events during the four-day trip are all presented as apprehended by this nine-year old, a sensitive, impressionable child, his young mind unencumbered by adult notions, by concepts frozen into set patterns by the flow of time. "Time itself," Chekhov tells us at noon of the first day of the trip, "seemed suspended, as if it had stopped and a hundred years had elapsed since that morning."[25] With this note of temporal arrest, space, as if immobilized, comes to reign supreme in Egorushka's imagination. His wonderment over the boundlessness of the land mounts and his pristine, primitive impressions coalesce, step by step, into an image of the steppe as a gigantic living being held in captivity, and of the people inhabiting it as oppressed as heavily as those living in Chekhov's fettering enclosures.

The heat is the oppressive power that holds the languishing, parched, thirsty land in its grip, stilling the air and immobilizing birds and insects. During the first midday stop of the trip Egorushka hears a mysterious, barely audible, plaintive song, "as if an invisible spirit hovered over the steppe." Before discovering that it is the voice of a woman standing by her house on the outskirts of a nearby village, Egorushka decides that it must be the grass, doomed and dying, that is singing dolefully, "trying to explain that she was in no way to blame, that the sun had scorched her needlessly, that she passionately wanted to live, that she was still young and could be beautiful, if it were not for the heat and the drought."[26]

Throughout, Egorushka's impressions of the landscapes are supplemented by impersonal digressions designed to intensify the sense of limitless expanses and to infuse the image of the steppe with additional attributes of a huge organism bound in immobility and powerlessness. In monotonous repetition, like a refrain, the words "you drive on and on..." introduces each of these digressions. You drive on and on and you are unable to tell where in the purplish haze of the horizon the hills end and the sky begins. At night, you drive on and on and you sense the passionate desire of this beautiful, austere land to live; you sense the steppe crying out that her strength and beauty are going to waste, neglected and untended; you hear her "calling mournfully and hopelessly for a bard to sing her praises."[27]

Toward sundown on the first day of the trip Egorushka witnesses a feeble, futile attempt of the steppe to free itself. The land, the hills, and the air, their strength and their patience worn, seem unable to bear the oppression any longer and attempt "to throw off the yoke." A strong gust of wind suddenly whirls across the steppe. Thunder growls in the distance. One small, final effort, it seems "and the steppe would win. But the invisible, oppressive force regained its grip over wind and air, smoothed the dust, and restored quiet. The wind died, the parched hills glowered, and the air grew still in resignation."[28]

Egorushka's uncle, the wool merchant Ivan Ivanovich Kuzmichev, is the principal character in control of the trip. He is all sobriety and business acumen. To seek for anything but pecuniary gain is beyond the range of his interests. Acquisitive greed is the invisible force holding him in its grip. He pays little attention to his nephew during the trip for he considers his sister's desire to provide the boy with a higher education as a foolish waste of time and money. Kuzmichev's mind is fully absorbed by his mercenary venture, by concern for the safety of his wool already en route in a convoy of carts, and by his intent to contact and to negotiate with the powerful and elusive Varlamov, a wealthy sheep breeder and dealer who is constantly on the go among his vast landholdings.

On the first evening of the trip Egorushka witnesses a real protest against the wrongs and abuses of monetary power, a protest just as ineffectual as the efforts of the steppe he had just watched to throw off the oppressive heat. The travelers stop at a tavern owned by the Jew Moses and Kuzmichev is told that his wool carts have passed as scheduled. When he hears that Varlamov is supposed to be stopping at a nearby farmstead, he decides to continue his pursuit of the local magnate without delay. Moses is the epitome of sycophantic deference and servility. After displaying hysterical jubilation over the visit of such rare and illustrious guests as Kuzmichev and Father Christopher, after expressing awe at Egorushka as a future savant, he subsides into moaning outcries of abysmal misery on hearing that the visit will be short.

A very different reception is in store for the travelers at the hands of Moses' brother and assistant, Solomon. Bringing the large tea tray into the gloomy room, he strains to display utter contempt for the guests, a derisive and arrogant smile frozen on his face. He is unimpressed at the sight of Kuzmichev emptying a large bag filled with money on the table to sort and count the ruble notes by denominations. Solomon's defiant demeanor stand in sharp contrast to his ludicrously puny build and skimpy, careless attire. The contrast is so glaring that Egorushka decides that "Solomon assumed a provocative stance and a sneering, scornful expression on purpose, in order to play the fool and to amuse the dear guests."[29]

But the earnestness of Solomon's countenance becomes apparent even to Egorushka when he hears him expounding his philosophy of life in response to Father Christopher's inquiry as to how he is getting along: "How am I getting along? The same as everybody else. You see that I am a servant. I am my brother's servant, and my brother is the travelers' servant, and the travelers are Varlamov's servants, and if I had ten millions, then Varlamov would be my servant.... He would make as big a fool of himself before me as Moses is making before you.... His [Varlamov's] whole life centers on money and profits, whereas I burnt my money in the stove. I need neither money nor land nor sheep nor people to be afraid of me and to take their hats off when I pass them. This means that I am wiser than your Varlamov and more of a human being."[30]

Agitated and embarrassed by his brother's arrogance and lack of respect for the distinguished guests, Moses hastens to blame such discourse on Solomon's deranged mind, adding plaintively that the imbecile did indeed commit an inheritance of six thousand rubles to the flames. Did Chekhov intend this puny, pitiful, and yet imperious and independent little man to mimic the gestures of Dostoevsky's Nastasia Filipovna in *The Idiot*—the proud, wronged beauty who throws a hundred thousand rubles into the fire as a challenge to the greed of her suitors, testing their eagerness to retrieve the money? But neither Kuzmichev nor Father Christopher comprehend Solomon's behavior, his words fall on deaf ears and his rebellious stance is brushed aside.

The carriage resumes its journey, Kuzmichev carefully guarding his bulging moneybag. Darkness has settled over the steppe when the briskly-stepping horses catch up with the lumbering wool convoy and stop alongside the caravan of carts laden high with bales of wool. Eager to continue his relentless pursuit of Varlamov and to free himself of the responsibility for his nephew, Kuzmichev bids the six drivers to let the boy spend the rest of the trip with them. Hoisted to the top of the last cart of the caravan, Egorushka finds that the bales of wool provide a comfortable bed and, on the following morning, an excellent vantage point from which to get a first glimpse of his travelling companions, whom he later comes to know more closely during rest periods.

There are six of them, each in charge of three carts and marching along their assigned vehicles. Chekhov gives us here a bird's-eye view of the Russian "tumbleweeds" roaming restlessly across the land. This phalanx strung along the road exemplifies successive stages of human life, each figure exhibiting a singled-out aspect of the human condition, its potentialities and frustrations. There is the old gray-haired Panteley, marching near the tail end of the caravan, a devout Old Believer, his face stern and pensive, his bare feet stepping stiffly as if they are used to very cold weather and even his lips moving in a frozen cadence as he expresses his approval of Egorushka's destination and then tells the boy of his own hard life and the tragedy of losing his wife and children in a fire. Ahead of Panteley walks Emelian, a man in the neighborhood of forty, strangely waving his right hand and the whip in his left as if he is directing a choir. He lost his beautiful voice after a severe chill that weakened his vocal chords and can no longer engage in his favorite pastime of singing in a church choir. Snatches of melodies, of religious chants, and choral prayers are now constantly passing through his head. Unable to communicate with his voice, he expresses his obsession with their polyphonous harmony and spirituality by directing an imaginary choir and by trying to find the right words to convince his companions in a hoarse, whispery voice of the beauty of the musical chords pent up in his soul and begging to be released. This recalls the novice Ieronim in "On Easter Night," who describes the beauty of religious canticles and music to the narrator.

While Emelian is trying to cope with the frustration of his

vocal deficiency, Vasia, the third driver, joyfully exhibits a rare gift. He is endowed with exceptionally keen eyesight, which permits him to observe the life of the steppe, the movements of animals and birds, in intimate and minute details hidden from normal human vision. "Thanks to such keen eyesight, besides the world which everyone could see, Vasia had another world, his own, accessible to no one and, no doubt a very pleasant one, for when he rejoiced in transport over what he saw, it was difficult not to envy him."[31]

Sheer animal vitality, strength, and recklessness distinguish Dymov, the fourth driver. In his thirties, broad shouldered and curly haired, he is the handsomest in the group. Bursting with pent-up energy, possessed of a rebellious, independent disposition, "his wild mocking eye roamed along the road, the convoy, the sky, never resting anywhere as if seeking, out of boredom, something to kill or to laugh at."[32] He shocks his companions and Egorushka by pouncing savagely and killing a harmless snake he detects in the grass. Eighteen-year-old Stepka and the stocky, blackbearded, abysmally stupid Kiriukha complete the drivers' group.

Chekhov masterfully differentiates the speech of these men. Like a forceful chorus it reflects and modulates the tonality of various modes of unhappiness and discontent. There is resignation and a simple faith in divine providence in old Panteley's approach to life. He has a kind word for everyone, his speech is tinged with ecclesiastical parlance and interspersed with frequent references to saints' images and religious celebrations, not unlike Father Christopher, whom—Chekhov tells us—Panteley resembles in "his gaunt and undersized build." A strain of hopelessness, born of nostalgia for his lost voice and hankering for the beauty of the music he is no longer able to reproduce, runs through Emelian's utterances. Vasia retreats into contemplating the creature-world of the steppe, deploring Dymov's cruelty in needlessly killing the snake and later lovingly commenting on the antics of a fox he alone is able to detect in the distance. Dymov and Kiriukha are, at times, the loudest in the group, Dymov shouting a string of obscenities into the wind and hooting ribaldly after discovering Egorushka's presence in the convoy that old Panteley had given birth to a boy during the night. As to Kiriukha, when his loud voice is carried by the echo of the steppe, "it seemed as if stupidity personified had rolled past, borne on heavy wheels."[33] During the first midday stop shared by Egorushka with the cart drivers, the various strains of malcontent are voiced and blended in such a crescendo as to convince the boy that he has landed in the midst of exceptionally unfortunate people. The plaintive song of the parched grass held captive by the heat which Egorushka imagined he had heard, the cry of the steppe for release, for life unfettered, for strength unleashed, come to mind.

The personage who holds sway over the steppe and its people comes briefly into Egorushka's view on the third day of the trip. When the boy awakes before sunrise he is told by Panteley that the man he sees talking to two of the drivers at the head of the convoy is Varlamov. Slightly built, past middle age, clad in a suit of cheap gray fabric, and mounted on an ungainly horse, wearing an expression as dry and businesslike as Egorushka's uncle, he yet exudes an air of importance and self-confidence and lacks Kuzmichev's constant expression of worry and fear. Egorushka witnesses a show of the powerful man's violent temper. A messenger, galloping at full speed from a settlement visible in the distance, arrived without bringing an important paper impatiently awaited by his master. Shouting angrily at the messenger to be gone, Varlamov menacingly swings his whip at him, a gesture that sends a tremor of cowed despondence through the culprit and spreads submissive dismay through the group of cart drivers watching the scene.

Chekhov does not tell us whether Kuzmichev succeeds in catching up with Varlamov. Kuzmichev does speak of profits made but frets that they could have been more substantial had he been better informed about differences in local price levels. It is Father Christopher who stands out in the story in his loving simplicity and serene contentment with the world. He is the only one pleased with the results of the trip. He is delighted with his wool sale, anticipating the pleasure of the profit the transaction will bring to his son-in-law, on whose behalf he has undertaken the trip. Full of solicitous concern for Egorushka and his education, he is the one who tends and comforts the boy when he arrives at his final destination, after having been terrified, drenched, and chilled in a violent thunderstorm, magnificently described, on the third day of the journey. Meanwhile, Kuzmichev settles arrangements for Egorushka's lodging and school enrollment and is anxious to start on the return trip, eager to continue at home his relentless pursuit of business deals.

With the exception of one episode yet to be discussed, "The Steppe" does not offer directional signals. Other, shorter stories of Chekhov's concerned with the image of a road and the flow of time reintroduced point more explicitly toward experiences denied within the confining walls of Chekhov's symbolic houses. The rare and momentous encounters when the barriers of isolation between Chekhov's characters break down, when the chilling paralysis of indifference is replaced by moments of warming human rapport and concern, all occur "on the road." "On the Road," in fact, is the title of the story concerning the chance meeting between the sympathetic young woman Ilovaiskaia and the dissolute middle-aged Likharev in a wayside inn—a meeting that just misses turning into a more lasting relationship.

While some of Chekhov's protagonists, trapped in domestic enclosures, become blind to temporal reality, immobilized by their inability to accept change and the flow of time, others move along a road and are granted realistic, retrospective glimpses of the passage of time, of the links between past and present. The old wood carver Petrov in "Grief" (1885) is driving his dying wife to the hospital in a snowstorm so severe that it is impossible to tell whether the snow is falling from the sky or rising from the ground. "When Petrov observes that the snowflakes landing on the woman's face do not melt, he realizes that she is dead. And the forty years of his married life suddenly spread before his eyes like a vast wasteland, an unending stream of drunken stupors and mistreatment of this meek and humble woman. A similar revelation comes to Iakov in "Rothschild's Fiddle" during the walk he takes after his wife's funeral—a startling assessment of fifty years spent in domestic wranglings, violent outbursts, and drinking bouts while opportunities for simple enjoyment were missed and the beauty of the surrounding countryside passed unnoticed.

It is when the image of a road is associated with the concept of light, the third recurrent symbol in Chekhov's fiction, that it acquires its greatest significance.

But what kind of light? A positive, inspiring use of light shining from a house is rejected in "A House with a Mezzanine." The lamp lit and later extinguished on the upper story where Misius lived heralded the conflict with her sister Lida. But before this confrontation, decisive and crushing for the heroine as it is, the light figures in a negative allegory in the same story, in the argument between the narrating artist and Lida about the value of personal endeavors to alleviate the plight of the peasantry by servicing local health and educational centers. Lida strongly supports the policy while the artist says that philanthropy on a local scale is ineffective, even harmful; it only adds new links to the chains, new financial burdens to be met by the people. "Teaching peasants how to read and write, books with insignificant precepts and mots, medical clinics, cannot reduce ignorance or the death rate any more than the light from your windows can light this huge garden."[34]

We have to look outside confining enclosures to find luminous symbols suggestive of release, guidance, liberation in Chekhov's fiction. Could the early story "The Lights" point the way? The title stems from workmen's shacks and barracks lighted along and around the half-finished embankment of a railroad under construction. The string of lights stretches as far as the horizon above a chaotic landscape of earth upturned, heaps of sand, clay and gravel piled high, pieces of equipment scattered about, and neat rows of slender telegraph posts rising incongruously above the disarray—the scene of beginning industrial advance that the narrator likens to "primeval chaos." "An important mystery seemed to be buried under the embankment, known only to the lights, the darkness and the [telegraph] wires."[35] Early in the story the lights and the scene they frame evoke a comparison with an ancient, Old Testament camp of warriors preparing for an early morning battle. The comparison is made by the young engineering student Von Stenberg, who is working as an assistant on the construction job. A confirmed pessimist and skeptic—"mental apathy" written on his face, according to the narrator—he expresses his view of the senselessness of human existence and his refusal to believe in anything, for "words can prove or disprove anything, and soon linguistic technique will be perfected to such an extent that mathematical calculations will prove two times two to equal seven."[36]

But the construction engineer Ananiev likens the lights to human thoughts. "You know," he says to the narrator, "the thoughts of every single individual are scattered just like this in disorder, they stretch in a line amidst darkness toward a distant goal and, having failed to illuminate anything, to light the darkness, disappear somewhere far beyond old age...."[37] This comparison follows upon Ananiev's story of his youthful adventure when he callously seduced a trusting and unhappily married woman and the startling discovery he made at that time of the power of conscience as an active agent stimulating thought and, in his case, arousing remorse for his dishonorable behavior, a behavior "tantamount to murder."

In the early morning of the following day the two comparisons concerning the lights made by Von Stenberg and Ananiev come to mind again. Ananiev's thoughts seem indeed to be scattered in disorder and to illuminate nothing. His actions no longer seem to follow the dictates of conscience as he claimed on the preceding night in his story. For he roughly and callously refuses assistance to an exhausted peasant who is vainly trying to deliver a cargo of railroad equipment, his horses starving after two days without food and futile trips along the line trying to find where the equipment belongs. Ananiev's insensitive and puzzling behavior occurs in the midst of a modern assault to conquer space with railroad tracks. But hasn't human behavior always been irrational, Chekhov seems to say, as irrational in modern times as it undoubtedly was centuries ago, in the military camps of biblical antiquity which the lights had brought to the mind of the young student Von Stenberg? The narrator's confusion and inability to provide a comprehensive analysis of what he witnessed and recorded is summed up in his concluding remark: "You cannot make head or tail of anything in this world."[38] The mystery that seemed to be buried under the railroad embankment remains unsolved. Lights as symbols of human thought, lights strung along a new type of road made possible through the advent of the machine age, have failed to dissipate darkness. Can they be used to suggest experiences beyond the realm of rationality and reason?

It is indicative of Chekhov's abhorrence of preaching, of presenting the reader with ready answers and spelled-out conclusions, that it is one of his least attractive protagonists whom he permits to deliver a loud and impassioned sermon on the function of light as a spiritual symbol. Misail's father in "My Life," the architect who has imposed his seal of tastelessness and mediocrity on the appearance of an entire town, addresses his son in an attempt to dissuade him from becoming a manual laborer: "Get it through your head...that besides brute physical force you also possess a divine spirit, a sacred flame that sets you far apart from an ass or a reptile and bestows upon you an affinity with the deity. This flame was nurtured for thousands of years by the best among mankind. Your great-grandfather Poloznev was a general and fought at Borodino, your grandfather was a poet, a public speaker, a marshal of the nobility, your uncle is an educator, and lastly, I, your father, am an architect. All Poloznevs nurtured the sacred flame just so you could extinguish it!... Anyone can work with his hands, even a complete idiot or a criminal. Such work is the hallmark of slaves and barbarians, while the flame is granted only to a few."[39]

Misail's reaction to these words is to strip them of any

impact or significance. He claims that his father's reference to "the sacred flame" is but an arrogant rhetorical pretext brought forth to disguise the shame and disgrace his father would suffer should he, Misail, become a manual laborer. But the accompanying elitism, the assertion that the sacred flame is granted but to a few prominent members of the human race, is removed from other protagonists of Chekhov's whose spiritual experiences are referred to as luminous and compared to the phenomenon of light. Moreover, Chekhov never speaks in this connection of a flame (*ogon'*) as Misail's father did; it is always the diminutive (*ogonek*) he uses—a glimmer, a flicker, a faint and unsteady glint.

Doctor Khruschev in *The Wood Demon* tells Sonia that he has found his *ogonek*—his love for her is his guiding beacon, the reward for all his misfortunes. "If you walk at night in the woods," he tells her in the second act, "and you see a small light far ahead of you, you will feel, for some reason, such well-being that you will forget exhaustion and you won't mind the darkness or the prickly branches that hit you in the face."[40] But by the time Chekhov reworked *The Wood Demon* into *Uncle Vania* the role of a beacon guiding man through a dark forest has changed. Though, like Khruschev, Astrov tells Sonia in the second act of the bracing effects a distant light glimmering in the forest can produce, he continues in a different, despairing key, for he himself has stopped looking and searching: "But I see no *ogonek* in the distance. I no longer expect anything for myself, I do not like people.... It's been a long time since I loved anyone.... Spontaneous, pure, unfettered attitudes toward nature, toward people, no longer exist."[41]

In "Ionych" an agonizingly brief flare-up of an inner glow takes place in Doctor Startsev's consciousness. He meets Ekaterina Ivanovna four years after her refusal to marry him. Though he is no longer in love with her, he is overcome by memories of the night she had proposed a rendezvous in the cemetery and then failed to keep it, memories of the intensity of his desires on that long past, aborted tryst. "He remembered everything that had happened, he remembered all the minutest details, how he wandered about the cemetery, how later, toward dawn, exhausted, he wended his way homeward, and he was suddenly overcome with sadness and nostalgia. A small light began to glimmer in his soul."[42] The light grows stronger as the memories crowd about him. He shares them with Ekaterina Ivanovna and then shifts to complaints about the doldrums of his present existence. But when he remembers the pleasure he experiences in the evenings counting the bank notes collected from his patients, "the glimmer in his soul is extinguished."[43] He takes his leave, resumes his routine, and continues, unchecked, on his way of physical and emotional deterioration. His physical and moral decline is measured throughout the story by his growing inability to wander on foot "in a dark forest"—as the Wood Demon did seeing the glimmer of his love for Sonia ahead of him—and his reliance on showy, elaborate means of transportation, ending with a troika driven by an impressive coachman.

So far, we have seen Chekhov's use of lighting effects bringing no sustained illumination. Neither lights burning in a house nor lights symbolizing intellectual experiences nor glimmers suggestive of emotional stirrings in Chekhov's fiction are strong enough or durable enough to serve as substantive, arresting spectacles and inspirational beacons symbolically linked to roads. Bonfires are such beacons. In "Three Years" we are given a passage hinting at their function. Julia, the heroine, is visiting an art exhibit with her husband and stops before a small landscape. In the painting, a log bridge leads across a brook to a footpath that disappears in a field. On the right there is a bonfire near a stretch of forest, and in the distance a sunset glows in the darkening sky. Julia feels strangely attracted by the quiet scene. She begins to feel that she has already seen this very same landscape with the fire blinking in the distance "a long time ago and frequently." She longs to relive the experience, "to go on and on along the path; and where the sunset glowed, there lay the reflection of *something unearthly, eternal.*"[44] (Italics are mine.)

Burning freely in open spaces, contrasting with the darkness closing in all around them, the glow of Chekhov's bonfires reaches far beyond the bounds of the respective stories in which they can be seen. What is spoken and acted out around the fires stands like separate, independent scenes lifted out of the drama of human existence, stages set to voice and illuminate issues central to Chekhov's view of the world. In each case, the seasonal setting, the environmental background, the nature of the road leading to it, even the intensity of the flames are all atune with the thoughts voiced and the mood that prevails.

The first such beacon in Chekhov's fiction is the bonfire on the warm summer night in "The Steppe." The "actors" are the boy Egorushka and the cart drivers to whose care Egorushka has been entrusted for the remainder of his trip across the steppe. The midday stop and the bonfire lit to cook a noontime meal serve as a prelude to the scene, orchestrating the mood of unhappiness and dissatisfaction of the participants which will prevail at night. Before darkness settles over the site Egorushka notices two dilapidated crosses nearby, flanking the road. They mark the graves of two merchants, he is told, who were robbed and murdered on this spot. These "stage props" contribute to the atmosphere of gloom and mystery and steer the conversation among the drivers to horror stories of hideous killings by gangs of bandits and tales of miraculous escapes, all obviously embellished by the imagination of old Panteley, who is the teller, yet readily accepted as truth by his audience assembled around the fire. For "real life is terrifying and wondrous" and Chekhov goes on to comment that the unreality of a fable or a fairy tale pales before the true facts of life in Russia and easily blends with actuality.[45] This is an arresting echo of Dostoevsky's conviction that reality is infinitely more fantastic than anything the human imagination is capable of creating.

Approaching footsteps rustling in the grass and snapping brittle weed stalks usher in the scene. The flames burn so brightly that the surrounding darkness is intensified and hangs like an impenetrable divide. And then, as if a stage curtain had been lifted, a man steps into the circle of light.

Strangely, the first thing that everyone notices is not his face and not his clothes but his smile. "It was an incredibly warm, broad, and gentle smile like that of a wakening child, one of those infectious smiles which it is difficult not to reciprocate."[46] The stranger turns out to be a man of about thirty, distinguished neither by good looks nor by any other remarkable characteristics. Invited to share the meal, he joins the group and starts to eat absent mindedly, still smiling, apparently absorbed in some very pleasant thoughts, not caring about the taste of the food and oblivious of his surroundings. A few questions about his identity bring him back to reality. Warming to the interest he aroused he tells the cart drivers that he has been married for just eighteen days and that his wife has gone to visit her mother for a short while. He finds the separation unbearable and wanders now aimlessly around the neighborhood awaiting her return. Now hardly able to contain his happiness, brimming over with exuberant joy, excitement, and triumph, he tells the men the story of his courtship. It took him three years to win the girl, three years of agonizing endeavors and attempts at persuasion. And it was finally "words" that won her consent, he says, "a whole hour of words." But when he is asked what kind of words he used, he does not remember— just words that poured forth "like water out of a gutter."[47] Since then he feels speechless in her presence.

Everyone now clearly understands that "this was a man in love, a happy man, happy to the point of distraction; his smile, his eyes, his every gesture expressed close to unbearable happiness." And everyone fell silent, pensive and sad, reminded of his own loneliness and dissatisfaction with life and longing to feel what this stranger who had stepped up to the bonfire feels. For it is a fable turned to reality, a pure vision of love that stands there in the circle of light, a vision of that magic force in human life, that supreme expression of man's total self which cannot be defined in words, a vision magic and yet real and pure—pure because it is so young and so new that it has not yet been touched by the malfunction of marriage so prevalent in Chekhov's fiction, not affected by pain, disappointment, resignation or marred by a sense of entrapment, even devoid of any indication whether it is reciprocated or not.

The scene ends and the curtain falls as the fire dies down. In the glow of the last red coals the two crosses by the wayside become clearly visible again and gloom returns to envelop the stage. In the distance another fire burns where someone else is probably cooking a meal. As the drivers get ready to continue their trip, the man in love bids them farewell and sets off toward the distant glow. "And he soon vanished in the darkness, and for a long while his steps could be heard receding in the direction where the light shone and where he would tell other strangers about his happiness."[48]

Autumnal chill, a feeling of desolate dampness, and a foreboding of approaching winter prevail in the second bonfire scene, in the story "In Exile." The two convicts, old Semen the Sensible and the Tartar "whose name no one knows," are warming themselves by a fire on the river's bank. Ice has begun to form on the water, the first snow has been falling intermittently since morning, and soon the ferry that connects the two river banks will stop operating and the two convict exiles who work as oarsmen will be out of work and forced to go begging or seeking occasional employment in the neighboring villages.

Ill and desperately homesick, the young Tartar bemoans his unfair lot which separated him from his beautiful wife, while old Semen, stimulated by the vodka he is consuming, expounds his conviction that "if you want to be happy you must, first of all, wish for nothing." He tells of a convicted gentleman he knew who refused to submit to his fate and who was rewarded with bitter disappointments and paid with growing debility for his futile efforts to better his lot. The "sensible" Semen delights in relating the pain and harm inevitably resulting from such foolish grapplings with fate. But the Tartar strenuously objects. In his halting and faulty Russian, groping for words, trembling and stammering, straining to make himself clear, he voices his readiness to endure any amount of suffering if God would only grant him just one day, or even one hour, to be with his wife. Better one day of happiness than nothing.

As if to strengthen Semen's arguments, the traveler whom the ferry is summoned to transport from the opposite bank turns out to be the gentleman whose misguided efforts at exerting his own will Semen has been discussing. Gloomy and obviously distraught, he tells Semen of new misfortunes he is trying to ward off. Semen delights in the sight of the desperate, desolate man and his living proof of the futility of human desires and personal endeavors to give life a volitional direction. But the Tartar "looking at Sensible with hatred and disgust," bursts out again, interspersing his broken Russian with Tartar words: "He good...good, and you—bad! You bad! Gentleman a good soul, excellent, and you a beast, you bad! Gentleman alive and you dead...God made man to be alive, have joy, have sadness, have grief... and you want nothing, so you not alive, you a stone, you clay! Stone needs nothing and you need nothing. You a stone— and God no love you, but love gentleman."[49]

More than the other bonfire scenes this one depends on the "stage" effects of sounds. We hear chunks of ice striking against the sides of the barge. We hear the laughter of the ferrymen exploding over the Tartar's naive and inarticulate defense of desires. We hear his weeping that "sounds like the howling of a dog" after the ferrymen leave him alone by the fire and go to their hut to catch some sleep. We hear Semen's final verdict, "he will get used to it," in response to the weeping. And we hear a gust of wind flinging the door of the hut open, the door that no one bothers to close. All these sounds intensify the sense of remoteness of the scene, of desires neglected and their value ill understood. The road that brought the actors of this scene to the bonfire is long indeed, reaching all the way from distant Russian villages to this Siberian outpost. But it is the solitary, weeping figure of the nameless and destitute Tartar, lit by the bonfire, and his artless but all the more poignant defense of human will, courage, and the need to wish that stand as the luminous finale of the scene.

The third momentous bonfire is to be found on the Good

Friday described in "The Student," a joyous sequel to the gloomy scene of "In Exile." A raw, penetrating wind intensifies the cold of the early spring evening. The flames of the fire are bright but not as bright and blinding as those in "The Steppe." They illuminate, in a wide circle, the ploughed land of two village garden plots, the soil tended and ready for spring planting and a new growing season. The garden plots belong to two widowed women who are present at the scene, Vasilisa and her daughter Lukeria, two figures brightly differentiated by their age, character, and even by their posture. Vasilisa, a tall and stout old woman with mild and friendly ways and a measure of refinement in her speech, with manners acquired while she was employed as a nurse in a gentile household, stands lost in thought and gazing at the flames. Her daughter Lukeria, small and pock marked, taciturn and reticent, beaten down by mistreatment at the hands of her late husband and retaining her peasant bearing, is sitting and washing the cooking utensils used in preparing their supper.

It is warmth rather than light that the fire offers to the divinity student Ivan Velikopolsky, who steps up stretching his numbed fingers toward the flames and greets the two women whom he knows well. Chekhov introduces him by name only once, at the beginning of the story. Throughout the rest of the narrative he is referred to as "the student." The first part of the scene at the bonfire is even closer to being a monologue than the episode of the man in love in "The Steppe." The only word coming from the two women is a brief, affirmative reply by Vasilisa when the student asks whether she has attended the noon service of that holy day. It is as if Ivan wished to recreate a passion play in drawing a parallel between the present environment and the first Good Friday nineteen centuries before, a play that turns into a wordless revelation of portentous import for "the student."

It is not the drama of the Crucifixion he dwells on; it is the tragedy of human weakness, of faltering virtue of the saintly figure of the Apostle Peter, his triple denial of Jesus after he was betrayed by Judas and led away to the high priest that

Ivan describes. It was cold then too, Ivan tells the two women. There was a bonfire in the yard of the high priest and Peter was warming himself just the way he, Ivan, is doing now. And it was by the light of that bonfire that people recognized Peter and drove him thrice to deny knowing Jesus. In stark, simple words, drawing on quotations from the Gospel which, as a divinity student, he knows so well, Ivan conveys the depth of Peter's despair, pain, and remorse and his foreboding that something terrible is about to happen on earth. "He loved Jesus passionately, to distraction, yet witnessed now from afar how He was being beaten.... The Gospel says," continues Ivan, "and Peter went out and wept bitterly! I can just see it: a very quiet and very dark garden and in the stillness—barely audible, suppressed sobs."[50]

The women's response is wordless but overwhelms Ivan with its intensity and depth of feeling. Vasilisa suddenly utters a sob and large tears start to streak down her cheeks. She shields her face from the fire with her sleeve as if ashamed of her tears. Lukeria stops washing the spoons she holds, turning red, staring at Ivan and seeming to be suppressing an acute pain. Ivan takes his leave and is immediately surrounded by darkness again. The cold wind is still blowing but he is filled with new joy and vigor, inwardly warmed by his experience, by the spectacle, illuminated by the fire, of the majestic bond, the luminous thread, that appears to span the centuries. He knows that it was not his eloquence that made Vasilisa cry and touched Lukeria's heart. The emotions displayed by the two women, so different in age and temperament, bore proof of their compassion and closeness to the Apostle Peter and the events in the Garden of Gethsemane. It was not thought of prayer, of inspiring religious exploits, that caught the imagination of the two women. No emulation occurred but rather a reliving, a sharing of remorse, a rush of tender pity for a show of human weakness in a saint's earthly path, his will stumbling and erring as painfully as that of any ordinary mortal. This scene is one of Chekhov's highest tributes to the basic tenet of Russian Orthodoxy—the stress on compassion for the weak, on mercy for human failings.[51]

It is this blend of human and divine, this evidence of the never-ceasing intersection of the eternal and temporal worlds, the continuous link between past and present, that filled Ivan with such joy that he had to stop for a moment "to catch his breath"—like Ieronim in "On Easter Night" perhaps, speaking of the breath-taking beauty of the holy phrase? Ivan felt that "...what happened nineteen centuries ago was relevant to the present, to the two women and, probably, to this forsaken village, to himself, to all human beings."[52] And he saw this continuity as a chain: "It seemed to him that he had just seen both ends of the chain; he had touched one end and the other end had moved."[53] These words are almost identical with those of Dostoevsky's Father Zossima, who likened the connection between temporal and eternal worlds to an ocean: "Everything flows and touches—a touch in one place reverberates in another end of the world."[54]

It is difficult to say whether the barely glimmering glow of the dying bonfire by the wayside in "In the Ravine" is more memorable than the bright and warming flames illuminating the other three scenes. The fading light imparts an aura of visionary irreality to the setting. Death rules the center of the stage. Lipa sets out on this Calvary at sunset carrying her dead infant, scalded with boiling water by her jealous sister-in-law Aksinia, home from the hospital. The light radiating from the red coals is barely sufficient to guide her toward the old man and the boy who are getting ready to extinguish the fire, to hitch their horses to their two wagons, and continue on their way. Trying to lighten the burden of her grief, Lipa tells the old man about the tragedy. His response is slow and measured. Only after helping the boy to find a missing shaftbow does he approach Lipa by the light of a glowing coal he had picked up and blown on to fan a flame. Only his eyes and nose are lit for a brief moment before the flame dies and darkness spreads, as the boy stamps on the glimmering ashes of the bonfire. But the brief flicker of the flame suffices to let Lipa see pity and tenderness in the old man's eyes. Though the ensuing exchange takes place in darkness, the thoughts and words spring from that fleeting instant of illumination and continue to blend the sublime with the pedestrian.

"Are you saints?" rings the humble, naive voice of the young mother, holding her dead child in her arms and groping for emotional succor in her boundless grief, drawn by the old man's silent and compassionate though seemingly casual stance. "No, we are from Firsanovo," comes the simple answer, and the tone is set for Chekhov's poetic answer, removed from the realm of terrestrial, temporal causality, to the same question that tormented Dostoevsky's Ivan Karamazov and drove him to a rational revolt and intellectual rejection of a God who permitted the suffering of innocent babes. Even if he is not a saint, perhaps the old man has an answer to that question. Why should a sinless child suffer for a whole day before dying? asks Lipa after accepting a lift. No one knows, he replies, as if eliminating all possibilities of finding a solution on the level of human rationality. For a half hour they drive in silence and then the old man picks up the thread of his calm and humble thoughts on human limitations. "It is not possible to know everything, how and what for," he begins. "A bird has only two wings and not four because two are enough to fly with; and man may not know everything, but only one half or one fourth, just enough to get through life."[55] And the old man launches into a hymn of praise for life, its richness, the vastness of earthly space, the innumerable roads open to exploration, the inevitable blend of good and bad, sorrow and happiness. And in the background there is the accompaniment of nightingales, cuckoos, and frogs singing and shouting of the joy, the ecstasy, and the brevity of existence.

And Lipa heeds the words of the old man, though he is not a saint; she apprehends the mystery of life, the vista he opens before her eyes of a world unknowable beyond the realm of reason, of time and space. Of all the principal "actors" in the bonfire scenes she remains in our field of vision the longest; in fact, she ranks high, perhaps highest, in the roster of Chekhov's immortal creations. The man in love and the student of the eternal drama of weakness and remorse vanish into darkness after leaving the stage, and our last glimpse of the Tartar defending human will is that of a huddled figure weeping and howling like a dog. But Lipa marches on along the road of life in a nimbus of all-forgiving pity and humility. At the end of "In the Ravine," three years after the murder of Lipa's child, the last rays of a setting sun light her way down the winding road which leads to the village at the bottom of the ravine. She is returning from a day's work at the brick factory, free and at peace with the world, singing merrily as she walks along, looking up at the sky "as though triumphant and exultant that at last the day is over and time for rest at hand."[56] Just before the last glow of the sunset vanishes she sees her father-in-law coming toward her, in whose house the murder of her child was perpetrated. He too is now destitute and driven to begging by the same villainous Aksinia who had poured boiling water over the baby. Neither rancor nor ill will mar Lipa's greeting him. With a deep bow she thrusts some food into his eager hand and continues on her way, crossing herself as she goes, an embodiment of the humility which, according to Dostoevsky, was the highest form of freedom and the most powerful force on earth. It is the highest crescendo of the melody of freedom which we hear from her lips.

Notes

[1]   IX, 198.
[2]   Ibid.
[3]   IX, 278.
[4]   VIII, 121.
[5]   VIII, 124.
[6]   VII, 460.
[7]   IX, 189.
[8]   XII, 171.

9   XII, 151.
10   X, 127.
11   Ibid.
12   VII, 32.
13   Ibid.
14   XIII, 182.
15   VI, 365.
16   Ibid.
17   Ibid.
18   Letter to Stanislavsky, Nov. 5, 1903, L., XI, 298.
19   XIII, 199.
20   XIII, 252.
21   XIII, 247.
22   XIII, 252.
23   XIII, 178-9.
24   VI, 263.
25   VII, 26.
26   VII, 24.
27   VII, 46.
28   VII, 29-30.
29   VII, 36.
30   VII, 39-40.
31   VII, 56.
32   VII, 36.
33   VII, 78.
34   IX, 185.
35   VII, 106.
36   VII, 138.
37   Ibid.
38   VII, 140.
39   IX, 193.
40   XII, 156.
41   XIII, 84.
42   X, 38.
43   X, 39.
44   IX, 65-66.
45   VII, 72-3.
46   VII, 74.
47   VII, 77.
48   VII, 79.
49   VIII, 49-50.

[50] VIII, 308.

[51] See Georges Florovsky, *Christianity and Culture*, Ch. VI, "The Social Problem in the Eastern Orthodox Church."

[52] VIII, 309.

[53] Ibid.

[54] Dostoevsky, *Sobranie Sochinenii*, 10 Vols. Moscow, 1956-57, IX, 400.

[55] X, 175.

[56] X, 180.

Epilogue:

Silence

In all four bonfire scenes the speech of the protagonists is relegated to an auxiliary role, supporting but not dominating the impact sought by the author on the reader. The central effect is visual, not oral. The burning fires, leaping briskly or glimmering dimly in the surrounding darkness, illuminate in Rembrandt-like fashion human experiences, thoughts, and emotions.

The faces grouped around the bonfire in "The Steppe" are dazzled by the radiant smile of "the man in love" who steps so suddenly into the circle of light, displaying his total immersion in ecstatic happiness. He recalls the decisive hour he spent pleading with his woman, the whole hour of words that "gushed like water from a spout" and swayed her finally to consent to marry him. But he no longer considers this verbal exertion as relevant and cannot even remember what it was that he said, feeling now "speechless in her presence."

The young Tartar in the second bonfire scene champions human desires and endurance in spite of his abject misery. He is illiterate and couches his thoughts in jumbled, stammered outcries, barely intelligible in his stumbling search for the right word, which he finds intermittently in his native tongue.

The soliloquy by the bonfire in "The Student" is considered by the speaker himself to be lacking in significance. He feels that the impact of his words rests with the content and not with the delivery. It is the biblical event itself, conjured in the consciousness of his two listeners that brings their mute but moving response.

In the fourth scene, the pity of the old peasant from Firsanovo for Lipa's grief is revealed in the brief flicker of a glowing coal; and the artless words of the "saint," filled with tender compassion and intuitive reverence for the mystery of life and the universality of pain, words that refute any possibility of finding sustaining answers in rational analyses of life's vicissitudes, is preceded by a half hour of meditative silence.

Would Chekhov have agreed with the avant-garde composer John Cage that there is no such thing as silence? Since there is no such thing as an empty space or an empty time? Since there is always something to see and something to hear? Cage argues that silence in a musical composition of the eighteenth or nineteenth century was a pause inserted into an otherwise continuous stream of melodically linked notes. This, he claims, forces the listener to respond in a special way to the musical performance. Experimental music, on the other hand, differentiates between sounds notated and sounds not notated and originating in the surrounding environment, such as clatter of machinery, the patter of rain drops, gusts of wind, and scores of other sounds sprung from nature or the handiwork of man. This frees the listener's perception from predetermined judgment, allowing him to find the way for his own individual experience while listening to the performance.

There is an arresting parallel between Cage's endeavors to reach beyond the barriers set by a notated musical score and Chekhov's treatment of the limitations of human speech. Chekhov's "pseudo-silence" is a gateway leading beyond mere cognition to an intuitive perception of his writing, inviting the reader to experience what the author has to say rather than just reading about it. Speech must be lived, not merely spoken and heard. Whenever Chekhov wishes to touch the innermost recesses of his reader's imagination, he resorts to the magical spell of his unspoken imagery—the blank page of an absent ending, a future shrouded in the mists of the unknown, a mute rapport between his protagonists. For this is where genuine freedom is born and nurtured—in the one-to-one confrontation between the reader's consciousness and reality as presented by the artist, the moment of individual reflection, choice, conclusion, where the intellect can be consigned to its proper bounds and a hymn to intuition be sung. Chekhov leaves no doubt, for instance, that "Ionych" is doomed, immobilized by obesity and immersed in selfish pursuits. But will Nina the Seagull reach her goal and become an accomplished, recognized actress? Will Gurov and "the lady with the dog" attain their aim of an enduring, legitimate union? Chekhov does not tell us and leaves the answer to the reader-jury to formulate.

The antipode to the pseudo-silence, to the blank page, the unanswered questions in Chekhov's writing is empty words, words devoid of reflective substance and content, loud, voluble, and superficial discourse, doctrinaire, opinionated utterances and ideas pressed tyranically upon the reader or listener and mindlessly accepted. These Chekhov relentlessly rejected from the very beginning of his writing career. He seems to place empty words on a par with religious rites and symbols stripped of inner substance and meaning.

His first published story, "Letter to a Learned Neighbor" (1880), gleams with silliness, burlesquing the thoughts of a "humble" landowner who deems himself a fierce devotee of science. He has filled his "miserable skull" with "complete sets" of erudite knowledge and speaks of the human species as "respiratory beings." The whole of the epistolary farce is generously spiked with spelling errors.

In Chekhov's last story, "The Betrothed" (1903), the heroine Nadia awakens to the empty rhetoric and clichés used by all those whom she looked up to in the past. She recoils from the hypocrisy of the trite remark of her fiance that "idleness is a sign of the time." She discovers the vapidity of her mother's statements, for instance, that the constant turnover taking place in human life is comparable to the turnover of matter occurring in nature. And then Nadia becomes disenchanted by the verbosity of the revolutionary Sasha, who reiterates the need "to turn life over" without supporting his words with any actions.

In his correspondence Chekhov frequently deplored the political clichés and dogmatic narrow-mindedness he found prevailing in contemporary literary publications. "Clannish, party-oriented boredom reigns in all our literary monthlies," he wrote in January 1888 to the writer and publisher Pleshcheev. "It is stifling! A party line, especially if it is dry and lacking in talent, dislikes freedom and a sweeping elan (*shirokovo razmakha*)." It is surely no coincidence that Chekhov wrote these words precisely at the time when he was also working on "The Steppe," his first major exploration of open space and the lure of doors flung open, his gaze veering away from the confinement and stagnation embodied in his symbolic use of the house.

To light the path of the human individual toward freedom was the supreme goal of his art. He rejected the tyranny of empty words, the aggressiveness of party programs, the mirage of political slogans, all pressures impinging upon independent individual thought and free judgment. It was the censure of flamboyant "fireworks" that struck Leo Shestov and led him to overlook Chekhov's bonfires, to claim that the concept of "Nothing," of a void, reigned supreme in Chekhov's world. But the ideals which Shestov believed to be withering and dying in Chekhov's hands were vibrantly alive and glowing in his art, transposed beyond the reach of mere cognition, beyond transmission by language alone.

It is illuminating, while examining this issue, to draw a comparison with Tolstoy and Dostoevsky, the two giants of the nineteenth century, with whom Chekhov's literary heritage has been linked in an early chapter of this book. The massive productivity of both authors showed little concern for limitations of human speech. Martin Luther's *"Ich kann nicht schweigen"* is applicable to both. Yet each had recourse to silence in a momentous scene. The two are poles apart.

When Anna Karenina, pursued by Vronsky's perseverance, finally yields to his passion, the ecstacy of their first sexual union is left to the imagination of the reader. For close to a year Vronsky's desire to possess Anna had eclipsed all other desires. To signify the gratification of this desire Tolstoy shows us Vronsky, his face pale, lower jaw aquiver, bent over Anna, who is torn between the sensations of guilt, joy, and horror. We are told of his strained voice beseeching her "to calm down, he himself at a loss why she should and how." A scene infinitely more evocative than an explicit description of the sexual act itself.

From the realm of the flesh we soar to the sphere of the spirit in Dostoevsky's supremely affecting finale to Ivan Karamazov's Legend—the wordless kiss bestowed by Christ on the bloodless, aged lips of the Grand Inquisitor, a silent response, awesome in its spiritual compassionate majesty and power to shatter the resolve of the Great Unbeliever to burn Christ at the stake. Flinching under the kiss, the old man opens the door of the dungeon and tells his prisoner to go and never, never to return. The supreme idea of redeeming liberation cannot be expressed in words. But it triumphs over the lengthy rationale of unbelief.

Restraint in depicting scenes of sexual love in fiction was an accepted practice in Tolstoy's lifetime. But his silence was not motivated by conventional considerations. And it was most certainly not an act of prudery. Tolstoy's silence was an act of condemnation. He continues the scene by showing Anna overwhelmed with humiliation and transmitting her sense of shame to Vronsky. To look back to the cause of such a burning sense of shame, Tolstoy tells us, is "horrifying and repulsive." This was a preface to the idea of a divide between carnal existence and spiritual life which was going to be expounded by Tolstoy the moralist in years to come, extolling love as a rational activity and reaching the point of banning copulation, even in wedlock, as a debasing concession to man's animal nature. But Anna Karenina was a supreme creation of Tolstoy the artist; glowing with vitality and humanness she is an immortal figure in world literature and one of Chekhov's favorite heroines in Tolstoy's works. In Chekhov's world love could never be compressed in rational bounds, it was carnal as well as spiritual, it soared, it transformed, it ennobled those who experienced it, and in its totality it reached beyond definitive forms of articulate expression.

A glance at Chekhov's distance from Tolstoy's silence on the sexual act also reveals his nearness to Dostoevsky's. Dostoevsky's silence was an act of glorification. Christ's kiss was the living stillness of a starlit sky, a tribute to the inexpressible dimension of faith. This supreme creation of Dostoevsky's genius sprang from the roots of the Russian Orthodox religion, a religion of freedom which addressed the individual directly, calling for volitional, individual striving toward active emulation of Christian ideals here, on this earth, engaging not merely the rationality but the totality of a human being. Chekhov's art aimed at the same goal. It strove to charm, to attract, to evoke free judgment and free choice rather than to persuade and compel. The World Beyond shone through the delicate verbal filigree of his writing.

But the imaginative maturity of Chekhov's contemporaries did not permit his readers to see this. Searching for collective answers, steering toward violent solutions for unresolved imbalances and deep chasms, the Russian public was not prepared to focus on the individual, to hear Chekhov's melody of freedom, to sense that a man is free only if he is able to apprehend God's nearness around him, in all parts of creation.

"Not By Bread Alone" was the title of the first cry of

spiritual liberation that resounded in Russia half a century after Chekhov's death, a half century of stupendous growth of unfreedom, but also a period when the heroic dimensions of a human being, his strength, valor, courage, will, and endurance, shone in unprecedented proportions during the crucible of the Second World War. It is against this background that Vasily Grossman formulated his tribute to Chekhov as the first standard-bearer of freedom in Russia.

BIBLIOGRAPHY

G. Andreev, "Zagadka Chekhova" (The Enigma of Chekhov), in *The New Review*, New York, 1975, No. 118.

G. Berdnikov, *A.P. Chekhov*, Moscow and Leningrad, 1961, 1974.

Nicolai Berdiaev, *The Destiny of Man*, London, 1937.

____, *O rabstve i svobode cheloveka* (On Human Slavery and Freedom), Paris, 1939.

Isaiah Berlin, *Russian Thinkers*, New York, 1978.

____, *Against the Current*, New York, 1979.

Petr. B. Bicilli, *Anton P. Cechov, Werk und Stil*, Munich, 1966.

Valentine T. Bill, *The Forgotten Class: The Russian Bourgeoisie*, New York, 1959.

E. Broyde, *Chekhov, myslitel', khudozhnik* (Chekhov as a Thinker and an Artist), Frankfurt, 1980.

W.H. Bruford, *Chekhov and His Russia*, London, 1948.

Martin Buber, *I and Thou*, trans. W. Kaufmann, New York, 1970.

Sergius Bulgakov, *Chekhov kak myslitel'* (Chekhov as a Thinker), Moscow, 1910.

A Bulgakov Anthology, ed. J. Pain and N. Zernov, Philadelphia, 1976.

Ivan A. Bunin, *O Chekhove* (About Chekhov), New York, 1955.

——, *Osvobozhdenie Tolstovo* (Tolstoy's Liberation), Paris, 1937.

John Cage, *Silence: Lectures and Writings*, Wesleyan Univ. Press, 1961.

Anton P. Chekhov, *Polnoe sobranie sochinenii* (Complete Edition of Works and Letters), Moscow, 1974-83.

Chekhov i Lev Tolstoy, ed. L.D. Opul'skaia and others, Moscow, 1980.

Chekhov v vospominaniakh sovremennikov (Chekhov in the Eyes of his Contemporaries), Gosizdat Moscow, 1960.

A.P. Chudakov, *Poetika Chekhova* (Chekhov's Poetics), Moscow, 1971.

Fedor M. Dostoevsky, *Sobranie sochinenii*, 10 Vols., Moscow, 1956-58.

Dostoevskii i russkie pisateli (Dostoevsky and Russian Writers), ed. V. IA. Kirpotin, Moscow, 1971.

Boris Eikhenbaum, *The Young Tolstoy*, trans. and ed. Gary Kern, Ann Arbor, 1972.

Victor Erlich, *Russian Formalism*, The Hague, 1965.

Georges Florovsky, *Puti russkovo bogosloviia* (The Ways of Russian Theology), Paris, YMCA Press, 1937.

——, *Christianity and Culture*, Belmont, MA, 1974.

Joseph Frank, *The Widening Gyre*, New Brunswick, NJ, 1963.

John Gardner, *On Moral Fiction*, New York, 1977.

N.I. Gitovich, *Letipis' zhizni i tvorchestva A.P. Chekhova* (Chronicle of Chekhov's Life and Work), Moscow, 1955.

R.L. Jackson, *Chekhov, Collection of Essays: 20th Century Views*, Englewood Cliffs, NJ, 1967.

Simon Karlinsky, ed. with M.H. Heim, *Anton Chekhov's*

Life and Thought; Selected Letters and Commentaries, Berkeley, 1975.

V.O. Kliuchevsky, *Sochineniia* (Works), Soviet Edition, 8 Vols., Moscow, 1956-59.

Karl D. Kramer, *The Chameleon and the Dream*, The Hague, 1970.

M. Kurdiumov, *Serdtse smiatennoe; o tvorchestve Chekhova* (The Troubled Heart; On Chekhov's Work), Paris, 1934.

Nadezhda Mandelstam, *Hope against Hope*, New York, 1970.

Rollo May, *Symbolism in Religion and Literature*, New York, 1960.

_____. *Love and Will*, New York, 1969.

Dmitri Merezhkovsky, *Tolstoii i Dostoevsky*, 2nd. ed., 2 Vols., St. Petersburg, 1903.

E.B. Meve, *Meditsina v tvorchestve i zhisni Chekhova* (Medicine in Chekhov's Work and Life), Kiev, 1961.

Eric Mount, *Conscience and Responsibility*, Richmond, VA, 1969.

V tvorcheskoi laboratorii Chekhova (In Chekhov's Creative Laboratory), ed. L.D. Opul'skaia and others, Moscow, 1974.

George A. Panichas, *The Burden of Vision: Dostoevsky's Spiritual Art*, Grand Rapids, MI, 1977.

Z. Papernyi, *A.P. Chekhov*, Moscow, 1960.

_____. *Zapisnye knizhki Chekhova* (Chekhov's Notebooks), Moscow, 1976.

David Park, *The Image of Eternity: Roots of Time in the Physical World*, Amherst, MA, 1980.

Renato Poggioli, *The Phoenix and the Spider*, Cambridge, MA, 1957.

E.A. Polotskaia, *Chelovek v khudozhestvenom mire Dostoevsovo i Chekhova* (Man in Dostoevsky's and Chekhov's Creative World), in *Dostoevsky i ruskie pisateli* (Dostoevsky and Russian Writers), Moscow, 1971.

George Poulet, *Studies in Human Time*, trans. Elliot Coleman, Baltimore, 1956.

_____, *The Interior Distance*, Baltimore, 1959.

Marcel Proust, *The Past Recaptured*, Vintage Books, 1971.

Ronald Rayfield, *Chekhov, the Evolution of His Art*, New York, 1975.

G. Selge, *Anton Chekhov's Menschenbild* (Chekhov's Image of Man), Munich, 1970.

Leo Shestov, *Chekhov and other Essays*, Ann Arbor, MI, 1966.

Vladimir Soloviev, *Smysl liubvi* (The Meaning of Love) New York, 1947.

Logan Speirs, *Tolstoy and Chekhov*, London, 1971.

Walter T. Stace, *Time and Eternity*, Princeton, NJ, 1952.

——, *Religion and the Modern Mind*, Philadelphia, 1960.

George Steiner, *Tolstoy or Dostoevsky*, New York, 1959.

——, *Language and Silence*, New York, 1977.

Rev. M.M. Stepanov, *Religia Chekhova* (Chekhov's Religion), Saratov, 1913; reprint University Microfilms, Ann Arbor, MI, 1975.

Allen Tate, *Collected Essays*, Denver, 1959.

William York Tindall, *The Literary Symbol*, New York, 1955.

Lev N. Tolstoy, *Sobranie sochinenii*, 20 Vols., Moscow, 1960-65.

N. Ulianov, "Mistitsism Chekhova" (Chekhov's Mysticism), in *The New Review*, New York, No. 98, 1970.

Volzhskii, *Dostoevsky i Chekhov* in *Russkaia Mysl*, 1913, second pagination, No. 5.

Rene Wellek and Austin Warren, *Theory of Literature*, New York, 1956.

INDEX

273